Renegade Women

*Gender, Identity, and Boundaries in the
Early Modern Mediterranean*

ERIC R DURSTELER

The Johns Hopkins University Press
Baltimore

This book was brought to publication with the generous assistance of the Gladys Krieble Delmas Foundation and a Lila Acheson Wallace–Reader's Digest Publications grant from Villa I Tatti: The Harvard University Center for Italian Renaissance Studies.

The Johns Hopkins University Press
2715 North Charles Street
Baltimore, Maryland 21218-4363
www.press.jhu.edu

Library of Congress Cataloging-in-Publication Data
Dursteler, Eric.
   Renegade women : gender, identity, and boundaries in the early modern Mediterranean / Eric R Dursteler.
      p. cm.
   Includes bibliographical references and index.
   ISBN-13: 978-1-4214-0071-6 (hbk. : alk. paper)
   ISBN-13: 978-1-4214-0072-3 (pbk. : alk. paper)
   ISBN-10: 1-4214-0071-5 (hbk. : alk. paper)
   ISBN-10: 1-4214-0072-3 (pbk. : alk. paper)
   1. Women—Mediterranean Region—Social conditions—Case studies.
2. Conversion—Social aspects—Case studies.   3. Conversion—Christianity—Case studies.   4. Conversion—Islam—Case studies.   5. Mediterranean Region—History—1517–1789.   I. Title.
   HQ1149.M43D87   2011
   305.409182'20903—dc22   2010046794

A catalog record for this book is available from the British Library.

Special discounts are available for bulk purchases of this book. For more information, please contact Special Sales at 410-516-6936 or specialsales@press.jhu.edu.

The Johns Hopkins University Press uses environmentally friendly book materials, including recycled text paper that is composed of at least 30 percent post-consumer waste, whenever possible.

Per Whit
And in memory of
Henry Y. K. Tom

CONTENTS

PREFACE

O N ITS SIMPLEST LEVEL, this is a collection of stories or, perhaps more formally, of microhistories. Their setting is the eastern Mediterranean, along the lengthy frontier between the Ottoman and Venetian empires—from Venice to the Dalmatian coast, from the islands of the Ionian and the Aegean to the megalopolis of Istanbul. The time is the decades between the great battle of Lepanto in 1572 and the outbreak of the War of Candia in 1645, a period characterized by generally peaceful relations between the two states. The protagonists are women—mothers, wives, widows, girls, nuns— all of whom inhabited this rich and complex historical space. Unlike so many women of the early modern era who remain wholly imperceptible in the documents, these left scattered and often barely perceptible archival traces in Venice, Rome, Greece, Croatia, and Istanbul, which, when linked together, allow us to recreate in unusually rich detail pivotal moments that profoundly influenced the course of their lives.

The women whose tales I recount were all renegades. In the languages of the age, *renegade* referred to an individual who "rebelled against the faith."[1] The label was almost always applied to Christian conversions to Islam but was also used occasionally in other religious and political contexts. I have taken liberties with the term and have expanded it to encompass not only women who converted from Christianity to Islam but all women who transgressed boundaries of any sort—political, religious, gender, social—and in any geographical, ideological, or theological direction. Modern scholarship on renegades has focused disproportionately on men, but here my focus is on the different and much more elusive experiences of renegade women.

In many ways, the Mediterranean is also a character in these tales; it functions as a channel of division, as a corridor of escape, and as a means of connection. While there is a growing body of literature on the Mediterranean, the women who inhabited its islands and coasts have received little attention. When scholars have considered them, it has only been within very narrow religious or political contexts. This book attempts to remedy this oversight, but even more, as the subtitle suggests, these tales provide greater insights into the experiences and conditions of women specifically, and culture and society more broadly, in the early modern Mediterranean.

My intention has been to keep the women and their stories center stage; thus, this preface and the analytical passages of the three core chapters are kept at a minimum, so as to reserve the foreground for the narrative. As a result, the reader will not encounter the traditional format of historical prose—introduction, body, conclusion. I address my central ideas and arguments in the narrative chapters, but the conclusions hinted at in the text will be dealt with more explicitly and completely in the conclusion. For those who prefer a map before departing on a journey, I recommend going in through the out door, beginning with the conclusion then returning to the body of the text.

ACKNOWLEDGMENTS

THIS BOOK BEGAN as a conference paper at the 2000 meeting of the Renaissance Society of America in Florence, Italy. On a lark I gathered a few leftovers from the research I had done for my doctoral dissertation and wrote a short article, mostly so I could go to the conference. After delivering the paper, I received an e-mail from an editor at the Johns Hopkins University Press, inquiring whether the article was part of a larger book project. This was the first time I considered that the stories I had gathered might add up to a book, and I am grateful to Henry Tom for helping birth the idea. Henry passed away unexpectedly as this book was going to press, and I will miss his sharp intellect, his unwavering good cheer, and his friendship. This book is dedicated to his memory.

Many colleagues generously contributed their time and knowledge at all stages of this project, which, given its broad historiographical scope, was essential to its completion. These include Palmira Brummett, Matteo Casini, Valentina Cesco, Diogo Ramada Curto, Sabine Florence Fabijanec, Cristian Luca, Anthony Molho, Gerassimos Pagratis, Leslie Peirce, Claudio Povolo, Natalie Rothman, Scott Taylor, and Matt Vester. Special mention goes to Holly Hurlburt, Craig Harline, Don Harreld, and Monique O'Connell, who read the manuscript and gave pointed and useful (and occasionally painful) advice on improving the final product. Edward Muir, Margaret King, Palmira Brummett, John Jeffries Martin, and Anthony Molho all wrote more letters of recommendation than I care to admit asking for, and these led to significant funding that made the book possible.

A project of this scope requires extensive travel and research in numerous archives and libraries, as well as time to write. A number of institutions generously supported my work at various stages, including the National Endowment for the Humanities, the Gladys Krieble Delmas Foundation, and, at Brigham Young University, the David M. Kennedy Center, the Women's Research Institute, the College of Family, Home, and Social Sciences, and the Department of History. I was also fortunate to spend the academic year 2006–2007 as a fellow at Villa I Tatti—The Harvard University Center for Italian Renaissance Studies, where Joe and Françoise Connors created a warm and welcoming environment for my research and my family that we will never forget. Thanks also to the wonderfully kind teachers and students of the Scuola Superiore Michelangiolo and Scuola Elementare Cairuoli, who welcomed my children so warmly during our year in Florence.

I had the opportunity to explore early versions of parts of this book in several stimulating settings, including Wake Forest University, the European University Institute, the Folger Shakespeare Library, West Virginia University, and the David M. Kennedy Center and Women's Research Institute at Brigham Young University. I am grateful to my hosts and to all those who provided helpful criticism and encouragement.

I have been fortunate to spend my professional life in the shadow of the Wasatch Mountains at Brigham Young University. I can imagine no more welcoming and generous academic community. Many individuals and entities in Provo have played key roles in all stages of the creation of this book. Dean David Magleby of the College of Family, Home and Social Sciences has been very supportive and encouraging. George Ryskamp of the Center for Family History and Genealogy offered timely advice on using the voluminous genealogical records at Brigham Young University. Amy Harris provided a helpful primer on the historiography of childhood. Julie Radle, who, with indefatigable good humor, makes everything in the Department of History run smoothly, was endlessly supportive in too many ways to count. Special thanks to the lunch crew at El Gallo Giro, the best Mexican food in Provo—Shawn Miller, Kendall Brown,

Donald Harreld, Chris Hodson, Karen Carter, and Craig Harline and his much mourned Beachcomber van. Almost nothing about this book was ever discussed during our lunches, which was immensely helpful in its creation.

A number of BYU students assisted in various aspects of this project, including Phil Cannon, Clay Hansen, Aileen Christensen, Candela Romero, Spencer Orton, and research assistant extraordinaire, Greg Jackson. Dan Francom, Shaun Hartman, Peter Wright, and Adil Uskudarli all spent long hours helping me work through the many linguistic challenges I encountered trying to navigate Greek, Romanian, Turkish, Italian, Spanish, French, English, and Croatian sources. And special thanks to the dedicated archivists who were especially patient and helpful in introducing me to the riches of unfamiliar collections: Giuseppe Ellero, Silvia Lunardon, Jadranka Delaš, Suzana Martinović, and Nella Pantazi.

As always, my greatest debt of gratitude goes to the members of my family, who have been my companions, my distraction, my motivation over many wonderful years. I am especially grateful to them for accompanying me to Florence at a critical stage in this project. Their courage, stoicism, and good spirits in adapting to a new language and to a year in Italian schools inspired and cheered me. Without them none of this would matter. When I began this book all three of my children were still at home. Now, Lauren is married and I am a grandfather in denial, Collin has moved on to college, and only Addy remains at home. I will miss the adventures we all shared together as the family of an impoverished graduate student and of a frenzied young professor, but I look forward to new experiences that no doubt await us in the next stage of our lives. As with everything I have ever written, and ever will write, this book is dedicated to Whit.

Portions of this book previously appeared in often significantly different form in several articles. I am grateful to the editors and journals for permission to use portions of these works: "Defending Virtue and Preserving Reputation: Gender and Institutional Honor on the Early Modern Dalmatian Frontier," *Journal of Early Modern History* 15 (2011): forthcoming; "Fatima Hatun née Beatrice Michiel: Renegade Women in the Early Modern Mediterranean," *The Medieval History Journal* 12 (2009): 355–82; and "Muslim Renegade Women: Conversion and Agency in the Early Modern Mediterranean," *Journal of Mediterranean Studies* 17 (2006): 103–12.

Renegade Women

CHAPTER ONE

Fatima Hatun née Beatrice Michiel

I N 1559, A SHIP set sail from Venice directed to the Albanian coast. On board were Maria Franceschina Zorzi Michiel and her four children, including the protagonist of our tale, Beatrice, who was perhaps five or six years old at the time. The family was headed to Budua—a castle more than a town, which was "small, weak and of little importance"[1]—where their father, Giacomo Michiel, served as chancellor to the local Venetian *podestà,* Giuseppe Bollani.[2] As they crossed the Adriatic, corsairs waylaid the ship and took Franceschina and her children captive. This was not an unusual event; corsairs and freebooters infested Mediterranean sea lanes, and the summer of 1559 was a particularly troubled time.[3] Unlike the majority of unfortunate victims, however, the story of the Michiel family would take a series of unexpected turns worthy of any Hollywood historical epic.

Franceschina eventually succeeded in ransoming herself and her two daughters and returned to Venice with them. She was unable to free her sons, however, who were sold into slavery and soon converted to Islam. The elder, aged ten or eleven, took the name Gazanfer, while his younger brother was known as Cafer. The two became trusted members of the household of the sultan-in-waiting, Selim, during his governorship in the Anatolian town of Kütahya, and at the death in 1566 of his father, Süleyman the Magnificent, the new sultan invited them to accompany him to Istanbul. There was a catch, however. Selim wanted them both to serve him in his inner palace,

Turkish woman
Cesare Vecellio, *De gli habiti antichi, et moderni* (Venice: Damian Zenaro, 1590)

The Eastern Mediterranean

which required that they be castrated in a risky operation.[4] Selim's request was unusual, since most eunuchs were emasculated as children; however, because eunuchs occupied an important place in the court culture of the capital, "castration was a means of advancement" for the ambitious young adult renegades too.[5] Thus, as the Ottoman historian Mustafa Ali reports, the boys decided that the "wicks of their night-candles should be cut off," and so they "were divested of their unblown buds" by the sultan's chief surgeon. Although there is some ambiguity in contemporary sources, it seems that both brothers survived the procedure,[6] and indeed the news was greeted with "letters of congratulation and presents" sent to the capital and verses composed to honor the occasion.[7]

We know relatively little about Cafer's life. In 1577 Murad III made him his *has oda başı* (head of the privy chamber), a position he held until his untimely death in 1582.[8] About Gazanfer Ağa, in contrast, we know much more. Once in the Ottoman capital, he became an ally of the *haseki,* Selim's favorite, the Venetian Nurbanu, and advanced rapidly within the imperial inner circle.[9] After Cafer's death, Gazanfer held simultaneously the two most important offices within the *enderûn* (inner service of the imperial palace): has oda başı and *kapı ağası* (chief of the white eunuchs). The Topkapi Palace in the early modern period was divided into three distinct areas: the first courtyard, which was open to the public; the second courtyard, the "semipublic theater of government," in which the imperial divan met; and the third courtyard, the "imperial harem," which was accessible to almost no one. This area included the sultan's private living quarters, the female harem with the household's women (the *valide sultan,* consorts, princesses, women servants), and the male harem, with its several hundred select boys being trained for government service, who were overseen and taught by the white eunuchs.[10]

As has oda başı and kapı ağası, Gazanfer supervised the palace and its staff and was "the person closest to the sultan, never leaving his side." He was literally the gatekeeper; his office was located at the Gate of Felicity, the entrance into the third court, which made him "the sole mediator between the Sultan and the world outside."[11] All persons or communications had to pass by him, which gave him tremendous political power and unprecedented influence over the sultans. In fact, it was widely held that Mehmed III always asked the kapı ağası "what he wanted him to write, and whatever he recommended, without any modification, was written."[12] During a troubled period of Ottoman history, Gazanfer preserved his position and his influence for thirty years in the service of three sultans— Selim II (1566–74), Murad III (1574–95), and Mehmed III (1595–

1603)—and was one of a small number of men and women who held effective power during the so-called sultanate of the women.[13]

As a powerful Ottoman official, Gazanfer became a great patron of literary figures such as the poet Gânîzâde Mehmed Nâdirî and the historian Mustafa Ali.[14] The latter dedicated his *Description of Cairo* to Gazanfer, "the breaker of the necks of the treacherous, the mentor of the well-spoken and eloquent, the lion of battle and warfare, the initiator of laudable and generous actions . . . the trustworthy prop among the pillars of the state."[15] Gazanfer also financed schools, fountains, mosques, and even the renovation of Muhammad's birthplace in Mecca. His most important work of patronage—a complex that includes Gazanfer's tomb, a madrasa, and a fountain—was completed in 1596 and is attributed to Davut Ağa.[16]

Although a youthful convert to Islam whose adult life and career were closely linked to the Ottoman dynasty, Gazanfer continued to identify, at least in part, as a Venetian.[17] As a result, after two decades of separation, in 1582 he reinitiated contact with his family and requested that his mother visit him in Istanbul. The inhabitants of the imperial palace received her "with much honor" and "great pomp," and she was "favored by all the grandees of this Porte." She remained in the Ottoman capital for two years, residing in her son's seraglio, before returning to Venice in 1584.[18] Because of Gazanfer's influence, the Venetian Senate granted Franceschina a personal audience at her return and declared itself "most ready . . . to give satisfaction to his mother and his relations." As proof of this, the Senate awarded her the proceeds of an office with a stipend of ten ducats monthly; the following year the income from an even more lucrative office was given to Gazanfer's sister, Beatrice.[19]

⤳

This brings us back to the real protagonist of our story, Beatrice Michiel. While her brother was scaling the Ottoman hierarchy, she had returned to Venice, where some twenty years later she married Angelo di Bianchi, scion of an elite *cittadino originario* family with deep roots in Venice.[20] The cittadini originari were a privileged minority beneath the patriciate who had near-exclusive access to the

Gazanfer Ağa and Sultan Mehmed III
Eğri fethi tarihi. H. 1609, fol. 27a. Topkapı Palace Museum,
Istanbul

most important bureaucratic offices, held key positions in the city's confraternities, and enjoyed other special honors. After 1569, the cittadini originari became an increasingly closed caste that practiced endogamy,[21] which suggests that the Michiel family, despite subsequent claims of nobility, more likely belonged to the citizen elite. At most, Franceschina may have been, as rumor had it, a natural daughter "from Ca' Zorzi."[22]

Beatrice and her husband settled in the parish of San Giacomo dall'Orio, where she gave birth to two sons. Baldissare was born in October 1584 and had two noblemen stand as his godfathers. He was followed several years later by Giacomo.[23] We know little else of this period in Beatrice's life, except that "she was very well known [and knew] many most honorable people . . . [and] because of her great virtue, goodness, and valor she was held in great esteem."[24] Tragedy struck the young family in January 1588, however, when Angelo died at age thirty-three following a yearlong bout with consumption. At no more than thirty years of age, Beatrice was left a widow with two young sons.[25]

Widows were legion in early modern Italy, and cultural attitudes, combined with economic realities, pulled them in contradictory directions. Francis de Sales recommended "permanent chastity" as "the highest ornament" of widowhood, and Savonarola encouraged widows to be chaste "like the tortoise," who spent "the rest of her life in solitary weeping" after losing a mate.[26] In Florence, a woman who remarried and threatened her children's well-being by reclaiming her dowry was a "cruel mother," and Venetian widows were pressured not to recover their dowries for the same reason. Charivari and other ritual forms of humiliation were widely practiced to shame widows who did remarry.[27] At the same time, there was also pressure on widows to remarry. In Venice, single women, especially widows, were viewed as dangerous, and sexually active unmarried or separated women could be condemned as prostitutes. Despite this, single women constituted perhaps upward of 15 percent of the city's early modern population.[28] Three options existed for these widows: the convent, remarriage, or widowhood.

Beatrice chose remarriage, within little more than a year of Angelo's death. Her decision to remarry, and so quickly, was somewhat unusual. Although *popolani* women remarried more frequently, fewer than 10 percent of elite Venetian widows did so, as widowhood permitted them an attractive level of autonomy and economic independence. Remarriage after age thirty was less common as well.[29] Beatrice's new husband, Zuane Zaghis, was a Venetian merchant without citizen status who was described as "a discreet person and full of good will."[30]

Soon after the wedding, Beatrice gave birth to another child, a daughter, but already the new marriage was in trouble.[31] We do not know the intimate details of their relationship, but it appears Beatrice was growing uncomfortable with her husband's behavior in regard to her financial and family affairs. Zaghis was particularly aggressive in benefiting from the position and influence of his wife's brother, Gazanfer Ağa. Immediately following their marriage, Zaghis traveled to Istanbul where he attempted to profit from his new family's connections. For a fee he intervened with his brother-in-law on behalf of several jewel merchants who were owed over 100,000 ducats by the sultan, and he received a handsome commission for arranging a trade of eighty bales of the sultan's silk. Zaghis also pushed Gazanfer to support his efforts to have a debt canceled by the Venetian state and to be awarded an important office.[32] More significantly for Beatrice, there seem to have been serious issues regarding her dowry.

Beatrice had brought significant resources to the marriage, including a six-thousand-ducat dowry, extensive terraferma landholdings, and an annual two-hundred-ducat income from a Venetian office.[33] During this time, unskilled laborers earned sixteen to twenty ducats annually, a ship's master perhaps a hundred ducats, a well-off patrician about one thousand ducats, and the very richest noble perhaps ten thousand ducats.[34] By the standards of the day, Beatrice's was a large dowry; contemporary patrician dowries ranged from one to three thousand ducats for the poorest nobles, to twenty thousand ducats for the very elite. Cittadino dowries averaged three to four thousand ducats. Thus Beatrice's dowry, the maximum permitted by law, was well above average.[35] In Venice the dowry remained the wife's property, and if valued over one thousand ducats, it had to be registered with civic officials. A husband could legally administer his spouse's dowry for the benefit of the family, but he was expected to do so responsibly. At his death the full amount reverted to his wife, who could dispose of it at her discretion. A husband who wasted or "expropriated dotal wealth" could be disciplined by Venetian authorities.[36] Despite numerous legal and institutional protections, however, "husbandly rapacity" was common, and contemporaries described women as often the "hapless victims of men's greed."[37]

The *malmaritate* (unhappily married) of early modern Venice had some limited options through both ecclesiastical and secular courts to defend themselves within, and even free themselves from, failed marriages. About half these courts' cases dealt with economic matters, and a consensus existed that a wife might justifiably leave a husband whose actions threatened her financial well-being.[38] We should not, however, exaggerate women's ability to flee unwanted marriages; actual cases of annulled or dissolved marriages in Renaissance Venice are statistically insignificant. In a population of about 180,000 at the turn of the century,[39] scholars have found perhaps thirty-five cases of marriages dissolved by ecclesiastical and secular courts annually. In part, this was because women were discouraged from appealing to these courts, and elite men used their status to obstruct proceedings, making it more difficult for an upper-class woman to dissolve a marriage. Legal action was considered "inconvenient," and women were expected to wait a year and a day after a husband's death before requesting their dowry or pursuing legal action. And the legal process was almost always long and drawn out.[40] For most Venetian women, liberating themselves of an unwanted husband through the courts was neither an attractive nor a viable option.

Thus, it is not surprising that no record exists of Beatrice pursuing any institutional means to end her marriage. Instead, saddled with a relationship she no longer desired, confronted by Zaghis's intrusive interference in her financial affairs with the attendant threat to her and her sons' status, and possessed of limited options for dissolving the marriage satisfactorily, Beatrice took matters into her own hands. In late 1591 she left her husband and children in Venice and boarded a ship bound for Istanbul to rendezvous with her brother, whom she had not seen for over three decades, and her mother, who had migrated to the city a year earlier.[41]

On her arrival in the Ottoman capital, Beatrice was met by a large company of Ottoman officials. They ceremoniously conducted her from the port to Gazanfer's seraglio, where his more than one hundred slaves attended to her every whim. As she settled into her new surroundings, she was shocked to learn that her mother had died unexpectedly the day before her arrival.[42] This revelation must have been tremendously disorienting. Beatrice had expected to find her mother waiting for her and instead now found herself in an unfamiliar culture, with a sibling she barely knew and sequestered with no possibility of outside contact. Strongly encouraged by her brother, Beatrice converted to Islam within a few short days of her arrival. The ceremony was brief and simple; she raised her finger and uttered the profession of faith, the *shahadah*—"There is no god but God, and Muhammad is God's messenger"—and assumed a new name, that of the Prophet Muhammad's daughter, Fatima, the most common choice among renegade women.[43] She also traded her Christian attire for that of a Muslim woman as the final, external manifestation of her transformation.[44]

Fatima's bold action raises several issues, the first of which is motivation. There is a great deal of obscurity and mystery behind her seemingly precipitous decision, and the surviving records do not permit an entirely complete or satisfying explanation. One scholar has suggested that she "was sold by her husband to her brother in exchange of ready cash."[45] There is some evidence that supports this view; in the heat of battle over her Venetian estate, Fatima herself claimed that Zaghis had sold her for one thousand ducats in order to gain control of her large dowry and that she had subsequently been coerced into conversion.[46]

This explanation is problematic, however, because it makes Fatima a pawn and deprives her of any voice in the events that led to her conversion. And more importantly, it is not consistent with the documentary record. There is no doubt that Gazanfer wanted to surround himself with family members, that he provided encouragement and funds to his brother-in-law to bring his sister and mother to Istanbul, that he pressured them both to convert, and that he stood to gain in reputation in the Porte if his family embraced Islam.[47] But considering Fatima's dissatisfaction with Zaghis and the lack of remedies for her situation, it is equally likely that, rather than being compelled, she made the rational choice to come to Istanbul in order to free herself and to benefit her family.

When Fatima set out for the Ottoman capital in the summer of 1591, she traveled alone. Before her departure, questions already circulated in Istanbul and Venice about her husband's intentions and his relationship with Gazanfer. If Zaghis had conspired to deliver his wife to her brother, however, it is unlikely that he would have agreed to her making the perilous journey unaccompanied, both to protect her and to ensure her arrival. Because she traveled alone, if Fatima had harbored any suspicions about what awaited her in Istanbul, or had been constrained by her husband to leave Venice, at any time during the month-long voyage, she could have informed the ship's captain of her plight. Or she could have disembarked at any one of the ship's numerous ports of call in the Venetian *stato da mar* and made her situation known to local officials, some of whom she might have known from her connections in Venice, and all of whom would have undoubtedly been sympathetic to her situation. Moreover, Zaghis would have faced serious legal and ecclesiastical penalties in Venice if it were revealed that he had sold his wife into apostasy. One experienced observer, the Venetian bailo Girolamo Lippomano, postulated that Gazanfer had wanted Fatima to join him in Istanbul because of "the poor companionship that

[Zaghis] provided his sister." Lippomano thought it highly doubtful that "the kapı ağası would deign to retain [Zaghis] as his brother-in-law." Therefore, it would not seem unreasonable to assume that some sort of understanding may have existed between the unhappy couple to resolve their relationship issues in this unorthodox fashion. It is also possible that Fatima may have acted without Zaghis's knowledge of her ultimate intentions.[48]

The overwhelmingly positive experience of her mother in Istanbul certainly influenced Fatima's decision to visit her brother. As we have seen, Franceschina Michiel had spent two years in the Porte a decade earlier and had been treated with great respect both within the imperial palace and by the Venetian Senate on her return. In 1590, she went back to the Ottoman capital, this time accompanied by her new son-in-law, Zaghis, and she was once again received regally. Although Gazanfer attempted "with many tears" to induce her to convert, Franceschina—described as "full of Christian zeal"—categorically refused to imperil "her honor and her soul by renouncing the holy faith." When Gazanfer pressed for Fatima to join them in Istanbul, although some questioned his intentions, he claimed his sole objective was to "see and . . . enrich his only sister." Franceschina believed her son and helped convince Venetian officials to grant his request. When Zaghis set out for Venice to get Fatima in May 1591, Franceschina decided to remain in Istanbul, "perhaps forever," because she was "full of good intentions for her grandchildren" and felt she could benefit them through Gazanfer's influence.[49]

Financial factors also played a role in Fatima's decision to flee Venice. The day of her arrival in Istanbul, Bailo Lorenzo Bernardo reported that she had come "in hopes of acquiring riches." Bernardo's replacement, Matteo Zane, concurred, but he added that she had come to Istanbul motivated "by the hope of deriving great gain, and maybe also from being little contented with her husband."[50] In the view of both of these seasoned diplomats, Fatima had decided her own course of action. She came to Istanbul attracted by financial hopes, which, given Gazanfer's past generosity and his current promises, combined with her mother's own positive experience and encouragement, were perfectly rational. This monetary motivation was common among the early modern era's many renegades, the majority of whom were men. Tales of Ottoman economic and social opportunity abounded throughout the Mediterranean, and periods of increased migration and conversion often coincided with economic crises in Europe. Fatima's case demonstrates that women renegades could also be motivated by financial factors. As Zane suggests, however, her motives were not solely economic. Marital dissatisfaction was an equally compelling reason, and while familial motivations could also drive men to convert, as the cases of Fatima and the other women renegades we will encounter suggest, these seem generally more representative of Mediterranean women's experiences.[51]

Fatima's decision to convert to Islam may also have been influenced by some knowledge, perhaps conveyed by her brother or mother, of the favorable situation of women under Ottoman rule. That a woman would intentionally choose to convert may seem improbable, given the popular image of Muslim women as oppressed and powerless victims of patriarchy.[52] Ottoman women, however, had available to them "a wide field of action . . . despite an inherited gender system that prescribed women's subordination to men."[53] They enjoyed legal and cultural prospects greater than those available to many European women; indeed, the wife of the English ambassador, Lady Elizabeth Craven, observed that "the Turks in their conduct towards our sex are an example to all other nations."[54] Ottoman girls were considered imperial subjects at puberty, and both sharia law and tradition granted women specific legal privileges, including the right to control property without male interference and the right to assert their legal prerogatives in court and even before the divan, the sultan's imperial council. Ottoman women regularly availed themselves of the courts, which generally affirmed their rights. Non-Muslim Ottoman women also frequently had recourse to courts overseen by a kadi (judge) because they perceived them as more sympathetic than Christian or Jewish courts.[55]

Ottoman women could also end unwanted marriages more easily through divorce, separation, and annulment. Divorces initiated by the empire's women for abuse, abandonment, and failure to provide financial support became common enough that they attracted concerned social comment. For non-Muslim women whose traditions did not normally permit divorce, conversion to Islam was an easy and common way to liberate themselves from unwanted spouses.[56] "Conversion immediately freed a badly married Christian women of her regrettable husband" and voided all legal relationships, including marriage and paternity, that had fettered her prior to embracing Islam.[57] Among European Christians, in contrast, legal separation was rare and difficult to obtain, which gave rise to informal, communal means of escaping "wed-lock," such as wife sales or the more common practices of separation and bigamy.[58] Though not legally binding, such practices were often the only means available to dissolve a failed relationship.[59]

Fatima's understanding of the Ottoman world was certainly informed by the widespread popular interest in all things Ottoman. While there is much talk of early modern *Turkenfurcht* (fear of the Turk), the age witnessed a parallel *ossessione turca* (Turkish obsession), and Venice was the epicenter of information on Ottoman life.[60] Learned treatises, travelers' narratives, popular plays, and sensational pamphlets were widespread, and crude illustrations of Ottomans were common on the walls of Venetian homes.[61] The reading of the ambassadorial reports from Istanbul "drew crowds to the Senate," and dispatches from the Porte were circulated in popular weekly manuscript *avvisi*.[62] Renegades were a commonplace in this literature, and figures such as Ibrahim Paşa, Uluç Ali, and Cigalazade Sinan Paşa were well known in Venice. A few women renegades also achieved notoriety; the slave-to-sultana story of Süleyman the Magnificent's wife Hürrem, or Roxelana,[63] captured the imagination of Europeans through representations in literature, on stage, and in portraits and popular engravings that imagined the face of a woman few had ever seen.[64]

One influential Ottoman woman Fatima was certainly familiar with was Nurbanu, haseki of Selim II, mother of Murad III, and a close associate and benefactor of her brother, Gazanfer. Enslaved by the Ottoman *kapudan paşa* Barbarossa as a young girl in 1537, Nurbanu maintained, and Venetian officials perpetuated, the myth that she was of Venetian patrician stock. Contemporaries knew her as the Venetian sultana, and she was notorious for her political influence, especially over her son, Murad. She worked to prevent an Ottoman invasion of Crete; she was a central figure in the peace that ended the War of the Holy League in 1573; she ensured the peaceful ascension of her son to the throne in 1574; and she corresponded on diplomatic affairs with western rulers, including Catherine de Medici (to whom many contemporaries compared her) and Venice's doge. Nurbanu was, according to one scholar, "the glue that held the empire together" during a difficult period of its history.[65]

Popular literature in Venice at the time was also rife with examples of amorous renegade relationships. The tale of Disdemona and Othello, made famous by Shakespeare but originally published by Giraldi in his *Hecathommithi,* went through seven editions in forty years—including three Venetian editions in 1566, 1574, and 1580. Matteo Bandello's *Novelle,* which contains a similar tale about a Christian princess and a Muslim king, also had a Venetian edition in 1566.[66] In both stories, Christian women marry Muslim men but are able to retain their faith. Such stories may have influenced the calculations of Fatima, who we know was literate.

It is unclear whether Fatima's decision to convert was part of a premeditated plan or if she hoped to enjoy the benefits of her brother's power and wealth while avoiding conversion, like the women in these popular stories and even her own mother. She subsequently insisted that her brother had forced her to "turn Turk," and to be sure he did pressure her as he had done his mother, but this claim may have been more self-serving than accurate. Although the Qur'an (2:256) famously states there should be "no compulsion in religion," in the Ottoman Empire involuntary conversions did occur through the *devşirme*, occasional sultanic evangelical policies,[67] and to a degree among slaves, especially women.[68] In general, however, forced conversion was uncommon throughout the empire.[69]

Claims of compulsion, in contrast, were very common among renegades seeking reentry into their religious communities of birth, who had a vested interest in underplaying their own role in their apostasy.[70] Fatima's protestations of coercion genuinely may have reflected subsequent regrets about her decision; indeed, several years after her flight, whispers circulated that she was trying to obtain absolution from Rome by emphasizing "the force that was used against her" in her conversion.[71] The Venetian diplomats Bernardo and Zane doubted her claims and instead made her the active agent. They believed she had fled to Istanbul because "she was unhappy," and when she heard "the encouragement of her brother and others . . . she finally fell into the diabolical error of declaring herself a Turk. In fact, one can say that she was ravished by seductive self-deception, which had the power to cause her to forget the love of her own flesh, her children, and what is most important, her soul."[72]

Rather than having been "ravished by seductive self-deception," it seems most probable that Fatima calculated the costs and benefits and then chose conversion. By converting, Islamic law considered her marriage to Zaghis annulled (after a period of three menstrual cycles to ensure that he would not also convert),[73] and she was automatically freed from all legal and economic responsibilities toward him. Her claims of coercion were likely intended to protect her own reputation and to slander that of Zaghis, who aggressively and repeatedly petitioned Venetian magistrates to give him full control over the assets she had left behind in Venice. Zaghis argued that Fatima's conversion, which he doubted was authentic, did not terminate their relationship "because the marriage cannot be dissolved for this reason, it ends only at death. Nor with her conversion do I become free to marry again; nor is extinguished the hope or the possibility that, just as she abandoned the faith of Christ . . . she could not freely return to it." He was, he lamented, effectively "tied . . . and unable to console myself with a new wife or other progeny."[74]

Despite this compelling argument, Fatima ultimately prevailed, and the Senate acknowledged the dissolution of her marriage, and her remarriage, and refused to grant Zaghis's claims on her estate, even though, as he correctly argued, ecclesiastical law favored his rights as her husband. To add insult to injury, the Senate awarded the income from Fatima's office in Venice to her sons, rather than her former husband, and paid off a 350-ducat debt she had in Venice.[75]

Whatever her motivations, Fatima's did not fit into the classic Pauline model of conversion as an instantaneous, transformative metamorphosis. Hers was clearly a conversion of convenience, more instrumental than spiritual. In the subsequent years, both Muslims and Christians believed that "internally she [was] not a Turk" but rather preserved her Christian identity behind an artificial Muslim mask. Several Venetian diplomats described her as "most Christian (cristianissima) of soul, even if she cannot show it externally," and they claimed that "were it not for the great love that the kapı ağası has for her, she would endanger her life."[76]

This tension between an authentic, internal self and the external performance of an assumed identity may strike a modern observer as untenable, if not hypocritical; however, this kind of dualistic self-presentation was widespread throughout the early modern world.[77] Catholics converted to Protestant sects and claimed to preserve the "true faith" in their hearts, while Calvin decried timorous Protestants who "simulated the practices of other religions to avoid persecution or to live comfortably."[78] In the Mediterranean, renegades appearing before the Inquisition without exception claimed to have been coerced into conversion, while retaining "the Holy Christian faith" internally. They performed the ritual demands of Islam but secretly continued to observe Christian fasts and dietary strictures, and women often affirmed that they surreptitiously baptized children born from relationships with Muslim men.[79] Inquisitorial manuals held that "those who apostatized for fear of death, but who remained faithful in their hearts, are not, properly speaking, heretics," and their trials were almost always ritualized formalities that defaulted in favor of absolution.[80] The same facade of outward conformity, called *taqiyya*, also existed throughout the Islamic world, particularly among Shiites; Muhammad ibn Jarir Al-Tabari wrote that if anyone, fragile women and children in particular, "is compelled and professes unbelief with his tongue, while his heart contradicts him, . . . no blame falls on him, because God takes his servants as their hearts believe."[81] Among Mediterranean Jewish communities, there was a diversity of opinion. Many rabbis condemned dissimulation, but Maimonides held that "force removed culpability" in instances in which Jews were compelled to convert outwardly. The most notable (though certainly not the only) example of Jewish dissimulation was in Spain, where conversos were widely suspected of, and Marranos widely engaged in, the practice.[82]

Whatever factors motivated Fatima to flee Venice for Istanbul, the decision seems clearly to have been a product of rational reflection. In her calculus, the "hoped-for-benefits" that awaited her in the Porte outweighed the potential "opportunity costs" associated with lost relationships and abandoned faith.[83] By relocating to Istanbul, Fatima positioned herself to profit from her brother's wealth, power, and protection, which he had used in the past to her benefit. As she herself indicated, Gazanfer had openly enticed her with promises of financial rewards, and she was aware of the economic opportunities that her transfer would make available to her family. In addition, Zaghis's interventions in her finances represented a serious threat to her economic and social status, and that of her sons as they prepared to enter into Venice's marriage market.[84] Her canniness in navigating both her conversion and her subsequent life in the Porte make it difficult to envision Fatima as simply a dupe in a game in which only her brother and her husband were players. She seems to have accepted the external sacrifice of her religion and the abandonment of her home as the price of defending herself from her grasping second husband and as a means to benefit herself and her two sons, whose welfare was one of her chief considerations.

Following her arrival in Istanbul, Fatima lived with her brother in the imperial palace until 1593, when she moved into another seraglio that Gazanfer had constructed to accommodate her. Because of her brother's status, many suitors sought her hand, and Gazanfer was eager to marry his sister as a means of establishing alliances with important individuals and families in the Porte, a common practice across the Mediterranean.[85] One suitor was a former *begler-begi* of Tripoli, who was already married to the daughter of the late Venetian kapudan paşa, Hassan; his hope was to obtain the admiralty through Gazanfer's support.[86] Fatima, however, "refused him" and other suitors for more than a year and a half. Gazanfer respected her wishes in part because sharia law required a previously married woman, unlike a new bride, to "express audible assent" to remarrying. Gazanfer was also invested in his sister's happiness—Venetian sources describe him as "lov[ing] her most cordially"—indeed, as we shall see, he fulfilled almost any request she made on behalf of herself, her sons at home, and even Venice's political interests.[87]

Fatima's single status could only be temporary, however, because Ottoman society, as much or more than Venetian, did not admit the possibility of a woman remaining unattached.[88] By June 1593 she had wed Ali Ağa, a protégé of her brother about whom relatively little is known. Contemporary sources describe him as "a private man, a scribe in the divan," a Circassian *sipahi* of the sultan, and the Ottoman biographer Mehmed Sürreya suggests Ali may have been Gazanfer's groom.[89] While we know little about the relationship between Fatima and her new husband, one observer described him as "lost in love" with his wife and noted the great influence she exerted over Ali, who did "nothing but what she desires."[90]

After their marriage, Ali advanced rapidly in the Ottoman hierarchy over the next decade. In 1596, when for the first time since Süleyman's reign, the sultan took personal command of his armies, Ali accompanied Gazanfer to Hungary and served as Mehmed III's personal messenger. In the grand parade on the departure to the front, Ali was regally dressed and carried a baton with heron feathers, an important Ottoman symbol of imperial status. He rode a "beautiful horse, black as night, with its rear covering completely embroidered in hammered gold with a scimitar, arrows, and a bow."[91] Following the Hungarian campaign, in early 1597 Selânikî reports that Ali became "chief doorkeeper." Later that year he became the *buyuk mirahur* (equerry-in-chief), in charge of the sultan's stables, animals, and carriages, as well as a staff of several thousand. In 1598 Ali hosted a banquet for the sultan and grand vizier near Istanbul, and later that year he and Gazanfer equipped 150 troops to battle Michael the Brave, the rebellious ruler of Wallachia. The following year he participated in a delegation that received several important visitors from the Iranian Safavid court.[92] In 1602 he briefly served as Ağa of the Janissaries, a position "of the first importance." With this he became a member of the Council of State, had precedence over all officials below vizier rank, rode at the sultan's side in military campaigns, and was Istanbul's police chief. Ali was unpopular with the Ottoman soldiery, however, in part because of his reputation for greed, and he only held this position for a few months.[93] During his years of influence, he was also an important patron of the arts: the great Ottoman poet Gânîzâde Mehmed Nâdirî composed his *Divân* at Ali's request and repeatedly praised him as the "great ağa."[94]

Fatima's adjustment to her new life, both before and after her marriage to Ali Ağa, was not without its challenges. Venice's chief diplomatic representative in Istanbul, Bailo Girolamo Cappello, described her as "most unhappy," with "continuous tears," and even suicidal over her "most abhorred state." For months she sought to console her guilt through "offerings, prayers, and continually asking God for forgiveness" and by seeking absolution from Rome.[95] At the same time, there is ample evidence that Fatima began to adapt, and even thrive, in her new setting; while she mourned the life she had left behind, she also exaggerated her desperation to retain the sympathy and support of Venetian officials.

As an aggregated member of the Ottoman elite, Fatima spent all her days enclosed in either her husband's, her brother's, or the sultan's seraglios. She was not permitted to move freely about the city and could only leave her velvet prison with chaperones and protection.[96] This was to be expected; Ottoman women of social standing were inevitably kept segregated, most often in a harem. This institution has attracted seemingly endless erotic curiosity in the West and has functioned as an iconic image of the powerless, objectified status of women in Islam.[97] Such voyeuristic fascination, however, ignores the complex functioning and status of the harem in early modern Ottoman society. Harem women wielded significant influence, which was a direct result of their cloistered status. When the sultans retreated into the harem in the latter sixteenth century, their mothers (the valide sultans), wives, consorts, and sisters, and other elite women grew in influence. Harem women patronized important public projects and charitable works; they also played an active and decisive role in affairs of state, including foreign relations. Instead of marginalizing them, their enclosure inside the harem ensured royal women regular access to the sultan and conferred on them great power in the early modern Ottoman state.[98]

As a cloistered member of the imperial inner circle, Fatima maintained regular outside contacts, both in Istanbul and in Venice, and she was able to use her enclosure and her newly acquired status as a means of exercising power in ways similar to the women of the imperial harem, though on a much more modest scale.[99] Fatima was clearly politically savvy; Venice's baili, the most experienced and capable members of its famed diplomatic corps, described her as "a woman of great valor and judgment," who ably navigated the corridors of power in the Porte. Over time she became conversant in the language and culture of the court, and for more than a decade, she enjoyed unusual access to the powerful women of the imperial palace and harem. Girolamo Cappello reported that she had "tremendous access to the seraglio and to the queen, where she does not fail to observe that which touches on the interests of [Venice]. She is very reserved however in speaking so as not to make herself more suspect, but where she is able she does not fail to serve and to warn."[100] During her years in the seraglio, she bore the honorific title of *hatun* (lady), with its connotations of dignity and status.[101]

Because of her access to the inner palace and other restricted

Harem scene
"Memorie turche" (MS Cicogna 1971, c. 24r). Biblioteca del Museo Civico Correr, Venice

spaces, and through her participation in the court's "female networks [which were] sustained through formal visiting rituals," she provided a perspective not normally available to Venice's male diplomats or their functionaries.[102] In a 1594 note to the bailo, for instance, she reported on discussions regarding the Ottoman military that she had overheard in the imperial harem. She provided an informed analysis of the situation of the sultan's fleet, its leadership and potential targets, and she supplied information about Ottoman military finances, including concerns in the Porte that cash flow problems and the failure to pay the military might lead to unrest. She also sketched out the many political rivalries within the palace.[103]

In 1596, Fatima sent a handwritten note to Marco Venier warning that the haseki's Jewish *kira* (lady-in-waiting), Esperanza Malchi, was trying to convince the sultan that Venice was assisting the

Austrians in their war with the Ottomans. She wrote, "I do not know what the Jews have found out about [Venice's actions], but they agitate greatly the sultana who is full of fire, and from what I have heard this Jewish woman . . . says that [the Venetians] are traitors; other particulars I really do not know, except that [Esperanza] is making every effort" to damage Venice's reputation. Based on this report, the bailo arranged a secret meeting with another influential woman in the harem, who sat hidden from view but confirmed through her kira what Fatima had written. The woman told Venier that Fatima "had worked vigorously with the queen in [Venice's] favor by cutting off the voice of whomever spoke against" the republic. This situation eventually boiled over into a heated argument "in front of the sultana" between Fatima and Esperanza.[104]

Fatima also prodded her brother to favor Venetian interests more consistently. For years Venetian baili had tried to enlist Gazanfer's support, but they were repeatedly rebuffed because he feared supporting his *patria* would compromise him politically. Even an impassioned request from his mother fell on deaf ears.[105] However, Fatima—who was reported to possess "supreme authority" with Gazanfer—was much more successful in influencing her brother. Her self-described technique was to play on his sympathy for her, particularly her loneliness for her sons, and to appeal to his vanity by suggesting how favoring Venice would raise his reputation in Christendom. This proved effective, she reported, "because these men delight in worldly recognition (*fumo mondano*), and they must be humored."[106] The results were indisputable: Gazanfer freed Venetian slaves, protected Venetian merchants, defended the sultan's Latin-rite Christian subjects, instructed the baili on navigating the ever-changing political world of the Porte, and worked behind the scenes to have Venice's friends in the Ottoman hierarchy placed in positions of power and its enemies neutralized.[107]

Gazanfer's pro-Venetian attitude was exemplified in 1594 when, at his sister's urging, he agreed to an unprecedented, secret, face-to-face encounter with Marco Venier inside the imperial seraglio. During their meeting, the kapı ağası described himself as "a true patriot" and encouraged the bailo to contact him directly at any time regarding any matter, promising it would immediately be taken before the sultan. Similar visits were arranged from then until the final week of Gazanfer's life.[108] There was, to be sure, a strict reciprocity to this relationship; Gazanfer expected Venetian officials to benefit his sister and her sons, to support his own political machinations, and to solidify his prestige by providing luxury goods and foods for the sultan and other dignitaries.[109]

~~

Even as Fatima worked to serve Venice's interests in the Porte, she was not averse to using her influence to benefit the social and financial standing of her family in the lagoon. The legal status of her sons, Baldissare and Giacomo, following the death of their father in 1588 is not made clear in the documents, though it is likely that Angelo would have made Fatima the children's guardian, as was the practice. If he died intestate, Venetian law required the mother and representatives of both families to resolve the question of guardianship in court, but judges usually decided in the mother's favor. Fatima's remarriage to Zaghis, however, posed a potential threat to her guardianship, as widows who remarried could lose custody of their children who "belonged to the lineage of their father" and therefore often lived with his family. In Venice, however, no law prevented a mother from continuing to raise children from a first marriage after remarrying if the families involved agreed, and examples of such arrangements were not uncommon.[110] This was the case for Baldissare and Giacomo, who remained with Fatima after their father's death, and after her remarriage to Zaghis as well. Their legal disposition after their mother's flight is murkier; they quickly became estranged from their stepfather, and while it seems reasonable to assume they passed to the care of their father's family, there is no archival evidence to prove this.

Whatever their legal situation, it is clear that Fatima remained closely involved in her sons' lives following her flight. After arriving in Istanbul, and before her marriage to Ali, Fatima arranged for two important Venetian patricians to serve as the boys' guardians. She was particularly attentive to their financial well-being. Before her flight, Fatima had been awarded the proceeds of an office through her brother's influence, and after her arrival in the Porte, she had Gazanfer intervene to ensure that its income of two hundred ducats a year be used to provide for her children. She subsequently negotiated for other important and lucrative Venetian administrative offices and pensions for her sons. She sent large sums of money, expensive jewels, and other goods to them, and in 1607 she used a portion of those funds to purchase a house in Venice from the nobleman Antonio Trevisan for 2,700 ducats. In 1595, Fatima engaged the prominent Venetian merchant Pasqualin Leoni "to take care of and to govern her two sons" in the place of their original patrician guardians. Leoni's relationship with Gazanfer and Fatima gave him extraordinary access to the imperial household, where he provided many luxury goods. In one instance, Fatima's intervention probably saved Leoni's life, which was threatened because of his role in the escape of several slaves. When Leoni returned to Venice in 1598, Fatima gave him "most ample liberty and authority" to manage her estate in Venice. Once Baldissare and Giacomo reached their teens, Fatima had her holdings placed in a partnership in which her sons each held equal shares that they could neither divide nor alienate.[111]

In addition to managing her financial situation in Venice, Fatima and her husband had extensive investments in Istanbul. Ali was involved in economic activities from international commerce to breadmaking, and he had a reputation among both Venetians and Ottomans as being "tyrannical and greedy," which contributed to his eventual downfall.[112] In early 1595, he invested sixteen thousand ducats with two Venetian merchants well known to Fatima, Agostino and Bernardino Agazzi, and he funded the purchase and refitting of a merchant ship with an additional eight thousand ducats.[113] Partnerships with Ottomans, though not uncommon, were forbidden by Venetian law. This was ignored, however, because although Ali contracted all the dealings, Fatima initiated the partnership herself for the benefit of her sons, and some portion of the investment funds came through her contacts within the imperial harem. The relationship quickly soured due to the Agazzi's fiscal mismanagement, compounded by the boat's shipwreck in 1599, and Ali and Fatima ultimately lost two-thirds of their initial investment. Furious at the loss, Ali used all his political connections to try and recoup his investment. The fallout caused concern in Venice that the affair might negatively impact Veneto-Ottoman relations, particularly after 1600 when the Agazzi brothers fled Istanbul and abandoned 200,000 ducats of merchandise.[114] The controversy continued after Ali's death in 1603, when the *baş defterdar* (head of finances) tried unsuccessfully to collect the debt on behalf of the sultan,[115] and as late as 1610 Fatima was still trying to recover eight thousand ducats and some of the investment in the ship, "which were rightfully hers as Ali's heir," from the Agazzis, who were now wealthy merchants living in Venice. In all these economic activities Fatima was supported by Gazanfer, who in fact used her connections to move some of his own wealth out of the reach of imperial confiscation.[116]

As these examples suggest, Fatima remained involved in the lives of her sons despite the distance that separated them. (Her daughter by Zaghis appears to have died in infancy.) Baldissare and Giacomo were both under ten at the time of her flight and so were sent by their noble tutors to a boarding school, known for its upstanding character, in the parish of San Barnabà in Venice.[117] From the time of Fatima's arrival, Gazanfer had desired to have his nephews join him in Istanbul. In part he seems to have wanted to surround himself with his family; in part he may have wanted to mollify his sister who suffered from ill health and was often disconsolate over the sons she had abandoned. Another factor was his sister's inability or unwillingness to produce children with Ali. In 1593 Gazanfer and a number of powerful allies exerted intense pressure on Venice to allow the boys to come to Istanbul to visit their mother. The Venetians responded with a series of improbable explanations about why the boys could not leave, including evoking Venetian law which prohibited "minors" from traveling to the dangerous Levant. The pressure became so great that the Venetian bailo secretly warned Fatima her children's souls were in danger, and she needed to "desist . . . from desiring" that they join her, which she did.[118]

During the winter of 1600, however, despite her wishes, Fatima's son Giacomo was kidnapped in a brazen act that became notorious throughout Venice.[119] The plan was hatched in Istanbul when Gazanfer met Zuanne Bustrone, a Cypriot nobleman, adventurer, and alleged renegade who was in the capital trying to avoid several debts owed in Venice. Bustrone had been captured during the 1571 siege of Cyprus and had for some years served the great Ottoman commander Lala Mustafa Paşa.[120] Gazanfer engaged Bustrone and another Cypriot refugee and commercial broker in Venice, Pietro Sansonetto, to spirit away his nephews. To gain access to the boys, Sansonetto enrolled his son in their school, and the young man and Giacomo, who thought his new young acquaintance "was a gentleman," quickly became fast friends. On the penultimate day of carnival in 1600, the two friends dressed in costume and went to Murano to celebrate. While eating dinner in a private home, Bustrone and his gang burst into the room armed with harquebuses and announced to Giacomo, "Sir, you need to come away with us, we want to take you to your mother in Constantinople."

The company set out in a small boat and rowed for four days before landing near Zara. From there they traveled thirty miles by foot across the frontier to an Ottoman castle, where Bustrone revealed to the conspirators that he had converted (probably reconverted) to Islam. Once in Ottoman lands, Gazanfer's name ensured them supplies and safe passage, and the party set out by horse for Istanbul. Initially, Giacomo resisted his captors, but after Bustrone told him "he was going to Constantinople to see his mother, and he would receive two or three million in gold, and then he would return to Venice," he quickly warmed to the adventure. The company traveled overland for two-and-a-half months before reaching the Golden Horn. On arrival, the kidnapers took the boy directly to his uncle's seraglio where he was kept incommunicado, and within days "they made him raise his finger and become a Turk." While in subsequent years Giacomo claimed to have been forcibly converted, there is no evidence of resistance on his part; indeed, he convinced Sansonetto's son to follow his example, describing "the delights and greatness" he enjoyed following his conversion. When he was finally permitted to meet the mother whom he had not seen for a decade, Giacomo told her "that he regret[ed] not having come here five years earlier."[121]

Following this initial enthusiasm, Giacomo, now called Mehmed, settled into a rather unremarkable existence. He was placed in the imperial palace and trained in its prestigious school, under his uncle's direct supervision. Gazanfer clearly had high aspirations for his nephew; however, despite being "flung into such a prominent position by the favorable influence of most partial Fortune," he quickly revealed himself to be "of obtuse intelligence" and ultimately proved a disappointment to his uncle.[122] On the heels of Gazanfer's death in early 1603, Mehmed left the seraglio, was awarded an office, and traded in silk and then grain, though with minimal success.[123] When his older brother died in 1614, Mehmed attempted to assert his claim to their mother's estate, claiming disingenuously that he could not "return to his patria, which has always been his will and firm intention," because of the "peril in which he would place himself," though he intended to do so "as soon as he is presented with a good opportunity."[124]

By 1633 Mehmed was bey of Kassandra, in Greece, but his bad luck continued, and due to a series of legal and financial problems, two of his three houses, one in Istanbul and one on the Black Sea, were looted and given to the kapudan paşa. In these years, Mehmed became a boon companion of Sultan Murad IV: Ottoman sources describe him as a member of a small circle of "foreigners" who goaded Murad on in his wine-fueled revelries, and in fact the Venetian was present when the sultan drank himself to death during Ramadan of 1640.[125] This is the last mention we have of Mehmed Bianchi, though it has been suggested that he lived on in the figure of Bekrī Muṣṭafā, a drunken buffoon character in Turkish and Arab shadow theater.[126]

The life of Fatima's son Baldissare, on the other hand, followed a decidedly more pedestrian path. After his brother's kidnapping, Fatima wrote Venice in a fury over the failure of her sons' wards to protect them. She requested that Baldissare, who had been formally engaged before a patrician witness a few months before his brother's disappearance, be married as quickly as possible. So Baldissare, though still quite young, wed Laura de Franceschi in the church of San Barnabà in June 1600.[127] The de Franceschi were cittadini originari with a long record of official service and have been described as one of the half dozen "formidable families" of the Venetian Chancellery. This was an auspicious marriage for a young citizen, especially one with a renegade mother.[128]

After his marriage, Baldissare moved in elevated circles, though there is no indication he requested formal recognition as a cittadino originario or took up a position in the chancellery. In 1609, he negotiated the marriage of his sister-in-law, Marina, to Girolamo Alberti, who in a curious coincidence had been posted to Istanbul from 1582 to 1599 as a dragoman and secretary and had certainly known of Gazanfer and Fatima. Baldissare paid Marina's dowry of four thousand ducats and provided her a splendid, large pearl necklace valued at over one hundred ducats. The 1610 wedding, and the subsequent baptisms of two nephews, Gasparo and Giovanni Battista, brought out an array of noblemen and the grand chancellor of Venice, and Baldissare's role in the marriage hints at his social and economic status among the Venetian elite.[129] He died in November 1614 with no surviving heirs.[130]

~

Fatima, her brother, and her son Mehmed were only together for several years before they were caught up once again in dramatic events. The turn of the century was a time of profound distress in the Ottoman Empire. The sultans were engaged in expensive and drawn-out wars in Hungary and Persia and faced major revolts in the Danubian principalities and in Anatolia. The economy saw rampant inflation, repeated coin debasements, and hemorrhaging imperial coffers. At the same time, the empire's population had doubled

in a century, producing large-scale migration and forced disloca-
tions. The sense that political inertia and ineptitude were only com-
pounding matters seriously threatened the centuries-old Ottoman
dynasty.[131]

Disgruntled members of the sultans' armies, outraged over long
campaigns, poor leadership, and payments that were in arrears or
devalued, repeatedly threw the capital into upheaval. The city's bur-
geoning coffeehouses were especially popular among the military
and were "centres of sedition" that religious and political leaders
tried repeatedly, but unsuccessfully, to control or ban.[132] In April
1600, soon after Mehmed Bianchi's arrival in the capital, soldiers
rioted over unpaid wages and murdered Fatima's nemesis in the
harem, Esperanza Malchi, and her son and dragged their mutilated
bodies through the city's streets. According to Selânikî, Gazanfer—
who with the valide sultan was perceived as the de facto power
behind the throne and was derisively called *sultan Gazanfer kapı
ağası*—only avoided the fury of the horde by promising to stay out
of government affairs.[133] His luck ran out, however, three years later.

Naima records that in the first days of January 1603, a mob of
imperial cavalry penetrated the palace and demanded an audience
with the sultan to consider "the state of the empire, everywhere torn
and afflicted with rebellion and insubordination."[134] The soldiers
complained to Mehmed III about military setbacks and the failure
of his advisers to address these problems, charging that his ministers were deceiving him about the empire's truly dire situation. The
rebels demanded reforms, including the exile of the sultan's mother,
who they believed was usurping his authority. When Mehmed refused this blatant insult to his honor, the soldiers countered with a
demand for Gazanfer's head. When the sultan tried again to refuse,
the infuriated mob demanded either the kapı ağası's life or the sultan's throne. Mehmed had no choice but to accept their demands.
Gazanfer was brought into the divan and stripped to the waist. He
begged his sovereign, whom he had known since Mehmed was a boy,
for mercy. The sultan attempted to stay the execution, but when the
soldiers saw the sultan's "fervent love, [they] refused, sayeng they

wold have his headd only, and all the rest of their lives should be spared." Mehmed issued the order, and according to Naima, the fifty-five-year-old Gazanfer was executed with "a sword the colour of water and as sharp as fire." His head rolled to the sultan's feet, and while the rebellious soldiers cheered so loudly it was heard across the Golden Horn, Mehmed wept fiercely "for having seen murdered before his very eyes the dearest person that he had in the world."[135]

The echoes of the downfall of the Venetian kapı ağası reverberated widely; all the major European diplomats in the Porte reported on the event,[136] as did the chief Ottoman chroniclers.[137] Gazanfer's death greatly affected his extensive patronage and kinship networks, particularly his sister and brother-in-law. His house was looted, and his great fortune (estimated at 500,000 ducats in cash and the same in jewels) reverted to the sultan. In addition, he became a convenient scapegoat among the ruling elite for many of the empire's ills. As an intimate ally and relative, Ali was in great danger and so "fled desperately with a single servant," leaving his wife Fatima behind in his seraglio. For a time, officials blanketed the city searching for him, but after passions died down, Ali met secretly with the revolt's leaders in a mosque, and with several well-placed bribes, he convinced them of his innocence and was able to return home. One evening several months later, however, he made the mistake of venturing out after dark. He was arrested and strangled between the doors of the seraglio on the orders of the sultan, who was in desperate need of funds and believed the rumors that Ali had a vast fortune squirreled away. These reports were proven accurate when the sultan's men dug up Ali's garden and broke his house apart, and discovered containers of cash, jewels, and other goods valued at almost 200,000 ducats.[138]

As these chaotic events unfolded, Fatima remained cloistered, no doubt fearing for her life. One report stated that she had "been blinded without knowing the reason," but this is uncorroborated, and it seems more likely that she was able to avoid retribution.[139] Indeed, despite claiming over the years that she desired to return to

Christendom, she made no effort to flee Istanbul. In part this was a practical decision. For over a decade she had been a wealthy and privileged court woman, and Islamic law dictated that she inherit a portion of her husband's (and perhaps even her brother's) estate. But because Ali had been executed for criminal acts and Gazanfer died without direct heirs, their wealth reverted to the sultan, leaving Fatima in a precarious financial position.[140] She remained in the city with her son, in hopes of receiving some reward from the bereaved sultan. After the disorder in the capital had subsided a few months later, in recognition of the loss of his friend and adviser Gazanfer, Sultan Mehmed gave her son an office with an income of fifty aspers daily, and he awarded Fatima a house in the capital so she could live "honorably."[141]

With this, Fatima fades from the historical record. We can assume that with the execution of her brother and the death several months later of Mehmed III, her access to the imperial harem, and therefore her political influence, came to an end. The Venetian baili who had lauded her so highly during her first decade in Istanbul fall conspicuously silent about her life. Notarial records, however, make occasional reference to Fatima's management of her estate in Venice. She rented the house she had purchased in 1607 to a lawyer for a hundred ducats annually, though she continued to hope it might be occupied by Baldissare, or even Mehmed if he were ever to return "into the bosom of our most holy Catholic faith." Two years later, in 1609 she directed her commercial agent in the lagoon to pass management of all her assets to Baldissare.[142]

The last mention we have of Fatima is a brief announcement of her death in 1613. She left a sizable estate, including her house in Venice; "three pieces of land" with walls, wells, and other structures; and thirty-two fields near Concordia in Friuli. As Baldissare had died without children and Mehmed remained in Istanbul, her will awarded her entire estate to three important Venetian religious institutions, the monastery of Santa Croce, the Hospital of the Pietà, and the Convertite.[143] Endowments of this sort to religious institutions were common among early modern Venetian women, and the large Franciscan convent Santa Croce was a regular recipient of women's bequests. The latter two beneficiaries, however, are more suggestive. The Hospital of the Pietà was the oldest and largest Venetian orphanage, charged, as one contemporary described, with the care of over a thousand "unhappy children, cast into whatever situation Divine Providence permitted" by the actions of their "iniquitous and unhappy mothers."[144] The Convertite was specifically dedicated to rescuing fallen women, particularly prostitutes and courtesans, and maybe even a renegade woman.[145] Perhaps in her last testament, Fatima was able finally to do her penance and find a degree of peace with her decision to abandon her home, her young children, and her religion for the prestige and fabulous wealth of the Porte.

CHAPTER TWO

Elena Civalelli / Suor Deodata and Mihale/Catterina Šatorović

FATIMA'S UNCONVENTIONAL LIFE played out on center stage in the eastern Mediterranean's two largest cities at the epicenters of its two dominant powers. Our next stories take us to the periphery of the Venetian and Ottoman empires, to the Dalmatian coast. The protagonists are two young women, girls really, both from respected families: Elena Civalelli, who was born in Zara in 1586, and Mihale Šatorović, born about twenty years later and 150 kilometers down the coast in the small town of Clissa. While the two girls shared much in common, what set them apart was a border; Elena was a Christian subject of Venice, Mihale a Muslim Ottoman. Though born on opposite sides of the political frontier and into different religious traditions, both girls were faced with similar circumstances when their parents attempted to arrange marriages for them at a young age. Both reacted by using the region's boundaries to withstand their parents' wishes and to follow a path of their own choosing. The tales of this Muslim and Christian girl illustrate some of the possibilities available to and limits upon young women in the early modern Mediterranean and the ways the region's political and religious boundaries could confer a degree of agency on them.

The setting for these stories was the fault line between the Ottoman and Venetian empires along the Dalmatian coast, whose physical space played a pivotal role in the dramatic lives of both Elena and

DALMATINA, O' SCHIAVONA.

Dalmatian woman
Cesare Vecellio, *De gli habiti antichi, et moderni* (Venice: Damian Zenaro, 1590)

Mihale. Dalmatia was where the Ottoman and Venetian empires adjoined most directly. Christians considered the region the *antemurale Christianitatis* (the breastwork of Christendom), and Fernand Braudel called it Venice's "limes." So close were the two that it was said that in Venetian Zara "you could hear the Turkish cock crow."[1] This simple binary view, however, ignores the region's complexity. In contrast to modern visions of well-demarcated, carefully defended political frontiers, the Veneto-Ottoman boundary in Dalmatia was imprecise and entirely porous, in constant flux both geographically and in the minds of the region's inhabitants. For people who had been pushed and pulled between the Venetians, the Ottomans, and the Habsburgs as they competed for their lands and their loyalties, the frontier often held minimal significance. Cross-border movement was regular and seamless. Ottoman and Venetian subjects mingled freely, and Muslims, though a minority in the region, were familiar sights in Venetian coastal towns.[2] In short, we should not make too much of Dalmatia's ephemeral borders; a shared culture characterized by similarity more than difference transcended the region's political and religious dividing lines.

To begin with, no one knew exactly where the actual border was located. Though a series of joint Venetian and Ottoman delegations in the sixteenth and seventeenth centuries tried to identify and mark the contours of this frontier, confusion led to an endless flow of letters between Venetian counts and Ottoman *sancak begs* and to the occasional redrawing of the official boundary.[3] On the ground, there was even greater confusion about, and indifference to, the political demarcations agreed to by rulers in distant capitals. Subjects on the frontiers of these composite states generally viewed the Veneto-Ottoman border as highly permeable and often ignored or actively manipulated its territories and jurisdictions.[4]

This lack of clarity gave rise to regular incidents along the confines. Animals were stolen, contraband moved discretely, children and adults kidnapped for ransom, punctuated by the occasional murder.[5] These acts elicited regular complaints from officials on both sides of the border. In 1591 the *beglerbegi* of Bosnia protested that

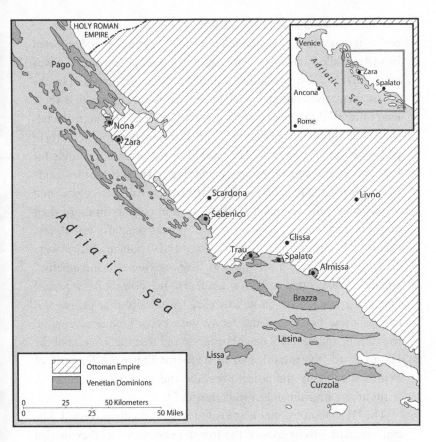

Dalmatia

"Franks" from Venice's Dalmatian fortresses were making "continual incursions" into Ottoman territory. Several years later, a number of important Venetian officials complained about Ottomans who came "to steal souls" and argued for the need to defend farmers in their fields.[6]

We should not assume, however, that conflict always characterized Veneto-Ottoman relations. Officials regularly reported that Venetians and Ottomans lived "in peace and quiet and with excellent understanding."[7] It is tempting to assign a broader significance to border incidents, but in many instances they were simply local criminal issues characteristic of liminal regions and possessed no real religious or political character. As one Venetian official reported in 1582, while violence was not unknown along the frontier, it was often carried out by "common thieves" who were "expelled by the Turks themselves because of their wicked nature. I say that these men cause all the tribulations along these borders." Ottoman officials similarly acknowledged the efforts of their Venetian counterparts in preserving peace and order.[8] In fact, the most persistent trouble for both Venetians and Ottomans in the late sixteenth century came from the piratical Uskoks who swarmed the Adriatic coasts[9] and unruly local populations that often acted in contravention of their metropole's policies.[10] While the detente was regularly tested, and occasionally broke down, both Venetian and Ottoman officials were charged by their respective rulers to "live together well and quietly," and indeed they often worked in tandem to preserve the *bona pace*.[11] One Ottoman official wrote in 1582, "We desire that people will live on these borders in the future with every kindness, in good friendship, and peaceful neighborliness, and that the subjects of the Happy Lord [the sultan], and of the Most Illustrious Signoria of Venice, may freely and peacefully come and go as good friends . . . without any impediment or molestation."[12]

The Dalmatian frontier was easily and continually traversed. The transhumant Vlachs crossed the frontier constantly as they herded their cattle, and in the region's conflicts, they variously sided with both the Ottomans and the Venetians, and even the Uskoks at times. Soldiers defending the Venetian frontier might live in Ottoman lands, Venetian subjects regularly crossed the border to work in Ottoman fields or to grind their wheat in Ottoman mills, and Ottoman subjects routinely pastured animals on, worked, and even rented Venetian lands.[13] So common was this that Venetian officials attempted repeatedly, but entirely unsuccessfully, to legislate against cross-border agricultural activity. Families, too, straddled the region's religious and political frontiers. The Dominican organist of the cathedral of Sebenico had numerous Muslim relatives in Ottoman territory, including his mother and a brother-in-law who was a "Turkish priest."[14] Friendship and marriage across the border were also so widely practiced that Christian officials warned such "familiarity presents an occasion for many sins."[15]

The cross-border trade was significant too; in the mid-sixteenth century it totaled 400,000 ducats annually. Dalmatian exports of "salt, salted fish, draperies, oil, spices, [and] worked wax" were valued at over 150,000 ducats and were exchanged for Ottoman "cheese, meat, honey, wax, slavins, and pelts." Cattle from Ottoman lands were an important part of the coastal cities' diets, but it was Ottoman grain on which Venetian Dalmatia was utterly dependent; in 1593 Zara could produce only enough to feed itself for several months of each year.[16] Dalmatian fairs attracted merchants from both sides of the border, and Ottoman traders were a common sight in Dalmatian towns, particularly in their taverns and guesthouses.[17] In Zara, the Ottoman commercial presence was so large that an Ottoman *emin* (official of the sultan) resided in the city to collect taxes and act as a sort of consular official.[18] Venice tried to limit this presence by requiring the Ottomans to turn over their weapons and forbidding them to stay in the city overnight "under the paine of imprisonment." For a time the Venetians also tried to funnel Ottoman merchants to a location outside Zara, called San Marco, "so that they do not have cause to come into the city," though as with other attempts, this met with little success.[19] Cross-border intellectual dialogue also occurred, as dialectical variations of the same language were spoken on both sides of the frontier. When the well-known Ottoman scholar Mustafa Ali went as secretary to the sancak beg of Clissa, he consulted on a thorny ethical issue with "Venetian, Serbian, and Croatian religious men."[20]

The Dalmatian border was not demarcated along religious lines either. Christians were in the majority on both sides of the frontier, with islands of Muslims and small communities of Jews. Conversions between faiths were not uncommon, though the difficult decades after Lepanto created a significant out-migration from Venetian territories of desperate and ambitious people into the Ottoman Empire.[21] Commenting on the inhabitants of Clissa, a Venetian official identified several factors that facilitated this religious nomadism: "They are of the Serbian faith, but because they practice their religion but little, and receive little instruction in it, and because of the lack of priests, their faith is rapidly weakening." In part this pliable faith resulted from a shortage of religious personnel; in 1579 Spalato had only twenty-eight impoverished priests for its five parishes, significantly less than other, similarly sized towns. In the end, the endurance of shared popular beliefs and practices blurred the distinction between Muslim and Christian. Muslim converts continued to "read the Gospels, circumcised their children, believed that Mohammed was the Holy Ghost, and drank wine even during Ramadan."[22] They made offerings and prayers to the patron saint of Zara, Saint Simeon, who they believed was a "great servant of God" and whose relics made Zara "impregnable."[23] In short, despite the occasional efforts by political and ecclesiastical authorities to define a clearly delineated boundary, the shared local culture and identity trumped distant political divisions and theological distinctions.

It is against this backdrop that Elena Civalelli's story had its beginnings. The Civalelli were an ancient Dalmatian noble family, one of fifteen that had politically dominated the fortified port city of Zara for centuries.[24] Since Roman times, Zara had been "the key of Dalmatia";[25] all ships that plied the Adriatic called in its "absolutely safe harbour," and as an archdiocese it was peppered with monasteries and churches, including the popular pilgrimage destination Saint Simeon.[26] In 1409, Zara came under direct Venetian rule, though the cities' destinies had long been intertwined. By the sixteenth century, Zara's most important role was military; its universally admired fortifications[27] made the city a bulwark of Venice's maritime defense network and, for some, of "all Christianity."[28]

These defenses were repeatedly tested in the sixteenth century as Venice and the Ottomans brawled over Zara. While the fortifications outlasted every attack, the peace of 1573 reduced the city to an isolated coastal outpost, with almost no hinterland, and this profoundly affected both Zara's ability to feed itself and its access to inland markets. Contemporary commentators decried Zara as "full of defects, shortages, and needs." Its urban population plummeted, and many rural villages on its outskirts were abandoned. Poverty rose, while the port silted up and docks collapsed, greatly diminishing the coastal city's commercial lifeblood. The population of the city and its countryside declined precipitously, from 23,829 in 1553 to 14,660 in 1573 to 13,774 by 1593. In 1596 the urban center numbered just 5,390 inhabitants.[29] Food shortages were endemic; whereas previously Zara "provided food for a large part of Dalmatia," it now produced barely enough to feed itself for four or five months out of every year and depended for the rest on shipments of Ottoman grain.[30]

The Civalelli's fortunes, and in turn Elena's young life, were closely linked to these broader developments. During the Middle Ages, the family had possessed extensive agricultural holdings and highly lucrative salt pans on the island of Pago.[31] Under Venetian rule, the Civalelli were regarded as among the *dominante*'s "most faithful subjects." Their men served Venice with distinction in the military,[32] and in the church as well; indeed, the "last male of the casa Civalelli" was Gregorio, bishop of Scardona (Skradin), who died in 1713.[33] By 1500, however, the family's fortunes had begun to shift. Venetian monopolization of the salt trade led to a 75 percent reduction in the Civalelli's salt pans between 1350 and 1450.[34] In 1555 the family's income was estimated at between four hundred and seven hundred ducats annually. Although this placed them among Zara's wealthiest noble families, such a distinction was relative in a region described as "universally very poor," and among a nobility who, "not wanting to cede their nobility nor deigning to do any industry, live in great misery and poverty" on lands that were "derelict and uncultivated." Some noble families, including the Civalelli, attempted to adapt by becoming involved in trade and shipping, but as one diplomat observed, in comparison to Zara's nobles, "the rest of the people [were] much better off."[35] Civalelli political fortunes were on the decline as well. In the mid-sixteenth century, the family provided one of the smallest contingents of cavalry for Zara's defense, only 3 of the 130 total.[36] Their reduced status probably fed their violent rivalry with one of Zara's most powerful noble clans, the Tetrici, which spilled into the streets in 1553, resulting in the murder of members of both families and threatening the peace of all Zara for a time.[37]

One Civalelli family member likely involved in this vendetta was Elena's father, Francesco Civalelli, son of Pietro Civalelli.[38] Francesco married Donna Isabetta, probably some time in late 1584,[39] and she gave birth to their first child, Elena, on January 15, 1586. The rector of San Simeon, the most important church in Zara, christened the newborn, an honor accorded only rarely to the most important Venetian and Zaratine families, and several of the city's nobles stood as her godparents. Isabetta gave birth to two more daughters in quick succession: Catterina in September 1588 and Geronima in April 1590.[40] Three daughters to dower presented a daunting proposition to any father, and by the time of Geronima's birth, Francesco Civalelli's finances were in dire straits.

Like many other impoverished nobles, Francesco was employed in Venice's large military contingent defending his hometown.[41] Among six or seven hundred soldiers, he was one of fifteen specially trained gunners, which provided a small income of fifty ducats annually that was the primary support for his young family.[42] In the inflationary late-sixteenth century, this meager stipend did not go very far, and many married soldiers supplemented their incomes by "gathering grass, firewood, and hay, which they then [sold]." Despite this, during "such penurious" years, many became heavily indebted "because of their small stipends," which were irregularly paid.[43]

These were difficult years throughout the Mediterranean, particularly in Dalmatia. In 1589 a ferocious summer storm destroyed four thousand fruit and olive trees, many vineyards, and "cast the grain to the ground." The following year was "extremely calamitous and scarce." An earthquake preceded "a terrible harvest of grain and legumes" and grapes, and the ensuing famine forced people to rely on Venetian handouts of "small, poor bread."[44] As was always the case, children suffered disproportionately in these hard times: in 1585 almost 15 percent of the 205 children born in Zara were abandoned.[45] Faced with his meager income and limited opportunities in Zara, as well as broader socioeconomic disruptions, Elena's father was poised to follow a course of action that would lead to the dissolution of his family, the abandonment of his children, and the eventual loss of his oldest daughter.

In 1588, Francesco Civalelli and Elena's sixty-year-old maternal grandmother set out from Zara for Istanbul. They came at the request of Isabetta Civalelli's brother, Omer Ağa. Omer was a renegade Christian eunuch from Zara, whose date and circumstances of arrival in the Porte are unknown. It is quite possible that he had been captured during the War of the Holy League in 1571, when Dalmatia was the target of numerous raids and skirmishes, and the city of Zara was besieged.[46] Many Zaratines were taken captive and sold into slavery in this period, which led to a precipitous drop in population.[47] However Omer had arrived in Istanbul, by the time of his mother and brother-in-law's visit in 1588, he had risen to a position of influence within the imperial palace. Selânikî describes Omer as "an apprentice" to Gazanfer Ağa in the palace's inner service who then replaced "taster Mehmet Agha of the kitchen management" before returning to the seraglio in 1597 as the *saray ağası* (ağa of the palace). Omer acquired a reputation as a "wise [and] shrewd person" destined for higher office, perhaps eventually that of his patron, Gazanfer Ağa.[48]

As saray ağası and one of Gazanfer's five chief lieutenants, Omer wielded great power. He was charged with the safety and order of the inner palace, commanded a guard of fifty eunuchs, and was one of the few ağas who was permitted to speak to the sultan.[49] As a result, Venice sought to curry his favor in return for his support of its political objectives.[50] He was at the center of many palace intrigues: for example, Selânikî assigns him a prominent role in the murder of the sultana's kira, Esperanza Malchi, in 1600. The next year he lost his position in the palace under pressure from members of the ulema, the *valide sultan,* and the army. He was able to ride out Gazanfer Ağa's 1603 execution, however, and was soon thereafter awarded a prime position in Anatolia; some suggested a promotion to paşa or even a vizier was inevitable.[51]

Soon after his mother and brother-in-law arrived in Istanbul in 1588, Omer requested that his sister (Elena's mother), Isabetta, be permitted to join them. Although there were suspicions about his intentions, because he had made no overt attempt to convert his mother and had even settled her in Istanbul's international enclave in Galata so she could attend the Latin-rite churches there, the Senate approved the request on the condition that the Civalelli's three young children remain in Zara as surety for their parents' return. Francesco returned to Zara in late 1589 to retrieve his wife, and though rumors about Omer's intentions persisted, in the end his reassurances and the couple's "most high hopes" of achieving fortune allayed these concerns.[52] This sort of nomadism was not uncommon among early modern Italian nobles, who in times of difficulty often placed themselves in the military service of other European (and Ottoman) rulers, regardless of their religious affinities.[53] And, too, the Civalelli certainly were familiar with Zaratine contemporaries who had migrated to Ottoman lands, found success, and then were followed by other family members.[54]

After leaving their young children in the care of a family member, Francesco and Isabetta set out for Istanbul, where they arrived in early September 1590 and were met with great acclaim and honor. A private boat conveyed them to the house of the influential Mustafa Ağa, and they began to settle in. Isabetta soon met her brother, whom she had not seen for years, who, despite his promises to the contrary, began "to tempt them lovingly to become Turks." When this failed, "the threats began." These too were unsuccessful, and so in a potent act of theater, Omer brought out his and Isabetta's mother, who converted in front of her daughter and son-in-law and then "began to beg [them] to do the same." (It was subsequently revealed that this scene had been staged; the woman had converted a year earlier and had conspired with Omer to bring her daughter to Istanbul and to convert her to Islam.) Elena's young parents nevertheless continued to resist for "a great number of hours." Eventually Omer, whose primary objective was clearly his sister, had her "taken away by force" and locked in isolation in Mustafa Ağa's seraglio. There, he alternately threatened and cajoled Isabetta, plying her with promises of wealth and power, and giving her gifts of expensive jewels and clothing. In the end, "after three days she was finally induced to become a Turk."[55]

When word of this reached the Venetian bailo, Girolamo Lippomano, he confronted Omer and accused him of lying and behaving in a way "contrary to humanity, [as] all religions find repugnant that anyone should be made to change faith through force." A furious Omer insisted "his mother and his sister had become Muslims voluntarily." To avoid scandal, however, the renegade agreed to release his badly beaten brother-in-law, who no longer served him any purpose as he intended to marry Isabetta to a sancak beg. As Elena's father left, "stripped, all lacerated, and despoiled, and bearing the face of death," his brother-in-law offered him five hundred ducats compensation for the loss of his wife.[56]

Francesco Civalelli was taken to the Venetian bailate, where he spent months recovering from his severe injuries. He appeared to all who saw him a "unique example of every sorrow," haunted by the loss of his wife, fearful for the safety of his children, and traumatized by the collapse of his fragile finances. He also was in danger; Omer Ağa had quickly repented of freeing his brother-in-law and began attempting to regain custody of him, no doubt because of his sister's refusal to acquiesce to a new spouse. For a time Francesco's life hung in the balance; fearing the worst, he dictated a testament requesting that the Venetian Senate continue paying his meager salary "for the sustenance of his children" and that they be "placed in the orphanages of Venice, and preserved in the Christian religion."[57]

This request took on unexpected significance when, in August 1591, after his injuries had healed, Francesco abruptly converted to Islam. This unanticipated turn of events was inspired by "the greatness of the promises" Omer had made him, but even more by the possibility of being reunited with his wife. Isabetta had embraced, or at least accepted, her new faith—documents describe her as "established in being a Turk"—but she had refused Omer's attempts to remarry her.[58] Under Islamic law Muslim women could only be married to Muslim men. In cases in which only one spouse converted, a "waiting period" was required before the marriage could be annulled; if the non-Muslim spouse converted in the interim, the law decreed "then their marriage continues."[59] So for Francesco and Isabetta, conversion was the only way they could begin to reconstitute their shattered family. Following the couple's reunion, Omer delivered on his promises; Francesco, now called Jusuf Ağa, was made a *çavuş* (member of the courier corps) with an income of six hundred ducats annually, and soon after he was awarded a timar (land grant) near Zara. He was also given oversight of several areas in Dalmatia in order to deal with the persistent problems with Uskoks, and eventually he became a member of the sultan's personal escort.[60] Civalelli's *in extremis* request to the Senate and his subsequent apostasy set in motion a series of events that would eventually result in a breach with his daughter Elena, her defiance of his will, and a diplomatic standoff over the direction of her young life.

When Elena's parents departed for Istanbul, they left their three daughters and a natural brother in the care of a relative in Zara, but "in great poverty." After Francesco and Isabetta's conversions, Omer Ağa began to investigate the possibility of reuniting his sister's fractured family by bringing her children to join them. To this end he freed a Zaratine slave in the Ottoman capital and promised him "a great prize" if he would "steal" Elena. The *provveditore generale in Dalmazia e Albania,* the chief Venetian administrative and military official in Dalmatia who was based in Zara,[61] caught wind of the plot, however, and Elena and her siblings were quickly moved to the care of the nobleman Colonel Ettore Martinengo, governor of the fortress of Zara, to whom the Civalelli were linked by ties of god-parentage.[62]

For Elena, this transfer was only temporary. In October 1591 the embassy secretary in Istanbul warned that given the ongoing threat

Casa delle Zitelle
Giovanni Merlo, *Vero e real disegno della inclita cita di Venezia,* detail (Venice, 1696).
Biblioteca del Museo Civico Correr di Venezia, Venice

to the children, Venice ought to take steps "to preserve to Our Lord
Christ those poor souls."[63] In response, the Council of Ten, Venice's
most powerful ruling body, decided in early 1592 to move Elena
from Zara to the lagoon, to the Casa delle Zitelle.[64]

If this had simply been a matter of Elena embracing the life of a
religious, there were five convents in Zara to choose from; however,
the primary issue was the young girl's protection. Zara's proximity
to the frontier, the continual presence of Ottomans in the city, and
the regularity of kidnappings on the frontier were all cause for concern. Additionally, an episcopal visitation found Zara's convents
crowded and in bad repair, noting that the nuns had the habit of
occasionally leaving the cloister and wandering through the city
"either for devotion or for recreation."[65]

In contrast, Venice's Casa delle Zitelle, founded in 1559, had a mission to shelter and educate poor, attractive "virgins in peril" of falling into a life of sin.[66] Located on the Giudecca, the house was geographically off the beaten path, and the girls were cloistered and watched over "every hour of the day." Thus, the Zitelle represented an attractive refuge for young Elena, in danger not of prostitution but of conversion. Normally, girls had to be nine to ten years of age to enter the house (in 1597, of the house's 184 wards, 60 percent were ten to nineteen, and 28 percent twenty to twenty-nine), but an exception was made for Elena, who was at most six years old when she was admitted. The majority of her fellow Zitelle residents were from Venice proper and, like Elena, came not from the absolute margins of society but from "families who had fallen on hard times."[67]

Daily life in the Zitelle was highly regulated. The girls dressed in identical cream-colored dresses and were instructed in basic religious doctrines, prayer, the rosary, and singing, to inculcate in them "true virtues, like humility, obedience, purity, and the mortification of their will." They were also taught to read and write, and they devoted part of their day to making handiwork, which was sold to help cover their expenses. The house was staffed entirely by women, and contact with all men, except the house doctor and confessor, was forbidden.[68] Unlike a traditional convent, the Zitelle was a way station that protected and prepared the inmates for the two options available to early modern Italian women: marriage or the veil. The house's constitution decreed that the young women were to remain in the house for not less than five years, after which "they could choose in absolute liberty marriage or the monastery." Most chose to marry; only 10 to 15 percent took the veil.[69]

Elena remained in the Zitelle until 1597, and she would have stayed longer had her unusual family situation not caught up with her. Despite their conversion, Elena's parents continued from a distance to oversee their lands in Zara and to play a role in their children's upbringing. Indeed, her two younger sisters at some point joined their parents in Istanbul, though the records provide no details as to how this came about.[70] In September 1597, Elena's father suddenly reappeared in Zara and informed the city's governors of "his intention" to see his daughter. He was no doubt shocked when he received a carefully worded reply, dated October 31 from the Venetian Collegio, informing him that his daughter could not meet with him because she had "already many days ago" taken vows to become a nun, and was now "on the verge of putting on the habit and cloistering herself in the convent . . . [therefore] she cannot leave there, nor does she wish to." The Collegio assured Civalelli that Elena would continue to receive "all necessary comforts and . . . every possible courtesy" from its officials and offered the prodigal father two suits of silk so he would "depart contented and [would] give a good report of the treatment he received to his influential brother-in-law Omer Ağa," whom Venice did not wish to alienate.[71]

Although the official position maintained that Elena had already taken her vows, the truth was that Venetian officials had hastily transferred her to a convent only after her father's appearance in Zara. This was done "to liberate the young woman from the danger that loomed over her," but not without ascertaining that "she was content to pursue this action." In fact, it was not until November 2, over a month after her father's initial inquiry, that an account book in the Zitelle noted, "Elena the Slav went as a nun to Corpus Domini."[72] Carrying out this rapid transfer required unusual measures; the patriarch of Venice, Lorenzo Priuli, had to intervene "with great charity" with the governors of Corpus Domini for her to be admitted into the convent in such an unorthodox fashion. The Senate in turn decreed it would be a "convenient and pious act" to assist Elena and awarded her two hundred ducats for her spiritual dowry, plus a ducat a month "for the rest of her life" for clothing and personal necessities. This was quickly raised to five ducats monthly and subsequently supplemented by several grants of fifty ducats to cover extraordinary clothing expenses.[73] Elena was now effectively a ward of the state.

While the Venetian Senate hoped that her entry into Corpus Domini would permanently resolve the matter, the contest for Elena was just beginning. Her father's sudden appearance in Zara and his insistent inquiries were not random occurrences. As the niece of an influential Ottoman official, Elena represented a valuable component in her family's political machinations, and Omer and her father intended to expand the family's patronage network, influence, and wealth by arranging a favorable marriage for the young girl. In the early modern Mediterranean, Muslims, Christians, and Jews all practiced arranged marriage.[74] Law and custom generally protected a child's right of refusal, but there were many instances of daughters (and sons) being forced or coerced into unwanted marriages. While somewhat less common in Islamic regions, in Christian Europe the practice was widespread enough that one of the major Tridentine reforms attempted to prevent "tyrannical fathers" from imposing unwanted unions on their children.[75]

Unwilling to relinquish their plans for Elena, her father and uncle tried to leverage Omer's influence in the Porte. Omer met with Venice's bailo in Istanbul and insisted that the family cared only for the girl's well-being, that her father intended to marry her in Zara to someone of her own choosing "who [would] be pleasing to her," and that he personally would provide her with a generous income. Venice's rulers, however, held firm; the decision, they responded, had been Elena's. She had "demonstrated a great desire and inclination to enter into this monastery," and since her vow was immutable, Venice's only option was to support her financially, which it did and would continue to do, out of its great respect for her powerful uncle.[76]

Undaunted, in the spring of 1599, Omer hatched an ambitious plan to marry Elena to Ioan (called Stefan) Bogdan, a pretender to the title of *voivode* (prince or governor) of Moldavia.[77] Born around 1570, Bogdan was the son of Iancu Şaşul, who briefly ruled Moldavia from 1579 to 1582, and Maria Paleologa, of the Byzantine imperial line. Following Iancu's assassination, the family resided for a decade in Poland before moving to Venice in 1593 to pursue Bogdan's claim as voivode. Soon after arriving, his sister, Voica, married Zuanne Zane, scion of an influential Venetian patrician clan. This unusual match had clearly been carefully planned, as Zuanne's relative, Bailo Matteo Zane, was quickly enlisted to use his position in Istanbul to advance the family's claims to the Moldavian throne.[78]

The Danubian principality of Moldavia was an important source of agricultural commodities and raw materials for the Ottoman Empire, indeed Selim II claimed that Moldavia produced "the majority" of Istanbul's provisions.[79] Since the late fifteenth century, the region had been a nominally independent Ottoman tributary state. Moldavia's voivodes were elected by an assembly of boyars and clergy and confirmed by the sultan.[80] By the late sixteenth century, however, bribes and political intrigue in Istanbul, Moldavia, and Europe were needed to acquire the office, and the voivode required an additional 650,000 ducats in annual gifts to the sultan and other officials in order to retain it. This produced a revolving door of voivodes; between 1590 and 1600 the office changed hands eight times among men who enjoyed little legitimacy and even less power. So severe was the disorder that in 1595 the Ottomans attempted (and failed) to bring Moldavia under their direct rule.[81]

As one of many pretenders, Stefan Bogdan was in constant search of allies and funds to pursue his tenuous claim to the throne. Following his Venetian interlude, he moved to Istanbul, where he attempted to use his connections and limited resources (including reputedly Attila the Hun's jewel-encrusted battle sword) to buy support among influential Ottomans and Europeans.[82] Key to his strategy was establishing kinship bonds through marriage to advance his claim— in Venice to the Zane, and in Istanbul to the Civalelli and, through them, Omer Ağa. Bogdan intended to use these ties, along with well-placed gifts and bribes, to obtain the voivodeship by imperial appointment, rather than trying to win election by the fractious Moldavian boyars.

In November 1594 Murad III appointed Bogdan to rule Moldavia's neighboring principality, Wallachia, in an attempt to quell unrest and restore order to this important region. After kissing the sultan's hand, Bogdan joined the Ottoman army raised to insert him on the throne and headed north.[83] On January 25, however, the smaller army of Wallachia's ruler, Michael the Brave, routed the sultan's army of fourteen thousand at Rusciuk (in modern-day Bulgaria). Over seven thousand troops were killed, including the Ottoman commanders Hassan Paşa and Mustafa Paşa, and Bogdan barely escaped the battlefield with a small band of men. He returned to Istanbul but found, not surprisingly, that he had fallen from favor with the new sultan, Mehmed III.[84]

Notwithstanding this setback, Bogdan continued his single-minded quest. Fortune did not smile on him, however, and following a series of political and financial reversals, in 1597 the cash-strapped young man was forced to take refuge in the Venetian embassy to escape the ambassador of Poland-Lithuania's intrigues to have him murdered or forcibly converted.[85] It was during this time that the scheme to marry Elena was concocted. All parties stood to benefit from the match: Bogdan hoped to win crucial support within the imperial palace for his claim; Omer Ağa sought to gain an important ally and extend his patronage network; and the Civalelli family hoped to see their daughter again.

The plan was set in motion in late summer 1599 when Bogdan set out for Venice. His first challenge was to contact Elena, who was "held in close custody" in Corpus Domini. With the assistance of his brother-in-law and other influential friends, Bogdan discovered that the girl had not yet taken her final vows and thus could still change her mind. Encouraged that he might still be able "to achieve his desired objective," the young man unsuccessfully struggled for a time to establish direct contact, but he eventually succeeded in smuggling Elena a letter from her parents by way of the convent's confessor, who read it to her in confessional.[86]

Following this initial contact, Bogdan had the Zane family and other interested parties exert pressure on young Elena to leave the Zitelle. According to her confessor, this created a "disturbance . . . in her mind." She expressed a willingness to accept as God's will "that which [her parents and uncle] had decided," but she refused to act without the doge's approval, as he had paid her spiritual dowry and was "her special protector." Heartened, Bogdan appeared before the

Signoria, whose members seemed initially "well disposed" to his proposal but then unexpectedly made an about-face when "enemies" whispered allegations that he planned "to take the girl to Istanbul to become a Turk, as he himself had done." Bogdan tried to counter these rumors in a second audience, but the Signoria, which was "very cautious especially in matters of the faith" involving women and children, balked.[87]

In an attempt to break the deadlock, Bogdan turned to his allies in Istanbul, to Omer Ağa and Bailo Girolamo Cappello. Cappello, who had become like a father to the young man during his two years' residence in the Venetian embassy, was initially skeptical of the scheme, until he learned that Elena had not yet professed. He wrote his peers that Bogdan was "totally constant in the most holy faith of Christ" and that his intentions toward Elena were entirely honorable. Beyond religion, Cappello urged the Signoria to consider the political stakes. Venice stood to gain not just an ally on the Moldavian throne but, more importantly, a friend in Omer Ağa, who enjoyed "great authority in the seraglio," possessed extensive connections to influential individuals in the Porte, and seemed destined for even greater heights. Elena's uncle, the bailo wrote, "desired nothing more than the conclusion of this marriage," and he had explicitly tied his continued support of Venice to this request. In other words, Cappello argued, the political benefits to be gained from acquiescing to the marriage far outweighed any unsubstantiated concerns about the soul of Elena.[88]

It took two months for Bogdan's October letter to reach Istanbul, and Cappello's reply did not arrive in Venice until February 1600, much too late to influence the debate. While Bogdan attempted to muster support for his case, Venice's rulers were mobilizing to ensure that Elena's desire to remain in the convent was respected. For despite her wavering and Bogdan's clearly optimistic report to Omer Ağa (who had already paid a significant advance on her dowry), Elena ultimately decided to continue on the path she had begun and to take her vows.

On October 30, the Collegio returned to the case when one of the patrician procurators of Corpus Domini presented two documents. The first was a fascinating letter from Elena, "written in my own hand," recounting the dramatic events of her young life: "For twelve continuous years . . . I have been overwhelmed by infinite dangers to my soul, . . . in 1588 I was deprived of my natural father, Mr. Francesco Civalelli from Zara, who was cunningly and with violence persuaded by his impious brother-in-law to distance himself from the faith of Christ. I, too, running the same risk . . . was received into the religious bosom of my dear natural prince, nourished and raised up in the true faith, and many times preserved from the hands of the demon." After entering Corpus Domini, Elena reported, she was "awakened by the Holy Spirit" and decided on a religious vocation. For eighteen months she lived as a nun and prayed continually "for the illumination of the blinded minds of my miserable mother and father." When her novitiate year had passed, she received permission from the patriarch to take her vows; however, "the tempter Lucifer did not fail to oppose my most affectionate desire" and permission was retracted when "a doubt was planted that I had not reached the necessary age." At the same time, her father, "distanced from his paternal duties," was "trying to contaminate my intention, and to distract me by way of diabolical ministers . . . from the dear religion in which I live most contentedly." She concluded by gendering her relationship with Venice, her new "father," and requesting that the Collegio defend her from her "natural father" by petitioning Rome for permission to take her vows, whether or not she had "the age [required] by the sacred decrees"—though, as she insisted, and as an inquiry formed by the patriarch had found, her age was "legitimate."[89]

The second document presented to the Collegio, was a letter from the vicar of the staunch reformist patriarch of Venice, Cardinal Lorenzo Priuli, who had met with Elena to ensure that neither religious nor government officials had manipulated the young girl in her decision.[90] During his visit that morning, he had found Elena "with excellent disposition and readiness to live as a religious, and she showed great desire to profess as soon as possible . . . She said to me with great steadfastness, and with very firm resolution, that she hopes, with the help of the divine grace, that she will be a good servant of the Lord." The vicar's assessment was that "the young girl will accomplish much good in religion."[91]

Venetian authorities were clearly proceeding with great caution in this matter because of the intersecting political and religious implications of the case. One of the major Tridentine reforms had established minimum age requirements for prospective nuns; novices had to be at least twelve to take first vows and sixteen for final profession, with a minimum of a year between the two. Venetian officials increased the minimum age of first vows to fifteen in 1592. A girl also had to make a formal statement of volition, as Elena had done, before taking any vow. The reforms were intended to prevent forced monachizations, though these admittedly proved "relatively ineffective."[92]

The Collegio faced a conundrum: contravene the religious aspirations of a young woman dependent on its protection and thus expose her to spiritual peril, or refuse the persistent demands of Omer Ağa with the attendant political cost. In the end, "to assure the soul and health of this servant of God, and our subject," the senators resolved to allow Elena to remain in Corpus Domini. Venice's ambassador in Rome, Giovanni Mocenigo, buttressed by Patriarch Priuli, was ordered to request a papal dispensation for Elena, emphasizing the "most urgent necessity . . . to free this soul from every peril."[93] Such requests were not unusual, though they were generally made by the patriarch and required considerable time; the direct and urgent intervention of political authorities was less conventional and hints at the unique character of Elena's case and the importance Venice attached to it.[94]

On November 5 Mocenigo was granted a papal audience and recounted the striking tale of apostasy, abandonment, and a young girl caught up in international intrigue. Although moved by the account, Pope Clement VIII refused to act until Elena's exact age was established.[95] Negotiations dragged on for two additional weeks, until November 20 when the pope finally granted a dispensation without the girl's actual age ever being established, in return for a political favor for a member of the Curia.[96] By the first of December, Elena had made her profession, taking the name Suor Deodata, and thus closed the door on any possibility of leaving Corpus Domini.

We should pause here to consider the question of agency in Deodata's case: to what degree did she assert a voice in the dialogue that shaped her future, particularly given her young age? Considering the patriarchal nature of early modern Venetian society, Deodata's age, and the powerful forces at play, it would seem reasonable to assume, as one scholar has suggested, that this was a clear case of forced monachization with little consideration of the actual wishes of the young girl, perpetuated by the organs of the state acting *in loco parentis*.[97] Certainly at her initial transfer to the Zitelle in 1592, Deodata was too young to participate meaningfully in the decision, and so Venetian authorities acted on their own to protect the young girl. In the subsequent drama, however, there is ample evidence of the active role she assumed in the debate over her future. Documents from powerful Venetian political and ecclesiastical bodies, and from Deodata herself, emphasize that she chose to take vows; indeed, there is no question that this decision created significant diplomatic difficulties that Venetian officials would gladly have avoided if possible.[98]

Deodata's active role in determining her destiny did not lack precedent. Recent scholarship has complicated the view of children as simply subservient to parental, particularly paternal, domination and has shown the degree to which early modern children were social agents.[99] Scholars have demonstrated how, even within "a patriarchal family unit," both women and children could achieve a level of self-discovery and "personal autonomy."[100] Examples of children acting against parental wishes are numerous, from the widespread practice of clandestine marriage ("the scourge of parents," particularly in Italy)[101] to the familiar theme in saints' lives of children taking religious orders in the face of significant parental opposition. Taking the veil was a common way girls rebelled against unwanted marriages; in fact, spiritual advisers sometimes promoted it as a means to avoid such matches. Parental authority did not lack limits either, and early modern girls "were not always the passive objects of parental strategies"; rather, they often were "the principal actors in the drama of their own lives."[102]

Deodata's decision to enter Corpus Domini voluntarily was not unusual either. The traditional view of convents as "nothing more than a prison" and "dumping grounds" for daughters "who were ugly, sickly, or otherwise unsuited for marriage"[103] has been challenged by more recent scholarship that shows many nuns were "fired by religious enthusiasm" and chose the religious life voluntarily, often against parental wishes.[104] Convents filled an important social role for women and girls, functioning as "an alternative family" and providing "real human affection," particularly for those from troubled family situations.[105] Convents were places of women's learning; they served as "a shelter from the uncertainties of an arranged marriage with an unknown man," and they provided a means of resistance and leverage against parents' plans for their daughters.[106]

In Deodata's case, Corpus Domini clearly functioned as refuge rather than prison. Her father had left her when she was barely three years old, and by age four she had been abandoned by both parents. She was shuttled between two families before being moved into a series of religious house at age six. These institutions, the girls that inhabited them, and the women who ran them became the only family that Deodata really knew. By the time that Bogdan—a man twice her age and utterly unknown to her—appeared in the lagoon in 1599, her memories of her parents, particularly her father, would have been minimal, if not nonexistent. Her decision to resist efforts by parents barely known to her to relocate her yet again and to marry her to a complete stranger seems understandable, even rational.

Once Deodata was safely ensconced in Corpus Domini, its abbess, Perpetua Bernardo, reported that she "lived with joy and with signs of a true religious." In addition, as the new nun herself stated in a letter to the Senate, she considered herself "no longer Jusuf Aǧa's but rather your Most Serene Sublimity's unworthy daughter" and had resolved "to never again accept letter, embassy, or envoy from that apostate Mahomettan" and to "forget that [she] was his daughter." This was because her father had "with false piety" initially agreed to meet her expenses as a nun, but when she refused "to obey or to listen" to his "promises of sublime greatness," he "cursed me and cancelled me from his grace, asserting that I should never again expect to have anything from him." Deodata was left alone and destitute, unable to pay for "the things necessary to a nun" or to set up "a humble cell," which led the Senate, in recognition of her constancy, to award significant additional funds for its ward's support.[107]

While these events played out, Bogdan remained in Venice and, according to an anonymous source, continued to threaten "the soul of that poor girl." He tried to press his case with Deodata by way of another nun, Francesca Bon, whom he visited disguised "in the clothes of a Venetian nobleman." The informant warned, "I assure you that the goal of this man is perfidious." An inquiry confirmed these allegations and found Deodata wavering in the face of Bogdan's persistence.[108] From Istanbul, Omer Ağa also kept up the pressure on his niece. Although he insisted that he wanted "nothing except that which pleases God, and if it will be the will of His Majesty that this girl remains [in the convent], no one will oppose it, and he [would] consider her as dead," he also pressed for Venetian officials to convince Deodata to meet with the papal nuncio in Venice, whom Omer Ağa curiously believed would encourage her to renounce her vows.[109]

Faced with this assault on her community, Abbess Bernardo took immediate action. She dismissed the confessor, ended Sister Francesca's access to the convent's windows, and reported the situation to the *provveditori sopra li monasteri*. Because there were rumors that "Bogdan had gone to Rome regarding this matter" and "because of the greatness and authority" of Omer Ağa, "for the public reputation and for the salvation of the soul of this poor creature preserved up until now from Lucifer's maw," Bernardo also referred the matter to the Council of Ten, the powerful and secretive body that dealt with Venice's most sensitive affairs.[110] These episodes proved to be the final gasps of Deodata's case, however, as Bogdan finally accepted the futility of pursuing his young bride-to-be, and turned to other schemes to gain the office of voivode.

Over the next decade he traveled throughout Europe seeking support in England and the Holy Roman Empire. Out of fear of Omer Ağa, who had turned against the young man after he failed to repay his dowry advance, he avoided Istanbul until 1602.[111] On his return, Bogdan was imprisoned in the Ottoman capital for more than two years, before escaping dressed as a woman in 1606. He returned to England and tried to arrange a marriage to the famed Lady Arabella Stuart as a means of obtaining his throne, though this plan failed too when rumors that he was already married to a Venetian woman resulted in public scandal for the "Prince of Moldavia, whom adversity hath rather made crafty than honest."[112] Bogdan returned to Istanbul in 1608 and took up residency in the English embassy, from which he conspired to obtain his throne through various schemes for several more years. When these all failed too, in an act of great irony given the concerns about his religious identity raised during his pursuit of Deodata, in 1611 Stefan Bogdan converted to Islam, took the name Ahmed, and was made a sancak beg in Albania.[113]

~⊃

As the intense activity surrounding her abated, Deodata settled into the predictable rhythms of the religious life of Corpus Domini. Founded in the late fourteenth century in Cannaregio, Corpus Domini was one of Venice's largest, wealthiest, and most eminent monasteries. Its Gothic church contained the hand of Saint Veneranda, which drew some faithful; however, the feast of Corpus Domini, with its large procession from St. Mark's to the convent and attendant festivities, was the high point of the nuns' year.[114] Patriarchal officials occasionally visited the monastery, and their reports provide a glimpse into Deodata's everyday existence.

Corpus Domini was a Dominican house and observed the rule

of Saint Augustine, which decreed a communal life of moderation, chastity, and prayer, organized around the daily liturgical offices.[115] There were seventy nuns in 1596; this number grew by a third in the next two decades, mirroring broader Italian trends.[116] The nuns regularly complained about the food; the bread, made with "*gran grosso*," was "at times horrible" and the wine quality inconsistent. Theoretically a community of equals, there were divisions between young and old nuns and squabbles over cell assignments. Several members of the noble Bassadonna family dominated the convent, and they and their allies received better medical care and the choicest wine.[117] The nuns were often lax in observing their rule; there were complaints that "silence is rarely observed" and that nuns wore "white shoes" or "silk veils on their shoulders." Some sisters kept pet dogs in their cells and others hens for their eggs. The dormitory doors were left unlocked at night and were never visited; thus, "many nuns [slept] in the cells of one another." And as Deodata's case illustrates, despite the efforts of ecclesiastical and political officials,[118] many inmates maintained outside contacts, primarily at the *ruota* (service wheel) where they spoke and touched hands with friends and family.[119]

The last meaningful glimpse we have of Suor Deodata is a letter from 1604. In May of that year an imperial çavuş, and friend of her parents, arrived from Istanbul to announce the coronation of Sultan Ahmed I, and he was able to deliver a message from the Civalellis to their daughter.[120] The letter was heartfelt and conciliatory:

My most dear and beloved daughter Signora Sister Deodata. It has been many years, months, and days that I have not had a letter from you, nor any note of how you are, and I, your poor father, and your mother, we are both afflicted from not hearing any news of you. And even though you became a nun, according to the will of our Lord God, nonetheless you ought not to forget the love that your father and your mother bear for you, and you ought to at least write occasionally so that with your letters we will hear of your health. We are at peace with the fact that you never would accept our will, neither allow yourself to be visited nor take that husband that we had arranged for you. If you had taken him, you would have eased some part of the suffering that we have because of you. May God be praised, in addition, if our lot has been to be separated [from each other]. At the very least, we pray you for the love of God not to fail to write us often regarding how you are . . .

Your mother and I salute you infinitely. Your sisters, now known as Maiadri (the elder) and Essecadri (the younger), are well, and both kiss your hands. Everyone at home salutes you much . . . We pray you anyway not to fail to write often because we want nothing more from you than that you pray to God for us, and to hear of your health. I end, and pray our Lord without cease to protect you from evil and to conserve you in his good grace.

The letter is signed, "Your most loving and dear father and mother, Jusuf Ağa, Müteferrika, and Atise, mother." A postscript mentions a gift of handkerchiefs "worked *alla turchesca*" that they had previously sent her via another friend and requests, "If you received them we pray you to let us know."[121]

Deodata's response, while brief and cautious, suggests that perhaps some of the wounds of her long and troubled relationship with her parents had healed on her part as well:

Dearest Father and Mother. I received your letters of the 9th of this past March, which were brought to me by Mustafa Ağa, to whom they were given by you, and I was pleased to hear of the state of health in which you find yourself. In return, I see your desire to know of me, about which Mustafa (to whom I will give the present letters) can tell you in person. I inform you that I live in this monastery most contentedly and full of every consolation, having first the Most Serene Signoria favored me with what I need to live and wear, and then having acquired the favor of all these Reverend Nuns and Sisters. I can say with truth that I do not lack anything that I desire. Thus I can

happily attend to praying the Lord God on behalf of my
benefactors, as I also offer to pray for you.

She concludes abruptly, stating that "the handkerchiefs" never arrived and their friend never appeared.[122]

I would like to think that the disobedient daughter and her way-
ward parents continued to correspond occasionally, but unfortunately no records of such communications survive. All we know of
Deodata after 1604 is gleaned from a few documents from Corpus
Domini, where she appears regularly in lists of the convent's con-
vocations over the next four decades.[123] The last word we have of
the young Zaratine girl, now become an old woman, is recorded in
an all-to-brief interview with Corpus Domini's abbess in 1651, and
is decidedly melancholic. The effects of her advancing years were
clearly foremost on her mind, and despite more than a half century
in the convent and her status as the fifth most senior nun, it is revealing that she still perceived herself as an outsider among the mostly
patrician, Venetian nuns.[124] Although of noble lineage herself, she
was also something of a scholarship girl in the convent, there only
through the charity of the Venetian state and tainted by the dishonor-
able status of her renegade parents. When asked by the abbess about
her impressions of the convent, the sixty-five-year-old Suor Deodata
responded, "I have poor eyesight and I can see little. I hear some
things. I am a foreigner. Since you can be informed [of the convent's
problems] by other nuns, I beg you to leave me be."[125]

With these final few words, Deodata disappears. There is no reason to doubt that she lived out the few remaining years of her life
in the monastery, bringing to an end the unusual tale of a girl whose
parents abandoned her then tried to reclaim her, but who in the end
crafted a life of her own choosing.

A case strikingly similar to Elena Civalelli's occurred two decades
later, 150 kilometers to the south of Zara in the coastal town of
Spalato. On December 22, 1621, the Venetian count and captain of
Spalato, Giacomo Michiel, reported two troubling incidents in his

jurisdiction.[126] A certain Hassan Turco had been wounded by an unknown Venetian subject, and more significantly, "a Turkish girl" had been kidnapped from her father's home.[127] Although Venice had been at peace with the Ottoman Empire for almost half a century, as we have seen, the Spalato border was a sensitive area where tensions occasionally flared, and the threat of the two events to the region's *bona pace* was certain to challenge the political skills of Michiel, a forty-three-year-old scion of one of Venice's leading families, who had only recently taken up his post.[128]

Venice had definitively acquired Spalato in 1420, and as with the rest of Dalmatia, the War of the Holy League had decimated the region. After 1573 Venice controlled a coastal area around the city barely ten miles long and two wide. There was no city in Dalmatia that had "more [Turks] close by . . . [it was] surrounded on every side by Turks"; thus, as in Zara, cross-border contacts were commonplace. Spalato's hinterland produced quantities of wine and figs, but the population (in 1583 numbering just 3,221) depended completely on Ottoman grain.[129] This situation produced "unhappiness and misery" and a "poverty of life," until the last decade of the century when a Jewish entrepreneur and several Venetian and Ottoman officials collaborated to transform Spalato into an important trading center.[130] As the terminus of the overland trade routes from Istanbul, the town became the "key point" in Veneto-Ottoman trade and essential to Venice's commercial life; by 1626, 25 percent of Venice's port activity passed through it.[131]

Five miles inland, only "a strong arm's throw away" from Spalato, was the Ottoman town of Clissa.[132] Situated at the mouth of the best pass through the Dinaric Alps, a medieval fortress universally described as "impregnable" loomed on an outcropping of rock, 360 meters above the town.[133] Clissa had been under Ottoman rule since 1537,[134] and a castellan and between 125 and 250 men buttressed by four cannon defended the fortress and kept watch over the two hundred houses and resident kadi in the town below.[135] Clissa was an Ottoman sancak in the *eyalet* of Bosnia and was further subdivided into four *kapitanije* (captaincies), whose heads were

Spalato and Clissa
Christofaro Tarnowskij, *Clissa principal fortezza del Turcho nella nella dalmacia et Chiave dil Reg° di Bosna Lontano da Spallato miglia 5* (Split[?], 1605). Newberry Library, Chicago

charged with administrative duties, policing, and border protection. According to a 1624 Ottoman survey, the sancak had a mostly rural population of about twenty thousand.[136]

The girl who had been kidnapped, Mihale Šatorović (Sattorovichia, Satorovich), came from one of Clissa's most "honored household[s]." Her mother was named Haisecaduna, and her father, Ahmed Ağa, was a "principal man in Clissa," not, as some reports claimed, the sancak beg or even the captain, but still an important figure in the garrison.[137] By 1627 he had become the *dasdar (dizdar) chlischi,* or castellan of the fortress, a position he occupied for over two decades.[138]

We know little about the Šatorović family. The extended clan possessed 170 acres of land, and its members were "among the richest noblemen" in the region. Records dating to the 1590s mention two brothers, Ibrahim and Ahmed Šatorović, who had converted from Christianity to Islam many years previously. Both were described as "principal Turk[s] of Clissa," where they were part of the Ottoman garrison, though several imprecise contemporary accounts suggest that the Šatorovićs' loyalties were pliable in the fluid political environment of the frontier. Despite such rumors, the family was well-connected both locally and in Istanbul.[139]

When Mihale's parents discovered her missing, they immediately feared she had been kidnapped and taken to the Venetian side of the border. This was a relatively frequent phenomenon along the frontier; in one two-year period, eleven children were kidnapped, and only two ransomed. The motivations for these abductions included ransom, which was a major source of income, and bride theft, which was practiced throughout the region, and indeed was often prearranged with the consent of the woman as a way to overcome parental opposition.[140] Cross-border flights and conversions were also regular occurrences; Venetian officials reported that "very often our subjects go to change their faith in Turkey, and their subjects come to our state to become Christians." As long as they acted of "their own free will," such conversions produced no "perturbation" and "no one spoke of them." It is not surprising then, that when Ahmed Ağa inquired "with great anxiety" about his daughter, Michiel had not heard anything. Realizing the gravity of the situation, however, he immediately issued "stern proclamations" to try to discover her location.[141]

It soon became clear that the girl (whose age is never established) had not been forcibly "kidnapped" but rather had "fled from her father's house" of her own free will, "with the resolution to become a Christian." After leaving home, Mihale slipped into Venetian territory and sought refuge in one of the Venetian castles that dotted the frontier. With the assistance of members of the garrison, and without Michiel's knowledge, Mihale was quietly transferred to the island of Lissa (Vis).[142] Lissa seemed an ideal refuge; the small, mountainous island was located 65 kilometers west of Spalato and had "very few," "very poor" inhabitants who worked its vineyards and peach orchards.[143] On Lissa, Mihale was taken into the home of Francesco Perović, a sixty-year-old married man without children, who while not among the island's few noble families, was nonetheless well respected and "comfortable in the gifts of fortune." Perović received the young woman "as the daughter of his soul" and treated her with "terms of paternal kindness."[144]

In mid-January, a month after her flight, Mihale was finally located and returned to Spalato. She was placed in one of the city's three convents,[145] most likely Saint Raynerius, the largest and most honored Spalatine monastery, which housed twelve noble nuns and was under the archbishop of Spalato's direct control.[146] This was done, according to Michiel, to ensure that "her honor was preserved from every injury," particularly in connection with her relationship to "a Turkish [servant] boy" from her father's household who had accompanied her on her flight. This theme of preserving Mihale's honor would recur throughout the course of the controversy. While it was claimed that she had left home to become a Christian, several sources hint that there may have been a romantic relationship with this servant, or even that the two intended to marry. For his part, Ahmed Ağa acknowledged that he had tried to arrange an "unequal marriage" for her; thus, once again the threat of parental interference in a young woman's life played a central role in precipitating a boundary crossing.[147]

Informed of the discovery of his daughter and her intention to convert to Christianity, Ahmed Ağa was "greatly aggrieved" and demanded to see her. Michiel agreed, and the Ottoman, his wife, and other family members traveled to Spalato "to assure that no violence was used against" their daughter in making her decision to convert and to try and discourage her "with their prayers."[148] In an intimidating scene, Mihale confronted her family and several Ottoman officials. "With a constant soul" she refused to return home and insisted that she wanted to become a Christian, "and with virility" parried all attempts to dissuade her from her decision. Her performance was impressive enough that Ahmed Ağa's superior, the captain of Clissa, affirmed in a letter his satisfaction that the girl was sincerely committed to her course of action and that she acted of her own volition. For their part, faced with their daughter's firm commitment, Mihale's parents left Spalato "confused [and] without saying a thing," but with plans to bring greater political powers to bear on the matter.[149]

Following their departure, Mihale was instructed in "the first rudiments of the Christian faith," and "moved by Christian and pious zeal," Michiel "agreed secretly" to her baptism request. He and the Spalatine nobleman Peregrino Capogrosso stood as godfathers, and she was baptized on Sunday, January 23, in Spalato's St. Doimus cathedral by Archbishop Sfortia Ponzoni and took a new Christian name, Catterina.[150] She received many gifts, and her baptism was accompanied by noisy festivities and cannon fire. While commonplace among both Muslims and Christians, given the combustible situation and the anger that especially accompanied the conversion of youths, this unwise celebration only served to intensify Ottoman anger.[151]

Michiel's mismanagement of this affair exposed him to intense criticism from Venice. The Senate excoriated him because he had not acted as "necessary in an affair of such importance, which additionally created enormous disturbance to our interests in the Porte, since this violence and the kidnapping of women is of extraordinary concern to the Turks."[152] Once the matter was resolved, the Senate used it as the basis for a new protocol for dealing with frontier conversions; because of the "closeness of the Turks on those borders," all Venetian officials in Dalmatia in the future had to receive permission from the chief government official in the region before baptizing any "Turk."[153]

The Senate's concerns proved well founded; from the outset, the incident fanned emotions on the normally tranquil Spalato frontier.[154] Immediately following Mihale's flight, eight Venetian subjects from the neighboring town of Trau were taken hostage in retaliation. There were repeated warnings that the Ottomans were massing on the border, "threatening depredations and damage to our subjects," and rumors circulated that the sancak beg had come from Livno to

Clissa to take matters into his own hands. These were not insignificant threats, as he could put some six thousand men and cavalry in the field, many more than the undermanned Venetians could muster.[155] Fearing that the tensions would produce "that which is usual in these sorts of incidents," Venice's forces were put on high alert, and the *capitano del golfo,* Leonardo Foscolo, anchored his six armed ships in Spalato's port to act as "a brake" on the Ottomans.[156]

As the Senate's criticism made clear, Michiel's missteps were particularly egregious because the case involved a Muslim woman. Whereas the shooting of Hassan Turco, which had occurred at the same time, created a momentary local disturbance, the flight of Mihale Šatorović was an extremely serious affair that dragged out over five years, and eventually engaged the Ottoman and Venetian military forces, as well as the highest officials in the region and in the respective imperial capitals. Clearly, there was something unique about incidents involving women and girls, at least those of a certain social status.[157] Venetian officials repeatedly emphasized that "violence [against] and the abduction of women are esteemed in an extraordinary fashion by the Turks" and such acts "very often caus[e] dangerous disturbances with vexing consequences."[158] Writing about Catterina's flight, Venice's highly experienced bailo in Istanbul, Giorgio Giustinian, warned that if word of it percolated up to the imperial divan, it would "cause great agitation in the souls of the Vizier and others, because . . . the abduction by Christians of Turkish women, especially young girls, is held by the Turks as one of the greatest and most execrable excesses that can be committed in offense against their law."[159] Although such abductions were not exceptional, and were committed by both Ottomans and Venetians, the status of Ahmed Ağa and the gender of the abductee combined to make this a particularly sensitive and potentially explosive case that required the most careful management.

Faced with Michiel's bungling of this delicate affair, the Senate called on one of its most senior officials, *Provveditor General da Mar* Giusto Antonio Belegno, who was based in Corfu and supervised all Venice's land and sea forces in the Levant.[160] The Senate ordered him to make a "speedy voyage to Spalato" and to organize a "top secret" inquest to identify "those who kidnapped the girl, . . . give them their deserved punishment, recover the girl, [and] return her to her parents."[161]

On March 15, the day after his arrival in Spalato, Belegno and Michiel met with an emissary from the sancak beg of Clissa, Ibrahim Paşa, who reported that "everyone in the sancak had weapons in hand so as to regain the girl taken from her home in Clissa." He proposed a second encounter between Catterina and her parents, who were convinced that at the first meeting their daughter "had been forced to say things contrary to her will." The Venetian officials agreed, though they insisted the audience take place in Spalato, out of fear that the girl might be taken away by force if the meeting were held on the frontier. They also requested that an Ottoman official be present "to verify once again her will."[162]

The meeting took place on March 18 in the home of "a most honorable gentlewoman." At Ibrahim Paşa's request, Catterina and her parents were to be allowed "to speak together as long as they want[ed]." He further stated that he would respect "that which the girl . . . desire[d]," and strongly urged Belegno to do the same. The meeting collapsed as soon as the parties sat down, however, when Ahmed Ağa and Haisecaduna demanded "to spend the night with their daughter." The provveditore refused, citing vague "health issues," though the real concern was certainly to prevent them intimidating the young girl. Incensed, Catterina's parents returned to Clissa, however, Belegno convinced the sancak beg's officials to go ahead with the meeting. Once again confronted with a room full of powerful male interrogators, the young woman indicated that "no one had kidnapped her or carried her away . . . [and] that she never want[ed] to return among Turks, . . . as long as she live[d]." She stated "with great consistency and fearlessness that her desire was the same as it had always been, to remain Christian and to never return home, as she had already expressed to her mother and father, and these words she repeated and repeated again, always in such a way that it was very clear that they came from her heart."[163]

Faced with Catterina's unwavering position, her parents' abrupt departure, intense Venetian pressure, and the testimony of his own officials, Ibrahim Paşa had the option of either escalating the confrontation or conceding. Charged by the sultan with preserving the peace on the borders and protecting the "reciprocal commerce so beneficial to both of their subjects in that region," he opted to resolve the matter locally. He declared, "From here on out there should be no talk of the young woman," and he had the kadi of Clissa issue a *hüccet* declaring the "enormous scandal" resolved.[164] Belegno's agreement to release the sancak beg's annual gift, which had been held in limbo during the standoff, made the decision more palatable.[165] Any lingering inclination to alter this decision disappeared in the maelstrom surrounding Sultan Osman II's assassination in May. By summer 1622 the case of Catterina Šatorović had disappeared from the minds of both Venetian and Ottoman officials.[166]

Though the matter appeared resolved, Venetian officials were anxious to transfer the young woman from the area "to avoid any new request by the parents and to remove any incitement of discord." At her request, Catterina returned to Lissa to the house of Francesco Perović, to whom she had grown very close. Her stay was once again brief; in late spring the Senate ordered her transferred to Venice in "honest company," in part out of concerns about Perović's intentions and the potential dishonoring of the girl. On her arrival in the lagoon, the provveditori sopra li monasteri were directed "to ensure that she is placed in a location appropriate to her status." Like Elena Civalelli, Catterina was taken to the Casa delle Zitelle, apparently Venice's preferred refuge for endangered girls from the Veneto-Ottoman frontier.[167]

❧

By all accounts, the young Ottoman girl settled comfortably into her new surroundings. Catterina demonstrated a real conviction for her new faith, evidenced by statements both before and after her baptism, and her commitment seems to have been sincere and even profound. There is a tendency to interpret conversion in entirely functional, rational, and self-interested terms, but as Catterina's case and many others suggest,[168] real religious conviction and sincerity were also possible and could provide powerful motivation in individual lives.[169]

For five years Catterina lived uneventfully, troubled only occasionally by letters from her parents, who made "every effort to persuade her to desist from her" chosen course. Then, in late May 1627, without any formal notice, her father appeared at the Zitelle and requested to see his daughter. The house's custodians responded that outsiders, particularly men, could not enter and suggested that he refer his request to the Collegio. Initially, Ahmed Ağa reacted with "tremendous perturbation," but he quickly calmed down and asked simply "if his daughter was happy, and if she had a smile on her face." The concerned father received assurances that his daughter was well and "very steadfast in the most holy faith."[170]

The following day, Ahmed Ağa appeared before the Collegio and requested permission to meet with his daughter. To buttress this petition, he presented a rescript from the sultan dated March 1627, which claimed that his "daughter was kidnapped by an infidel Christian of [Venice], taken to Spalato where, surrounded by thirty or forty religious and by an infinite number of Christian women who told her that our faith [Islam] is not good, she was taken to a church and there they made her kiss the cross and [then] took her away and gave her a Christian name." Ottoman merchants who traded in Venice had sworn before the kadi of Clissa that the girl was now held in a Venetian prison. The sultan concluded by evoking the "ancient friendship" and "good peace" that reigned between the two states and demanded that Catterina "be liberated from the prison in which she is held, and returned to her father."[171]

Venetian officials were faced once again with a knotty situation. The sultan's letter raised the threat that Catterina's case could escalate into a more serious diplomatic affair. But the reputation of Venice and its officials was also at stake. They had a moral and religious duty to protect a defenseless ward of the state who, if placed in her father's custody, would certainly be forced to return to Islam and potentially could face serious punishment for her apostasy.[172]

Before responding, the Collegio sought advice from several individuals, including the former bailo Giorgio Giustinian, who stated that the sultan's letter was filled almost entirely with "false information." The governors of the Zitelle also appeared and reported that the girl had corresponded with her father and had shown a "great desire to see" him. Indeed, she knew of his intention to visit and eagerly waited his arrival; every time she heard "cannon fire she thought in her heart that it was her father," and were she to be forbidden to see him, they were convinced that she "would fall into despair." The Collegio decided to proceed with caution and granted Ahmed's request, with the stipulation that he be accompanied by Venetian officials who were to provide "in writing most diligent notice of every particular" of the visit.[173]

So on June 5, 1627, Ahmed Ağa, his son-in-law, and several servants, accompanied by the house's noble governors and two Venetian dragomans, were escorted into the Zitelle. The party toured the facility, saw young girls doing needlework, and listened to the house's choir. Then, Ahmed was shown into a large room, and there, for the first time in over five years, he saw his daughter. He embraced and kissed her, burst into tears, and then after calming himself, began to interrogate her whether "she was in this place willingly or if she was forced to be there." He told her of the sultan's order, which could free her "if she desired it," but Catterina laughed, shook her head, and said she did "not want to leave heaven for earth." Her father and his companions pressed her to reconsider; they reminded her "of her mother's affliction, of his lack of progeny, and they then told her she was his sole and only heir." Ahmed promised that if she returned home, "she would be treated as a noblewoman, she would be married, and she would receive her opulent inheritance." Catterina responded patiently that in Venice she was treated as a gentlewoman and that she would not renounce "the salvation of her soul."[174] The encounter lasted for some time, and the father and daughter parted amiably, agreeing to see each other a second time.

Two days later they met again. Catterina led her father by the hand on a visit of the facility and its garden, and she sang and played for him to his great satisfaction. While profuse in his praise for the Zitelle, Ahmed Ağa still feared that his daughter was not being treated honorably, according to her rank. He questioned her simple dress and lack of jewelry, but he was told that all the women in the house wore similar clothing by choice. He was apprehensive about the quality of his daughter's companions and was pleased when informed that a girl from the royal house of Bosnia, whose family he knew well, was also in the Zitelle. Concerned about her education, he asked his daughter to demonstrate her ability to write; he also inspected her "hands, fingers, and fingernails," declaring them superior to her mother's and evidence of the good treatment she received and the noble and honorable quality of her lifestyle.[175]

Throughout their encounters, despite repeated requests that she address her father directly in Turkish or Slavic, Catterina insisted on speaking to him in Italian through an interpreter, using language to demarcate the boundary between the two of them, and between the past and her present life.[176] Clearly the issues that had led her to flee her father's home five years previous still strained their relationship. As their time together waned, however, softened perhaps by the passage of years and touched by Ahmed's tears and his solicitousness toward her, Catterina finally let down her defenses. As the two sat together in a quiet corner, she asked in Slavic, "Father, do you love me?" Ahmed, whose emotions had been close to the surface throughout what was potentially his last encounter with his prodigal daughter, "arched his eyebrows" and was silent for a moment, almost as if stunned by her question. In a rush of words, he then began speaking of his guilt over a "certain unpleasant situation that he feared he had committed against his daughter when she was a child," probably referring to his attempt to impose marriage on her, which had in part precipitated her flight. Before her father's words were translated for her, Catterina began to laugh, and she indicated to him that this was not the sole reason she had fled her paternal home. To alleviate his remorse, and as a sign of her willingness to reconcile with her parents, Catterina indicated that she would accede to a request he had previously made that if she did not want to return home, at least she could transfer to a convent closer to him and her mother. This time it was Ahmed who refused, saying that the Zitelle was "paradise" and that she should never leave "since there could not be a better place in the world." As their conversation concluded, Catterina performed a musical number on the organ for her father and gave him gifts of silk flowers and boxes that she had made. Father and daughter walked one last time in the garden, said their final goodbyes, and Ahmed departed.[177]

In a final audience before the Collegio, Ahmed acknowledged that he was at peace with Catterina's decision. "I saw my daughter in a very different state from what had been represented to me: beautiful, healthy, and virtuous, cared for by the most important gentlewomen in a very ample and spacious place." The doge promised that Venice would continue to look after his daughter in an honorable fashion, and satisfied with this assurance, Ahmed Ağa took his leave.[178]

With her father's departure, the matter of Catterina Šatorović seemed resolved. Venetian authorities remained alert for any change in his demeanor or a response from the sultan, whose rescript had been effectively ignored. While desiring to preserve peaceful relations with the Ottomans, "because of the demands of religion" and because "the girl was firm and constant in our most holy faith," Venetian officials were adamant that they would not "return her no matter what situation might arise." The honor of its officials and the reputation of the state were important enough for Venice to mobilize extraordinary political, diplomatic, and military resources and to expend significant political capital all to preserve the faith and honor of a Muslim girl from the Dalmatian coast. This investment was deemed "convenient to the piety of Our Signoria and to the honor of the Lord God." In other words, the pious reputation of Venice was inextricably linked to its actions on behalf of God, and the reputation of the city, its institutions, and its rulers was closely tied to its defense of the honor of its women.[179]

These precautions on the part of the Venetians proved unnecessary. Though his sultanic letter gave Ahmed significant leverage, and he certainly could have chosen to pursue the matter further, it seems he came to Venice genuinely desiring to ascertain his daughter's will rather than impose his own. He wanted to verify for himself that she was happy and well cared for and that she was still content with the decision she had made five years before. When he saw the quality of her life in the Zitelle, he effectively abandoned his attempts to rescue Catterina, took his imperial letter and returned to Clissa. His actions, like those of Suor Deodata's father, challenge our notions of the autocratic patriarch imposing his will on his children and suggest instead that the early modern prescription that "parents should rule with justice and firm love, not as tyrants" did inform parents' actions, and even perhaps transcended religious borders.[180] To be sure, both fathers did try early on to impose their wills on their daughters, but both ultimately accepted their inability to control them and sought to reconcile with their willful children.

There is no further record of subsequent visits or communications between father and daughter, though given the good terms on which they parted, I choose to believe that they remained in contact. While initially Catterina's intention was to enter a "rigorous and observant" convent, she eventually left the Zitelle and married a Venetian named Biancolini and had several children. The last mention we have of Catterina is when her children received an inheritance in Dalmatia in the early 1660s from the grandfather they most likely never knew, Ahmed Ağa.[181]

CHAPTER THREE

Maria Gozzadini and Her Daughters— Aissè, Eminè, Catigè

I N LATE MARCH 1637, the mighty galleasses of Venice's Mediterranean fleet dropped anchor in the horseshoe-shaped bay of the island of Milos. Commanded by forty-one-year-old Captain Pietro Mocenigo,[1] the fleet was tasked with keeping Venetian shipping safe in the corsair-infested waters of the Archipelago, as contemporaries called the islands of the Aegean Sea. At midnight on the fleet's eighth day in port, four women slipped aboard the captain's ship in the company of several "armed men from the galley." Except for the hour, there was nothing particularly unusual about this; Venetian ships often carried passengers, and several women were already guests aboard the captain's ship. These four women were far from normal passengers, however, and their flight from Milos produced a confrontation that would become a serious threat to the normally peaceful relations between the Venetian and Ottoman empires.[2]

Milos is situated at the western gateway to the Aegean. A small island, it is dominated by rugged mountains with rich mineral deposits, which also were the source of the island's famous white millstones.[3] The mountains loom over a fertile central plain that produced "grain, wine, legumes," cotton, and fruit.[4] Milos's most striking natural feature was its "brave port," which since antiquity had served as a way station for travelers, merchants, and pilgrims.[5] Because of its location on the liquid frontiers of the Mediterranean, where political authority was inconsistent, the island also functioned

Women of Milos
Joseph Pitton de Tournefort, *Relation d'un voyage du Levant* (Amsterdam: Aux dépens de la Compagnie, 1718)

as a base for corsairs.[6] At the request of its desperate inhabitants, Milos had passed to Ottoman rule in the mid-sixteenth century, but it enjoyed considerable autonomy;[7] in fact it was said that "the iland liveth freer than any other of the Turkes dominions, and hath indeed nothing but the name of servitude."[8] Milos's ties to its Ottoman overlords were limited to the annual payment of the *harac* (the tax required of all non-Muslim Ottoman subjects, which was apportioned and collected by the islanders) and the presence of a few officials charged with political, military, and legal affairs.[9]

Under Ottoman rule, Milos's population grew to between three and four thousand.[10] Almost all were Orthodox, with a few Roman Catholics and even fewer Muslims.[11] Evliya Çelebi reported that all of the island's inhabitants were "infidels," and a traveler in 1628 counted only "two Turkes on the Iland," the governor, the kadi, "and a few seruantes with them."[12] There were two chief towns, Apanokastro, near the port, and Milos (also Paleochorion), located

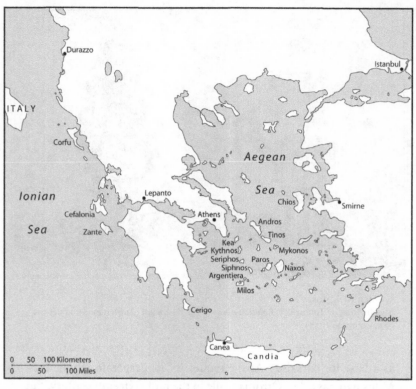

The Aegean and Ionian seas

three miles inland, in the central plain. The latter was home to the Greek and Latin bishops, as well as the kadi and a "few Turks."[13]

In addition to praising its port, travelers (inevitably men) regularly commented on Milos's women. Jean Thévenot described them as "very charitable to strangers." Phillipe du Fresne-Canaye was more explicit; "as soon as a ship arrives, the young girls with their mothers run to the shore, lovingly receive the strangers, and with an infinity of caresses they invite them to serve themselves with the girls."[14] Reinhold Lubenau thought Milos's women "of easier virtue than I have seen anywhere else in all Greece."[15] And the Jesuit Michele Albertino reported that on the island "a thousand sorts of sins and vices reign."[16]

It was not entirely surprising, then, that when Captain Mocenigo's quartermaster, Gratia Giobia, and a companion went ashore looking for wine rations, they were directed to the home of a Miliot woman named Maria Gozzadini, who lived with her three daughters. After discussing the sale of her wine, Maria proposed an altogether different transaction, entreating the men to "perform the charitable act" of helping her and her children—Aissè, seventeen; Eminè, nine; and Catigè, four—to flee Milos.[17]

Maria was thirty-seven and the widow of Hassan Ağa, a janissary from Rhodes, who had been the resident Ottoman military official on Milos. Born on the island of Siphnos, she belonged to the Gozzadini family, which had ruled the small islands of Kea, Kythnos, and Siphnos since the fourteenth century. She moved with her family to Kimolos (or Argentiera), an island a mile northeast of Milos sometime before 1613, probably in 1609 when a squadron of Ottoman galleys threatened Siphnos in response to endemic corsair activity in the area.[18]

Maria claimed to have been kidnapped at age thirteen, taken to Milos, and forcibly married to her husband.[19] Although abductions were common in parts of the Ottoman Empire, and Ottoman law stipulated harsh punishments for them,[20] it is more likely that her family had arranged the marriage. Even though religious authorities discouraged the "Satanic communion" of mixed marriages with threats of excommunication, the denial of Christian burial, and canon laws that forbade such unions, Orthodox parents not infrequently negotiated matches between their daughters and Muslim men.[21] Contemporaries reported that Greeks "marry one of their daughters to a Turk more willingly than to a Christian of the Roman faith, whom they hold as great enemies."[22] Non-Muslim families could advance their status through well-arranged mixed marriages, fathers could avoid paying a dowry and a groom gift, and they often received a bride-price from the groom.[23] Voluntary relationships between Orthodox and Muslim, often in the face of parental disapproval, were also not uncommon.[24] However, in Maria's case, even if she had likely not been abducted, she may well have been compelled to marry against her will.[25] Clearly, the marriage of one of the few Ottoman officials in the region, Hassan Aǧa, and the daughter of a prominent Greek family could benefit both parties, though the young Maria unquestionably felt otherwise.

Whether her marriage was voluntary or coerced, Maria never converted to Islam and by all accounts continued to live very devotedly as a Christian. She funded the construction of several churches on the islands of Nipoligo and Kimolos and "always had the desire to come to Christian lands." She claimed to have baptized her daughters without their father's knowledge and raised them secretly as Christians. Islamic law, however, considered the girls Muslim, and they acknowledged being brought up in their father's faith. Eminè stated, "for appearance we pretended to observe the Turkish rite, but secretly we observed Christianity's rite."[26]

The experience of Maria and her daughters illustrates again the confessional ambiguity of the early modern Mediterranean, particularly among the mixed populations of the Balkans.[27] In Bulgaria, Muslim Pomaks preserved Christian rituals, revered Christian saints, displayed the cross on everything from their bread to their door frames, and kept holy water obtained from village priests. Similarly, Bosnian Muslims incorporated Muslim, Christian, and pagan elements in their wedding, birth, and godparent rituals, and they observed Christian festivals and honored Christian saints.[28] Veneration of the Virgin "provided a bridge" between Muslim and Christian women; shrines and holy spaces were shared by worshipers from both faiths; and local processions and feast days in mixed communities regularly drew Christian, Muslim, and even Jewish participants.[29] The archbishop of Corfu wrote that Muslims often baptized their children as protection from leprosy, and contemporaries decried that Balkan Christians under Ottoman rule were "unlearning" their faith.[30] Intra-Christian religious lines were equally imprecise. On Corfu, individuals were indiscriminate in attending and paying alms to both Latin-rite and Orthodox clergy, who often celebrated religious functions in each other's churches. One official reported that "many farmers and simple people who do not know or understand the difference between the Latin and the Greek church go and confess" in one or the other. Latin women on Corfu often married Orthodox men, ate "meat on Saturday and other vigils to accommodate their husbands," and believed that they possessed a special dispensation to do so.[31] Maria's daughters' dissimulation was also common, as evidenced by crypto-Christianity, also known as "double faith," which was widespread throughout the Balkans and the Greek islands.[32] In short, the religious straddling and ambiguity of Maria's family was not at all peculiar.

The death of Maria's husband in 1634, shortly after the birth of Catigè, placed her in a difficult situation.[33] As the Christian wife of a Muslim, she already occupied a liminal position on Milos; the community's Greek leaders had obtained a sultanic order forbidding all "Turks" from inhabiting the island, with the exception of the kadi, and had repeatedly entreated the women to leave.[34] Her widowhood accentuated this troubled position; Islamic law gave women the right of *hidana* (caretaking) until age nine for girls, after which men were considered better able "to represent the interests of the child." When a father predeceased his wife, legal guardianship normally passed to his closest male relative; in some situations women were granted guardianship until a child reached majority, though this right could be lost through remarriage or "immoral behavior."[35] Hassan Ağa's closest male relative, a brother named Mustafa, resided on Chios and was in contact with the family, but there is no evidence he attempted to obtain custody of his nieces.

More important than custody issues was the status of Maria's eldest daughter, Aissè. At the age of nine, Aissè had been married by her father to Mustafa Efendi, Milos's kadi. Although quite young for Orthodox girls in the Aegean,[36] Islamic law did not set a minimum age on marriage. Nine was considered the age of puberty, which made a girl marriageable, though it was common for young married girls to remain in their parents' homes until reaching sexual maturity.[37] This may have been the case with Aissè; Maria affirmed that over the course of eight years of marriage, "by a miracle" the match with Mustafa Efendi was never consummated, even though

Islamic law allowed a man to insist on his conjugal rights as soon as a girl was able to "support intercourse."[38] This claim that Aissè's virginity was intact seems highly unlikely and was probably intended to make her more attractive for remarriage following the family's flight from Milos.

We know little about Aissè's husband, Mustafa Efendi. As kadi, he would have been trained in sharia and *kanun* law in one of the empire's many madrasas (religious colleges) in order to compete for a kadiship. These were limited and highly sought-after positions at the heart of the Ottoman legal system and dealt with "almost every conceivable area of life."[39] By 1637 Mustafa was well established in his career; he had been posted to the Danube region and several locations in the Archipelago, including perhaps eight to ten years on Milos.[40] As kadi, Mustafa was the island's most important government official and possessed significant legal and administrative independence and power. In addition, he had responsibility for several other small islands in the vicinity.

Given the limited marriage options for a Muslim girl on an Orthodox island on the periphery of the empire, Aissè's match with Mustafa was an extremely good one. Despite this, however, the marriage appears not to have been close at all. Mustafa was significantly older than his bride, his official duties took him away from Milos regularly, and he and his young wife may never have actually lived together. He seems to have known little about Aissè or her family; when questioned, he did not even know his wife's age.[41]

The precipitating factor in the marriage's dissolution, however, was Mustafa's pending transfer to a new posting in the Black Sea. Generally, Ottoman kadis were transferred regularly to discourage judicial corruption.[42] Maria and her daughters were able to take flight because Mustafa had already departed for his new position and had left Aissè behind temporarily. He had taken most of their household possessions and left these in the care of his brother, Mustafa, on Chios. His intention was to discourage Aissè from fleeing and to compel her to join him in the Black Sea.[43] In theory she had several legal options: she could refuse to move away from her family, she could have repudiated her husband at puberty, or she could seek a *khul* divorce.[44] Although the possibilities of divorce in the Muslim world were greater than in Christian regions, there remained not-insignificant limitations on Muslim women's ability to end an unwanted marriage. In a khul divorce, a woman could initiate the dissolution of a marriage; however, her husband had to consent, usually in return for some type of compensation. While a man could divorce without any recourse to the legal system, a khul divorce had to be processed through a court. Because Aissè was married to the local kadi, who would have had both to consent to and adjudicate his own divorce, her legal options were effectively limited.[45] In the end, instead of pursuing a divorce, the women chose to flee "because," as Maria explained, "I expected Mustafa Efendi husband of [Aissè] to return to claim her soul, [and thus] I fled with my three daughters, as I had wanted to do for many years." She preferred, she said, to "suffer martyrdom" rather than remain another day on Milos.[46]

The convergence of Mustafa's absence and the presence of the Venetian fleet created the ideal situation for Maria and her daughters. Touched by their plight, Quartermaster Giobia appealed to Captain Mocenigo on the women's behalf, who agreed to grant them passage.[47] Filippo Benin, Venice's self-proclaimed consul on Milos, facilitated their departure, acting as intermediary in arranging Maria's flight in the hope of gaining "considerable personal benefit." Indeed, Milos's communal heads ultimately held Benin responsible for "the disorder" that was to ensue.[48] Once aboard the captain's galley, accompanied by two servants, Pulimina and Fiorenza, the women settled into "the most comfortable" lodging on the ship, the quartermaster's cabin located near the mainmast. They brought with them just a few bags containing clothing and other personal effects, though the following night, with the captain's permission, crew members went ashore to retrieve three additional chests of belongings.[49]

Contrary winds forced the fleet to remain in Milos for several days, during which time servants and many of the island's prominent people visited the women.[50] When the winds changed, the fleet sailed for nearby Candia, where the women stayed in a monastery near Canea before setting out again toward Venice. Outside Cerigo contrary winds forced the ships back to Milos, where the captain anchored the fleet beyond the main port in order to avoid any unpleasantness over his special passengers. Nevertheless, several of the island's chief men quickly came to the captain's ship and requested the women's return so that no Ottoman officials would think "that this was done with the consensus of [the island's] inhabitants." Mocenigo initially claimed there were "no women of any sort on the galeasses"; however, when his visitors countered that they had spoken to Maria, he warned that even if he were "cut to pieces," he would not turn them over.[51] The women remained on board, and shortly thereafter the fleet set out again for the Adriatic.

In early July, three months after first leaving Milos, Maria and her daughters arrived at the fortified island of Corfu. Under Venetian rule since 1386, Corfu had a population of perhaps fifty thousand and was an important commercial and agricultural center.[52] Its two massive fortresses made it militarily "one of the keyes of Christendomme."[53] Before disembarking, the women met with Captain Mocenigo and thanked him for providing them passage and financial support, and "knowing [their] neediness," he gave them a final gift of money, a barrel of wine, bread, and oil.[54] Once ashore, they settled into a house in the center of Corfu's main town, which Maria had paid Quartermaster Giobia to find.[55]

As we have seen in each of these narratives, the Mediterranean at this time was a constellation of connected micro-regions. Migration scholars have described the early modern age as "highly mobile,"[56] and though older scholarship considered the Mediterranean a barrier to mobility, more recent work has portrayed it as a "connecting sea" that in fact facilitated movement.[57] The Mediterranean's "liquid landscape" of islands, rivers, lagoons, coastlines, and "interlocking coastal lowlands" created a space in which "human displacement" was unexceptional and deeply rooted "in the behavior and mentality of the population."[58] This mobility was in evidence throughout the Venetian and Ottoman empires,[59] and in particular among the peripatetic Greek population of the mainland and the islands.[60] Kinship networks, emotional ties, "political constraints," and simple economic necessity all could inform migration decisions. Gender and familial status were also factors; evidence suggests that historically women's mobility, particularly toward urban centers, increased among widows.[61] Viewed against this backdrop—and in conjunction with the exploits of Fatima, Deodata, and Catterina Šatorović—Maria's willingness to uproot her family does not seem particularly unusual.

Whether she had traveled there previously or not, Corfu was clearly not an alien space for Maria, and she proved highly effective at navigating the political, ecclesiastical, and social structures that she encountered there. On July 15, immediately after her arrival, Maria had Santo Burlion, "one of the chief gentlemen of that city" (and her soon-to-be son-in-law) represent her in an audience with the island's long-serving Roman Catholic archbishop, Benedetto Bragadin.[62] Clearly foreseeing many of the issues that subsequently arose in the intense negotiations over their status, Burlion presented the story of Maria and her daughters, particularly their flight from Milos, in the light most favorable to them. The narrative the archbishop heard emphasized several key points, to which Maria, her daughters, and their supporters returned repeatedly during the inquiries that would be held over the next months: first, the women were all Christians and possessed a profound faith; second, they had fled Milos of their own free will; and third, anticipating one of the key legal issues that would arise, they were in a state of profound poverty and had voluntarily left "many goods of value" behind in order to live in Christendom. Several witnesses, including three merchants from Milos and Quartermaster Giobia, appeared before the archbishop, and all corroborated the details of this account. Bragadin was clearly impressed by what he heard, and he ordered that an official letter of support be prepared for Maria, "to be used wherever it might be necessary."[63]

The decision to have Burlion, who was a well-respected member of the island's Latin-rite community, present her case before Bragadin suggests Maria's political savvy. She had always practiced the Eastern rite and portrayed herself (and there is no reason to doubt her claims) as exceptionally pious and committed to her faith. Thus, we might reasonably assume that on her arrival in Corfu she would have sought reconciliation with the religious community of her birth by meeting with the island's *megas protopapas,* or archpriest, who shepherded the great majority of the population, who were, like Maria, Greek Orthodox.[64] Instead, she chose to have her case heard by Archbishop Bragadin who, though he presided over a very small Roman Catholic population, nonetheless was the most prestigious and influential religious official on Corfu. Bragadin was made archbishop by Paul V in 1632 at age thirty-two and, like almost all of his predecessors, he came from an important Venetian patrician family. This gave him significant influence with the political officials who ruled Corfu, as well as important connections in Venice, all of which might prove useful for Maria if her sensitive case were to escalate, as she must have rightly assumed was a distinct possibility.[65]

Maria's decision to seek the support of the archbishop, then, seems perfectly rational; it is less clear why Bragadin was so willing to throw his weight behind the women after such a cursory examination. First, there was the issue of Maria's spiritual status. Although mixed marriages between Muslim men and Orthodox women were common, particularly in "frontier districts,"[66] clerical views toward the practice were generally very negative.[67] Bragadin's contemporary Marino Bizzi, archbishop of Antivari, considered women in such relationships as "living in disgrace before God." Although some clerics sympathized with individual situations, women in mixed marriages were nonetheless "excluded from the sacraments and from attending church, . . . [and] from confession because, having given birth to children, they had consented to sin." They were also denied Christian burial.[68] Though quite common, these relationships represented "unsettling phenomena in the confessional age," particularly for ecclesiastical and political elites tasked with defining and defending distinct borders. Renegades and individuals in mixed marriages were "people whose confessional allegiance was not entirely certain or stable," and their existence underlined the fact that "the boundaries between confessions were not as sharp or impermeable" as rulers and churchmen desired them to be.[69]

Second, Bragadin's action had potential political ramifications, which could easily have been perceived as usurping the position of the megas protopapas. In general, relations between the two Christian communities on Corfu were friendly: Clergy from both participated in each other's feast day processions and masses, and they often attended each other's funerals. Several Greek churches had Latin altars, and a group of Greek monks in Cassiope were dependents of the archbishop.[70] However, there was an imbalance in the political power of the two Corfiot churches, which was exacerbated by the more aggressive policy toward the Eastern-rite Church that the Roman papacy adopted in the decades following the Council of Trent. To try and dissipate the prospect of religious conflict, Venice's rulers adopted a policy of political expediency in the treatment of its Greek subjects, and were proactive in defending their religious prerogatives.[71] Despite these potential points of contention, once again Maria successfully avoided complications, and the speed and ease with which she and her daughters were assimilated suggests a subtext that the documents do not fully address.

Even before this meeting, on the day after Maria and her daughters went ashore, several of "the chief citizens" of the town had made proposals of marriage to the two oldest girls. These were propitious offers given that there were only about 130–150 Corfiot citizen families, less than one-half of one percent of the island's total population.[72] Clearly fortune, if we choose to see it as such, continued to shine on the marital options of Maria's family. A member of one of Corfu's most influential families, Orlando Calichiopoulo, sought Maria's hand. She refused, somewhat surprisingly, preferring the relative liberty of action that came with widowhood, as many early modern women of a certain elevated economic status did.[73] Instead she elected to enter "the Monastery of Our Lady called

Antivouniotissa," one of the island's oldest and most important ecclesiastical institutions. She took the name Sister Macaria, and her youngest daughter, Catigè, known now as Catterina, joined her in the monastery.[74] Eminè, now called Anna, was promised in marriage to Zorzi, the seventeen-year-old son of Dimo Trivoli,[75] head of "one of the principal [families] of Corfu" and a holder of important government offices.[76] The marriage took place two and half years later, in 1640, when Anna had reached a more acceptable eleven years of age.[77]

Aissè, now known by her Christian name, Margherita, reversed the more commonplace practice of Christian women converting to Islam to free themselves from an undesired marriage. On July 17, just days after her arrival in Corfu, she renounced her marriage to Mustafa Efendi by wedding Santo Burlion.[78] The Burlion were a Roman Catholic family active in trade and shipping whose roots on the island dated to at least the fifteenth century.[79] They were also politically influential, with members occupying the very highest government offices.[80] Burlion fortunes peaked with Santo. Born around 1590, he entered Corfu's Grand Council at age twenty; there his political skills were quickly noted, leading to increasingly important responsibilities at a young age.[81] He was twice elected Latin Syndic, the highest office to which a Roman Catholic Corfiot could aspire, and by Margherita's appearance in 1637, he had married and already been widowed.[82] Santo's fortunes turned, however; the union with Margherita produced no surviving male heirs, and when he died in 1650, he was a "public debtor" whose house in the ghetto was sold at auction for 430 ducats.[83]

The speed with which Maria arranged such quality marriages for her daughters, her own rejection of Calichiopoulo's auspicious marriage offer, and her ability to effortlessly enter a prestigious monastery, which normally would have required a substantial spiritual dowry,[84] are all surprising, if not suspicious, given the family's allegedly desperate financial status. From the moment of their arrival in Corfu, Maria and her daughters repeatedly insisted that they had fled Milos with only clothing and a few personal items, and that they were effectively impoverished. Skepticism about their economic situation abounded, however, both on Corfu and in Venice. Some officials expressed serious doubts, noting that the fact that the women had "found so easily a husband and protection indicate[d] otherwise" than the poverty that Maria claimed. The Senate ordered an inquiry into the finances of the women and their new husbands in order to find "if they possess goods, . . . and in short to penetrate the interests that may be involved."[85] The inquiry produced no conclusive evidence that Maria had a secret stash of funds, though it did identify personal items "of some value" in her possession, and several other reports indicate she possessed goods and cash sufficient to cover at least a portion of her own expenses.[86]

That the women were "without dowry" also gave rise to questions regarding the motives of the men who rushed to marry them, particularly as the Corfiot nobility was in general considered "poor and not very industrious," and at least one of the suitors, Santo Burlion, had serious financial problems.[87] Throughout the Greek and Latin Mediterranean in the early modern period, "a marriage without a dowry was almost inconceivable."[88] So for both Burlion and Trivoli to bypass this transaction was highly unusual and, in the opinion of the suspicious Senate, highly improbable. For their part, both men claimed they had contracted the marriages with "no other objective than to perform a work of charity."[89] It is certainly possible that Burlion and Trivoli did act out of real piety, in an attempt to protect the young women from being returned to Milos. In the end, however, it seems more likely that Maria had either hidden away assets brought from Milos that she used to provide dowries for herself and her daughters or, at the very least, that she made promises of delayed payments based on assets she had left on Milos.

However it was accomplished, arranging quick marriages was a clever move on Maria's part, as it effectively forced Venice's hand when the matter mushroomed into a major diplomatic controversy. For Venice, allowing these marriages to take place was seen as an error "greatly worse" than Mocenigo's taking the women on board his ship, as they "impede the execution of public decrees since the actions done are by their nature irrevocable."[90] Already, the patriarchal rulers of Venice recoiled at the thought of sending innocent Christian women back into Muslim hands, and the fact they had contracted legal Christian marriages, or entered a monastery, made deporting them nearly impossible, though some officials still entertained the idea. To close the door on any lingering thoughts of returning the women to Milos, within a month of her marriage, Margherita announced she was pregnant.[91] Whether this was true or not (and given how little time had passed since the nuptials, and the fact that Burlion died without heirs, the story was likely manufactured), the claim of pregnancy was another clever move on Maria's part to ensure that she and her three daughters would not be returned to Milos.

While the women undoubtedly hoped that they could now settle quietly into their new lives, the contest over their future was only beginning. News traveled relatively slowly in the early modern Mediterranean, but when word of the incident on Milos finally broke, it produced a flurry of frenzied activity in Venice and Istanbul; the case was even followed with interest as far away as Rome.[92] In the lagoon, the women's flight produced a significant institutional response—the Signoria mobilized numerous magistracies with jurisdiction over affairs throughout its stato da mar; monasteries were co-opted to house the women; Venetian couriers crisscrossed the region's sea and land lanes; ships and convoys were rerouted; and significant financial resources were expended.[93] The object of all of this action was to get a clear understanding of the details of the women's flight, and then decide what to do with them. The situation played out differently in Istanbul, where several influential Ottoman officials became deeply involved, but ultimately the affair ended up being treated more privately and outside official channels.

The figure at the intersection of the Ottoman and Venetian responses was Venice's chief diplomatic representative in Istanbul, Bailo Alvise Contarini. The bailo functioned as both a diplomat and a consular official, charged with defending Venice's significant political and commercial interests throughout the Ottoman Empire. Because of the sensitivity and significance of this post, contemporaries considered the bailo the most important position in the Venetian diplomatic corps, "requiring a man of great resolution and prudence."[94] When the news of Maria's flight broke, Bailo Contarini had just taken up residence in the Ottoman capital. Though new to the Porte, and at thirty-nine comparatively young for his job, Contarini already had extensive international experience and was a rising star in Venice's diplomatic corps.[95] The Milos affair would be the first major test of the new bailo's abilities in the unique diplomatic environment of the Porte.

Contarini first heard of the incident at the end of May, in a letter dated March 29, 1637, from the Venetian consul on Milos, Filippo Benin. Benin gave a detailed overview of Maria's flight, emphasizing that the women had fled "of their own free will" and had "left all their belongings, . . . and a sum of about 2,000 reals" in Milos. In a patently false statement intended to cover up his own complicity in their flight, Benin also claimed not to have known the girls were Muslims or that Aissè was the kadi's wife.[96]

Hard on the heels of Benin's initial dispatch, on May 28 Mustafa Efendi himself appeared in the Venetian embassy. His account of events mirrored Benin's in many details, but there were two key differences. First, and most importantly, he placed responsibility for the women's departure squarely on Venice, asserting that his wife and her family were "carried away . . . [and] seduced . . . by the people on the galleys." Second, he claimed that the Venetians had also taken property beonging to him—"clothing, furniture, and furnishings valued at a great sum." These were serious charges, and Contarini's dragomans thought it one of the "most scandalous cases that had happened in many years," particularly because of the importance given to moral issues by the reform-minded Sultan Murad IV, described as "most jealous and most cruel in similar matters" related to women's honor.[97]

At their initial meeting, Contarini feigned ignorance of the situation Mustafa described to him and suggested that either the women had been taken by the notorious Livornese corsairs, the Knights of St. Stephen,[98] or that his mother-in-law had "seduced . . . and persuaded and made [the girls] flee." Mustafa "immediately closed [Contarini's] mouth," however, by producing several statements from Milos, validated by the new kadi, that supported his version of events.[99] Contarini knew that these legal documents would carry great weight in the Porte, and Mustafa too had a clear understanding of "his advantages." The kadi, however, indicated that he preferred to resolve the matter privately, rather than escalating it to the sultan's divan, "so as not to publicize his shame and the damage that he would sustain from this affair to both to his honor and to his possessions." This represented an unexpected opportunity for Contarini, who had fully expected a protracted and messy diplomatic struggle, and he quickly agreed to the proposal. However, as a new bailo and "virgin to [such] travails," Contarini refused to act on such a sensitive matter without instructions from the Senate. Mustafa agreed, but he insisted that an extraordinary courier be sent to expedite the matter because, as he once again reiterated, this was a matter "of his personal honor and of that of his wife and his sisters-in-law."[100]

During the intense diplomatic pas de deux that ensued, this question of honor—that of the women and Mustafa but also of Venice and the Ottoman Empire—was a recurring theme. The Ottoman repeatedly "bemoan[ed] the disaster he received . . . to his honor" from the flight of his wife; similarly, Venetian officials were highly attentive to ensuring the honor of the women, the kadi, and the Venetian state.[101] The *couple infernal* of honor and shame, of course, has tormented scholars for decades. Although effectively jettisoned by anthropologists,[102] historians continue to see an analytical utility in the concepts.[103] They have argued that in the early modern period, female honor was tightly linked to sexuality—virginity before marriage and chastity after it were the basis of reputation.[104] Interestingly, evidence suggests that some contemporaries also equated religious conversion with female dishonor.[105] Male honor, in contrast, was associated with courage, integrity, and status. Central to this was men's ability to ensure "the chastity and fidelity of wives, the virginity of daughters and indeed the sexual conduct of their dependent women."[106] As Annibale Romei wrote in an influential sixteenth-century treatise, a woman "cannot offend without some fault in her husband."[107] Women were essential to male honor; their dishonor contaminated men's reputations.

As Mustafa's actions indicate, honor was a cross-cultural value; similar attitudes also prevailed in the Muslim Mediterranean. "Modesty and chastity," preserved through "gender segregation," at least at certain social levels, were as vital components of Muslim women's honor, and the virtue of wives, sisters, mothers, and daughters was integral both to their reputation and to that of the family's men. A man's ability to preserve his household's honor was the cornerstone of his reputation, and Islamic law penalized male heads-of-household for the infractions of its members.[108]

Throughout the Mediterranean, men's honor had a marked public quality; it derived from achievement in the family, the marketplace, and the halls of power. Reputation, in other words, "was the essence of honor." In Florence political offices were termed *onori* (honors), and the performance of these public duties was key to the construction and preservation of personal and familial honor.[109] Similarly, in the Ottoman Balkans, the sultan could exhort the paşa of Bosnia to be vigilant against any actions that might threaten the peace and bring "prejudice, if not the loss of your honor."[110] There was a highly paternalistic quality to early modern honor that was mirrored in the relationship of rulers and their subjects, which was likened to a father's responsibilities to his family, especially his wife and daughters.[111]

Ruling elites were thus invested in preserving and expanding personal honor through the defense of the reputation of their states. In Venice, insults, blasphemy, and gossip were perceived as threats to both individual and civic honor, and their prosecution was deemed essential to the maintenance of peace and order.[112] A similar nexus of honor and order is evident in Venice's prosecution of sexual crimes, which damaged individual and family reputation and thus the honor of the republic. Evolving laws and judicial bodies sought to empower the government to preserve honor through crime prevention and to rebalance society by "providing a socially acceptable vengeance."[113] The conservation or restoration of female honor was of particular importance and increasingly was seen as the duty of states and their ruling elites, who substituted for fathers and husbands as defenders of women's virtue. In Venice, patrician magistrates and ecclesiastics were tasked with ensuring the integrity of the city's many convents and nuns, who embodied "the honor, purity, and distinction of the nobility as a class."[114] This also manifested itself in the proliferation of new institutions, such as the Casa delle Zitelle and the Convertite, to house abandoned wives, prostitutes, widows, orphans, and poor girls whose virtue was endangered.[115]

In Islamic polities, the preservation of female honor was "a primary concern," and ruling elites "had a moral imperative to safeguard" women's sexual integrity and their children's legitimacy.[116] The importance attached to the sultan's role as protector of Muslim women's honor is evidenced in the case of two Ottoman girls in the mid-sixteenth century who were captured, converted, married, and became ladies-in-waiting to Catherine de' Medici. Despite repeated attempts over two decades, the two were only freed when Murad III refused to renew France's political and commercial capitulations until the women were released.[117] As the records in the Milos case make amply clear, Venetian authorities were fully aware of the importance the Ottomans attached to women's honor, which, combined with Venetian views on the implications of safeguarding women for their own individual honor and that of the state, makes the stance Venice took in dealing with Maria and her daughters much more comprehensible.

The mass mobilization of Venetian resources did not fully begin until Bailo Contarini's May 29 dispatch recounting his first meeting with Mustafa Efendi reached the lagoon at the end of June. Its arrival created a frenzy of activity because of the serious threat the incident posed to Veneto-Ottoman relations. The Signoria immediately set in motion its extensive bureaucracy and charged it with three objectives: first, find the missing women; second, establish what had actually led to their departure from Milos; and third, resolve the incident as quietly as possible. Instructions on how to proceed were sent to officials throughout the stato da mar and to Bailo Contarini in Istanbul.

Contarini and the Senate had hoped that news of the flight of Maria and her daughters could be contained; not surprisingly, however, given the seriousness of the affair, word spread rapidly. When the Venetian fleet first departed with its passengers, the new kadi of Milos, Hassan, had been away on the island of Siphnos. As soon as he heard of the women's flight, he returned to Milos and held an inquiry into the matter. His findings matched quite closely the story that the Venetians had reconstructed, with the key difference that the Miliots questioned by Hassan all claimed that the girls had been taken forcibly. Hassan fully understood the seriousness of the case and, fearing for his new kadiship, gathered several statements in support of his actions from other Ottoman officials in the Archipelago.[118]

Even before Hassan's inquiry, word of the case had already reached the ear of Bekir Paşa, the Christian renegade bey of Rhodes and a well-known figure in the Ottoman and international communities of Istanbul and the Aegean.[119] From 1636 he had functioned as the permanent representative of the *kapudan paşa* and thus the chief Ottoman official in the Aegean.[120] The report Bekir Paşa had received indicated that several of the chief men of Milos were responsible for the women's flight into the hands of "the perfidious Christians." Based on this information, in early May the *epitropi* (heads of the community) were ordered to appear in the Porte to explain what had occurred.[121] This caused such consternation on the island that when the Jesuit Michele Albertino passed through Milos a few weeks later, he reported that the Miliots "would not let us enter their city until they knew who we were." The city was "upside-down" because of the women's flight and the departure that very day of the island's representatives for Istanbul.[122]

The group of seven epitropi, led by Giorgio Tartaruchi, arrived in the Ottoman capital in July. They were unable to meet with Bekir Paşa, who was in the Black Sea in place of his master, the kapudan paşa, who was himself functioning as *ka'immakam*, or deputy governor of Istanbul, while the grand vizier was at the Iranian front.[123] Instead they met with Bekir's *kahya* (deputy), who reproved them for being slow in coming and asked why they had "allowed the women to be taken without stopping it with weapons." The Miliots attempted to defend themselves, claiming the incident had occurred under the cover of darkness and that "no one expected such an accident since the Venetians are friends and their galleys have been in [Milos] many times, [and] they have never done a similar thing. If they had been Maltese, or Livornese, we would have stopped them." The response was ominous: "You are ruined because you are to blame for the women having left." The kahya claimed he did not dare take the matter up with the kapudan paşa/ka'immakam, and he counseled the men to lie low for ten or fifteen days until Bekir Paşa returned "and then we will come to some resolution." He concluded with the warning, "Do not let the bailo see you."[124]

Despite the kahya's admonition, Tartaruchi did meet surreptitiously with the Venetian in order to discuss their common "interests." Armed with the Miliots' report, Bailo Contarini arranged a meeting with the kahya on the pretext of getting to know him better. Several gifts loosened up the official, who revealed that as the incident had taken place in his master's jurisdiction, it was not necessary to involve others and that he fully expected that Bekir Paşa "would take care of everything with little difficulty." In addition, the ka'immakam's secretary had caught wind of the situation, but with two hundred reals Contarini purchased his silence, at least until the return of Bekir Paşa. From these encounters—and the regular visits of the spurned husband Mustafa Efendi during which he decried "the calamities . . . to his honor and his property," all while seeking small handouts—the bailo became convinced that "neither the kadi nor Bekir's kahya cared so much about the women" as they did about resolving the matter privately and to their profit. Other informed sources reported that Mustafa Efendi was "a man of little authority, of lowly condition, and very greedy for money."[125] With the excuse that he was awaiting direction from Venice, Contarini kept the situation in check throughout the summer, though as time passed, Mustafa Efendi became increasingly impatient and began threatening to take the matter before the imperial divan.[126]

It was only after the arrival of Maria and her daughters in Corfu in mid-July that the political ramifications of their flight came into focus. On July 23, several days following Margherita's marriage, *Provveditore dell'armata* Zuane Mocenigo arrived at the Ionian port that functioned as his headquarters. He had already been informed of the situation in Istanbul in a letter from Bailo Contarini, and in Corfu he found letters from the Senate with instructions on how to address this very sensitive matter.[127]

Mocenigo immediately began an investigation. He first interviewed his kinsman and subordinate in the fleet, Captain Pietro Mocenigo, who tried to put the best face on what clearly represented a failure of judgment on his part. Captain Mocenigo insisted "the women had come on his galleass voluntarily with the sole purpose of becoming Christians, and without having brought anything with them." He also claimed that the inhabitants of Milos wanted the women off the island as no "Turks" except the kadi were permitted to live there. In fact, he claimed, the people of the island had praised his "great charity" in conducting "these innocent creatures to the bosom of the Holy Church." Mocenigo concluded with a mea culpa: "If I had had even the most minimal concern that this affair might create difficulty in Constantinople, I of course would not have agreed to give [the women] passage, even though Christian piety inspired me greatly."[128] Despite his earnest self-defense, Mocenigo was recalled to Venice and replaced soon thereafter.[129]

Zuane Mocenigo also convened a multiday hearing to examine Maria and her daughters, their servants, and members of the Venetian crew. The provveditore's line of questioning did not vary among any of those he interrogated. First, he attempted to determine whether the women had been coerced or forced to flee. All who testified concurred that their flight had been voluntary. Second, he tried to establish what the women had taken with them from Milos. Mocenigo ordered a full inventory of their possessions, which revealed only personal clothing items and a few small trinkets. Dimo Trivoli and Santo Burlion were also questioned. They supported Maria's protestations of poverty and further claimed to have provided Anna and Margherita with "bracelets, pearls, earrings, and rings" and "all the clothes . . . that [they were] presently wearing." Despite these findings, strong suspicions remained that the women had brought money, jewels, or other valuables with them and had hidden these away before the inventory. The insistent claims of Mustafa Efendi, as well as several reports from Venetian sources, reinforced these doubts.[130] A final focus of the hearing was the treatment the women had received while in Venetian care; to the relief of Venice's rulers, it was confirmed that the family had always been dealt with honorably.[131]

Immediately following the inquiry, on August 1, as directed by the Senate, Mocenigo sent Maria and her daughters to Candia, accompanied by Santo Burlion and several of his family members. Once again the security and reputation of the women was paramount. "A good escort of galleons" was sent to accompany them, and Mocenigo personally arranged "the most rigorous custodial care" for his charges. He ordered Venetian officials to ensure that they received "the most courteous treatment" and to be vigilant in "the preservation of the [women's] honor."[132] When Maria and her daughters reached Canea in late August, the rector of the city took personal responsibility for their care and placed them in the secure convent of Santo Spirito. There, while their case dragged on, they "passed their days with disgust and displeasure, as it seemed to them that they were more like prisoners." Constantly fearing that "they might be returned to their land," at one point "in desperation" Maria and Margherita threatened "they would rather take their own lives than return" to Milos and to Islam.[133]

The Senate wanted Maria and her family back in Candia so that two of its most senior and experienced officials—the *inquisitori di Levante,* Marco Contarini and Pietro Correr—could deal with what had developed into a case fraught with legal, religious, and political consequences.[134] The inquisitors' difficult charge was to get as clear a picture as possible of what actually had happened on Milos and in the intervening months and then, in close consultation with the Senate and Bailo Contarini, to decide what to do with Maria, Margherita, Anna, and Caterina.

Once again, a key objective of the inquisitori's investigation was to establish whether "pure inclination to return to the Christian religion led them to leave Milos" or, as Mustafa Efendi and other Ottomans claimed, they had been compelled.[135] Zuane Mocenigo's brief inquiry had persuasively indicated that the women's flight had been voluntary. However, "evidence strongly contrary" to this version of events also existed—the women had disappeared at night in the company of armed men, and Pietro Mocenigo had refused to release them when requested to do so by Milos's community chiefs. Most compelling was the legal weight of the *hüccet*s by Ottoman officials supporting Mustafa's claims, which Contarini and Correr realized would greatly outweigh Zuane Mocenigo's findings among members of the Ottoman divan.[136] To offset these documents, the inquisitors sent an agent to Milos who through a well-placed gift obtained a hüccet stating that the women had "boarded the galeasses . . . of their own free will, without assistance or violence by anyone . . . [and that] they left behind all their goods."[137]

Another vital issue in this final Venetian inquiry was the women's religious status. Maria had remained a fervent Christian throughout her years in Milos, but her daughters' situation was more ambiguous. All witnesses acknowledged the girls had been raised as Muslims. Maria claimed, however, and her daughters verified, that they had been baptized and had lived secretly as Christians. The question of whether the girls' decision to abandon Islam had been voluntary was pivotal; if they had acted of their own free will, there was a broad consensus that "it was not in the interests of the Republic's piety to return them."[138] Theologically, this was a murky question. Although forced conversions were widely decried, in the many contemporary cases of Jewish children who were baptized by Christians without the knowledge of their parents, ecclesiastical officials maintained that, whether voluntary or not, their baptisms were valid and irreversible. Venetian law attempted to prevent such occurrences by penalizing those who baptized children under age fourteen without parental permission, but it did not address the issue of secret baptism carried out by one parent without the knowledge or the permission of the other.[139]

While the Venetians struggled to resolve these issues, Islamic law, as Mustafa Efendi knew very well, was very clear about the girls' religious identities and the status of his marriage to Margherita. In the case of the two younger girls, Anna and Catterina, as Mustafa argued, Islamic jurists unanimously held that children of a mixed marriage were "born into the religion of their fathers." According to the Ottoman Hanafi legal tradition, at the age of seven a child became a minor with certain limited financial and legal rights. Minority ended at "the onset of physical maturity, and the ability to control one's own affairs," though actual practice varied depending on time and place. Because the two youngest girls were "not yet adults," he insisted, they were "not in a state to be able to change religion as they saw fit."[140] Even if children or minors renounced Islam formally, or if influenced by their non-Muslim mothers they ceased to consider themselves Muslim, the law nonetheless obliged them to remain in their birth faith. If they refused, they faced severe punishment, potentially even death.[141]

No one questioned Margherita's majority, and thus her ability to choose conversion, but her status as Mustafa's wife raised other issues. Because there were so many mixed marriages and so many apostasies in the Mediterranean, questions about the status of marriages in which one partner converted were widespread among Muslims, Christians, and Jews.[142] Islamic law permitted Muslim men to marry outside their faith, and such marriages were common. Muslim women, of course, could only marry Muslim men. Christian sects strongly discouraged cross-confessional matches but often found it necessary to accommodate them.[143] Regarding conversion there were also differences: Christians generally held that conversion did not nullify the marriage bond, but it could be acceptable grounds for divorce.[144] According to the four major Sunni legal schools, a spouse's conversion to or abandonment of Islam dissolved the marital tie after a brief waiting period, and there are many cases in which women used conversion, as Fatima did, as a means to liberate themselves from unwanted marriages.[145] Nevertheless, Mustafa insisted that Margherita remained his wife whether she was Christian or not. If, as Maria stridently claimed, Margherita had indeed been baptized as an infant, then as Mustafa rightly argued, her marriage to him at age nine remained in vigor and was unaffected by her flight, as sharia law allowed him to marry a non-Muslim.[146]

In the end, the legal nuances of the case were much less significant than its political and diplomatic implications. Because of the affair's potential to disrupt Veneto-Ottoman relations, Venetian officials debated intensely over how to proceed. Venice had long-standing capitulations with the Ottomans that, as Mustafa repeatedly pointed out, were operative in this case. Cases of cross-border flight were common enough that the capitulations directly addressed the issue of extradition. All Ottoman subjects who fled to Venetian lands were to "be personally and immediately returned" along with all the goods and possessions they might "have taken with them." The same held true for Venetian subjects moving in the opposite direction.[147] As officials in both Venice and Istanbul knew, however, the reality along the frontier was much more complicated than the stark language of the capitulations would suggest. As they had done in the case of Mihale Šatorović, the Venetians tried to argue "that given the friendship [between Venice and the Ottomans] these sorts of passages of subjects from one side to the other had been practiced by both without suspicion" or concern, and that the case of Maria and her family ought to be considered in light of this long precedent of turning a blind eye to the border crossings between the two states.[148] But because of the status of the women and the position of Mustafa Efendi, and because the issue had been escalated to both capitals, this attempt by the Venetians ultimately fell flat.

From his vantage point in Istanbul, Bailo Contarini wavered in his views on how to resolve the impasse with honor but also with the least difficulty. One possibility he explored in his communications with the Senate was simply to return the women to Milos and Mustafa and be done with the whole affair. Alternatively, he suggested that the only way "this matter [could be] resolved to public advantage" would be to claim that the women could not be found anywhere "and that they disappeared into the wind, as would unfortunately have been better had it happened to them, so as not to nourish the serpent in the breast of the Republic, at least until the memory of this affair dissipated." This plan, Contarini argued, would allow Venice to "preserve the public piety toward those souls" and at the same time avoid serious political ramifications.[149] In the end, however, Contarini's pragmatic position enjoyed little support. During the course of the summer and early fall, a consensus developed that Maria and her daughters would not be returned to Milos, even though Venice's officials clearly understood "the intention of public charity" not to turn over the women made for a "very difficult" diplomatic and political situation for *La Serenissima*.[150]

The unwillingness to deport the young women was motivated in part by the sense of duty Venice's male rulers felt to protect women (and children) and thereby preserve the city's honor and reputation. This paternalistic attitude was informed by schizophrenic early modern views of women's religiosity, which considered them "to piety more prone" but at the same time disorderly, incontinent, unreliable, intellectually weak, and irrational.[151] These liabilities, it was generally believed, made women vulnerable to heretical ideas[152] and "to the pressures of the Muslims," and thus more prone to conversion.[153] This spiritual peril was accentuated by Venice's view of the Mediterranean as a liminal and treacherous space (ideas paralleled by Muslim fears about the dangers of *dar al-harb* to their own women's weak faith).[154] The caricatured figure of the lascivious "Turk" lusting after both men and women[155] made the Mediterranean, in the minds of many, a place "given all to whoredome, sodometrie, theft, and all other most detestable vices," where "the liberty of Turkish living, . . . [could] make a saint a devil."[156] Thus, rulers attempted to prevent women from traveling in the region; diplomats tried to compel them to return home; and redemptionist religious orders gave priority to their liberation.[157] That Margherita and her sisters were guilty of apostasy (*irtidad*)—the punishment for which ranged from death to imprisonment and beatings "every three days until they return to Islam"—made it even more unthinkable that the women would be returned.[158] For Venice, the bodies and souls of Maria and her daughters were at stake, as was the honor of the city and its ruling elite.

The deliberations and negotiations dragged on for months. By late summer, Mustafa Efendi had become impatient and appeared poised finally to take the matter before the divan. Bailo Contarini used all his diplomatic prowess to stave this off, including buying time by giving gifts and small payments to the spurned husband. In mid-September, no doubt despairing that the matter would ever be resolved and needing to assume his new kadiship, Mustafa "let it be known" that he would be willing to settle the matter for two thousand reals. Still awaiting the Senate's final decision on how to proceed, Contarini took matters into his own hands to resolve "this most thorny affair." He ultimately negotiated the settlement down to five hundred reals and two suits of clothing.[159] In return, Mustafa produced a sworn statement "renounc[ing] every legal claim against the captains of certain Venetian galleasses" and acknowledging that the women had not been kidnapped but rather "had departed voluntarily, seduced by the aforementioned Maria, who was Christian."[160]

Because of the communication lag and Venice's desire to ensure the complete resolution of the matter, Maria and her daughters were kept in Canea for several more months. This proved wise as Contarini ended up paying an additional seven hundred reals to several other Ottoman officials, including Bekir Paşa, to prevent the case from flaring back up. Mustafa also had to make a significant payment to Bekir to assuage his anger at being left out of the negotiations. In November, Maria and her daughters were allowed to leave the convent of Santo Spirito and circulate about the city more freely.

In late December they received permission "to return in liberty to their [new] homes" on Corfu, but bad weather prevented them from sailing until March 1638, when they departed under the watchful protection of the inquisitori di Levante themselves. On April 5, almost exactly one year after they had fled Milos, Maria and her daughters finally returned to Corfu.[161]

In Istanbul, a relieved Bailo Contarini provided an epitaph to the affair. The women had "a great obligation to pray to God for the prosperity of the Most Serene Republic that gave them with the liberty of their bodies and also the means to save their souls."[162] Of course, this was only partly true. Margherita, Anna, and Catterina had their mother to thank as much as Venice for their new lives. Though the documents are silent on the details, it seems reasonable to imagine that as she sailed into the harbor of Corfu under the cannon of its great fortress, Maria may have enjoyed a moment of satisfaction, mingled with relief, at the successful resolution of her gambit to keep her family together and to free her daughters from "the vomit of infidelity."[163]

Conclusion

THE LIFE SKETCHES PRESENTED in these pages function, on the most basic level, as simple stories. They are, if I have succeeded, engaging tales that illuminate and breathe life into a distant, but hopefully not entirely unrecognizable, past. Rather than take a traditional historical monographic approach, I have chosen to place the women's experiences on center stage and to develop my arguments and analysis more obliquely. Although narrative may not always be the best vehicle for mobilizing an argument, I have attempted through these "thick narratives" to touch on structures and mentalities that may offer broader insights into the cultural world of the early modern Mediterranean.[1]

The obvious protagonists of this book are the women—Beatrice/Fatima Michiel, Elena/Suor Deodata Civalelli, Mihale/Catterina Šatorović, and Maria Gozzadini and her daughters, Aissè/Margherita, Eminè/Anna, and Catigè/Catterina. In many ways, however, the Mediterranean is itself a character in each account as well; the sea's "liquid landscape" and the terra firma backdrop of its islands, peninsulas, and coasts all play a pivotal role in the tales' development.

As a work of Mediterranean scholarship, this book fits into a long historiographical tradition, from Fernand Braudel's *La Méditerranée et le monde méditerranéen à l'époque de Philippe II*, one of the great works of twentieth-century historical erudition and imagination, to Peregrine Horden and Nicholas Purcell's equally weighty and more recent tome, *The Corrupting Sea: A Study of Mediterranean*

History. With their sweeping, multimillennial, interdisciplinary treatments, these influential works are primarily concerned with the elusive question of Mediterranean unity—whether the sea and its borders function as an analytical whole and, if so, what elements unite this diverse region and validate its study. Beyond these ambitious, "Olympian" historiographical manifestos, scholars have more often produced much more modest histories *in,* rather than *of,* the Mediterranean. These efforts narrowly treat a specific region, city, or topic, and they rarely address the broader question of Mediterranean unity.[2] Despite their proximity, these two approaches to Mediterranean research—histories *of* and histories *in*—have often only loosely informed each other.

What I have attempted here is to join these two historiographical strands in a study that focuses microscopically on the local yet places it into a broader, macroscopic Mediterranean context. Geographically, the book is Mediterranean in that the stories it presents range from Venice to Istanbul, from the Balkans to the Aegean, with tendrils of comparison reaching to Romania, France, Spain, and North Africa. It is also Mediterranean in that, while not explicitly engaging the debate on Mediterranean unity, one of its foundational assumptions is that amid great diversity and complexity, there are commonalities that make the Mediterranean a useful tool of analysis. I see the Mediterranean as "an arena of interaction, of encounters and exchanges" that allows us to move beyond the narrow *campanalismo* that can characterize national historiographies, to transcend the over-magnification of religious alterity and antagonism that often distort our understanding of Islam and Christianity, and instead to discern a more connected, multifaceted, and complex Mediterranean world.[3] By examining gender in this transcultural and transreligious context, these tales provide insight into the little-studied lives of Mediterranean women, and more ambitiously, they suggest ideas about the wider early modern Mediterranean and the ways the sea informed people's experiences.

At the most fundamental level, then, these narratives function in a compensatory role by attending to Mediterranean women: two girls from opposite sides of the Veneto-Ottoman border in Dalmatia, a Christian mother and her Muslim daughters who fled an Ottoman Greek island for a Venetian one, and a Venetian wife and mother navigating the halls of the Ottoman imperial palace. These are stories of women, both old and young, Muslim and Christian, who have remained generally unknown to us. While not "everywoman," they are also certainly not "women worthies"—queens, saints, great literary or artistic figures, the daughters or wives or mothers of great men. Rather, they are, like most Mediterranean women, on the whole unextraordinary, invisible, and forgotten by time.[4] Their "obliterated" lives are partly a byproduct of women in general being "systematically left out of the official record," a challenge that is even more accentuated when dealing with women who inhabit the interstices of the Mediterranean.[5] Sources to reconstruct these forgotten lives are elusive; reconstructing these women's stories required research in archives spread throughout the region, engagement with both Mediterranean historiography and the numerous national historical literatures, and navigating the Babel-like multiplicity of Mediterranean languages. Were it not for their social capital, which attracted the attention of political and religious institutions, as well as a dose of archival good fortune, these women, like so many others, would have inevitably remained unknown to us. And even as it stands, frustrating lacunae remain in all three cases, questions that call out for answers to which the surviving documents simply do not permit us to reply.

These stories are significant, then, because they recover the lives of Mediterranean women, about whom we know comparatively little. Even as Mediterranean studies have expanded significantly in recent years, the study of gender in the region has lagged, particularly in comparison with the rich literature on the Atlantic world.[6] There are ample studies that focus on gender in specific regional settings—Venice, the Iberian peninsula, the Balkans, the Ottoman Empire—but almost nothing in a broadly Mediterranean context.[7] While modest in its scope, this book represents an initial attempt to study gender from a truly Mediterranean vantage point. Each life story is re-created in specific individual detail but is then placed into a broader Mediterranean context. The perspective captured by this wide-angle approach helps address the historiographical lacuna on Mediterranean gender, but even more, it opens up rich and suggestive vistas that can be obscured by zooming in too narrowly. Looking at the lives of these women in detail and comparatively across the expanses of the Mediterranean, reveals many similarities in their experiences with marriage, divorce, motherhood, childhood, agency, patriarchy, honor, religious identity, dissimulation, conversion, and the manipulation of frontiers. These shared strands suggest the need for a more layered and fluid understanding of the Mediterranean and its women, one that transcends the stark boundaries that are too easily erected to divide the region into seemingly irreconcilable and antithetical blocks.

The physical space of the Mediterranean's islands and peninsulas, its lengthy coastal areas and hinterlands, its highways and waterways play an essential role in each woman's experience. Braudel described the Mediterranean as "an immense network of regular and casual connections,"[8] a position embraced and more fully articulated by Horden and Purcell, who identify the interconnectedness "of relatively easy seaborne communications" as the essential component of the region's unity.[9] With this connectivity inevitably came mobility, "the ceaseless circulation of humans" that was a defining attribute of Mediterranean life.[10] This connectedness and mobility created a Mediterranean characterized not by isolation and separation but by a culture of "widely shared attitudes and values." This evidence in turn necessitates a reexamination of the traditional vision of the sea cleaved along religious and political lines, the arena for the clash of great and eternally opposed civilizations.[11] Where frontiers previously evoked visions of a binary space of cultural collision, more recent scholarship has emphasized them as sites of cultural contact, hybrid zones, middle-grounds, places of much greater complexity than simple confrontation, collision, or, for that matter, assimilation or negotiation.[12] This new Mediterranean is "borderless," "uncentred," an *espace transitoire*, whose "edges are places not of barriers but of interaction."[13] This is evident in the work of "post-Orientalist scholars" who have replaced—or, better, supplemented—the vision of a conflictual Mediterranean with one in which there existed "shared patterns," not only in areas ranging from art, architecture, and cartography to food, science, and military technologies, but also in social practices and popular cultural attitudes regarding gender, honor, and religion. This new emphasis has effectively undercut the foundations of "the Orientalist notion of clear-cut religious and cultural boundaries in the early modern Mediterranean."[14]

The permeable, fuzzy boundaries of the Middle Sea's interconfessional space are evident in the experiences of the women studied here; their religious identities and practices were fluid, diverse, individual, yet also shared and communal. In the Mediterranean, "the certainty of faith" was often quite weak, and the view expressed by Carlo Ginzburg's famed miller, Menocchio, that "the majesty of God has given the Holy Spirit to all, to Christians, to Turks, and to Jews; and he considers them all dear, and they are all saved in the same manner," was widely shared.[15] In this quintessential "edge" situation, far removed from political and religious centers, there was great variability and imprecision in belief, which often caused religious elites significant concern.[16] Practice in this setting, more than theology, defined and marked communal and individual religious identities.[17] Political authorities, inquisitions, or muftis might attempt to demarcate orthodoxy and to inscribe fixed, unyielding boundaries of behavior, costume, foodways, and social conventions, but in reality these borders were porous and malleable.

Mediterranean connectedness played an essential role in the lives of each of these women. The sea that they inhabited produced a unique geographical context of "relative proximity . . . but also clear separation," what we might call proximate separation.[18] The sea, in other words, both joined and divided its constituent parts and created a familiar foreignness that made physical and psychological migration possible both to imagine and to execute. The sea's physical, political, and cultural boundaries all served as fulcrums by which women willing to transgress borders might prize themselves free from circumstances in which they normally had limited power to act and to refashion their lives.

Catterina Šatorović's flight required little more than a brief walk across a poorly defined border, and the language, culture, and people she encountered on the other side were entirely familiar. Maria and her daughters, crisscrossing among the Greek islands of the Aegean and Ionian seas, encountered equally recognizable cultural spaces. Fatima's escape represented a much greater leap, but she, too, found familiarity and acceptance among fellow renegades and migrants from Venetian territories amid the tremendous diversity of the Ottoman capital. The viability of travel and the anticipation of being able to understand, and even navigate, what might be encountered across a border, over a mountain, or on another island were essential to these women's ability to assert agency through their movements across frontiers.

Of course, to say women were agents, that they exerted what Stephen Greenblatt has described as "shaping power" over their own lives, is to say nothing particularly new or insightful.[19] The concept of agency has been debated extensively since the rise of social history in the second half of the twentieth century, influenced in no small part by structuralist views advanced by Braudel and many others. Some scholars, feeling a certain saturation with questions of agency, have expressed their reservations about the imprecision of the concept, which, as they rightly suggest, can obscure "the extent of choicelessness" and the very tangible nature of the abundant constraints, particularly on women, that existed in the premodern world.[20] This is certainly an important corrective, and I have sought to acknowledge such limitations throughout the text, but I am not convinced that we can elucidate and understand the experience of early modern women without recourse to questions of agency, particularly in the underdeveloped field of Mediterranean gender studies.

Historical scholarship over the past several decades has produced a rich and extensive body of literature revealing the extent and means of women's exercise of agency in the early modern era in a variety of settings.[21] This research has illustrated the broad-ranging and complex character of women's experience and roles in the home and family; in religious orders and institutions; in courts of law and the halls of power; in the marketplace and in the countryside; and in art, music, and literature. Although it is impossible to summarize such a rich and diverse body of work, scholars have been nearly unanimous in arguing that while there was a seemingly endless range of social, cultural, religious, and political constraints that weighed heavily on early modern women, they nonetheless had available to them "a wide field of action" and were "active agents in their own destinies."[22] The women's stories recounted here contribute to this discourse by illuminating the choices and modes of subversion available to women at the intersection of Mediterranean frontiers, and the ways that they used these as an escape, a defense, and a source of leverage.

Fatima's case presents a woman in a set of circumstances very common to the early modern period: motherhood, widowhood, and being trapped in an unhappy marriage. She responded to her situation, however, in a distinctively Mediterranean fashion. First, she maneuvered the political and religious borders between the Venetian and Ottoman empires to extricate herself from the troubled relationship with her second husband. She then converted and married an Ottoman official, her third marriage, which gave her access to the center of Ottoman power, the imperial harem, and provided her with greatly enhanced status, wealth, and influence. Finally, she used this new standing as leverage to benefit herself and the two sons she had left behind in Venice. In some ways, Fatima's is the quintessential renegade story: a Christian who "turned Turk" and seemingly "rebelled against the faith" by embracing Islam, though not for theological reasons but rather for very pragmatic economic and social ones.[23] There are two aspects of her tale, however, that make it unique.

First, the period 1500 to 1650 was the golden age of the renegade; they are estimated to have numbered in the hundreds of thousands and were "a sensational subject that inspired anxious fascination."[24]

Despite this, almost nothing has been written about renegade women.[25] In part, this is because existing renegade scholarship has been based nearly entirely on inquisitorial records, in which men appear disproportionately.[26] Women renegades surface much less frequently in these sources, in part because, as has been convincingly documented, many more men than women converted. Gender plays an essential role in this imbalance, however, as women were clearly less inclined or able to return to their birth faith due to ties to children and spouses in their adopted lands, and because cultural constraints and attitudes could make women's movement both in leaving and returning home more difficult than men's, though, as we have seen, not impossible. Thus, men's flight (or capture) was logistically more commonplace and straightforward than women's.[27] Women renegades may also have blended back into their birth communities more easily because they bore no external signs that marked them as converts, such as the circumcision that some male converts to Islam (and rarely Judaism) underwent.[28] Because there were fewer women renegades, and fewer still who returned to their birth religious community, their experiences appear more rarely in inquisitorial records, which primarily treat renegades who sought readmittance to the Christian body. If we rely solely on these sources, then the lives of women who permanently left their homes, their families, and their religions are forever lost to us. One of the challenges in excavating renegade women's lives, then, is finding viable documentary sources. The stories recounted here come not from inquisitorial sources but rather from a wide range of diplomatic, political, ecclesiastical, notarial, and historical records, and indeed the women's own voices occasionally filter through in rare documentary forms of "self-narration" such as letters and transcribed statements.

At its most basic level, then, Fatima helps us recover the often-ignored experience of women renegades. Her tale also illustrates how gender informed renegades' motivations in converting. While men's reasons for conversion were varied and complex, they were most often driven by hopes for greater social mobility and financial gain, which were widely perceived as being more available in the Ottoman world, or they converted as a means to escape social, political, and economic difficulties in their homelands.[29] In contrast, the circumstances that induced Fatima to convert fit patterns that scholars have tentatively identified among women in other settings.[30] These were often centered on complex familial situations—financially grasping or neglectful husbands, the inability to dissolve an unhappy marriage, parents trying to impose undesirable matches, or concerns over their children. Of course, these are not exclusively women's issues; nor, as Fatima's case shows, were socioeconomic or political matters components solely in men's conversions. Conversion was complex, multivalent, and motivated by a web of factors. Although women's history does not equate solely with family history, the cultural and biological realities of most women's lives made domestic issues—marriage, divorce, dowry, child-rearing—figure centrally in each of these cases.[31]

Many of the same themes in Fatima's story are mirrored in the experience of Maria Gozzadini and her three daughters. Theirs is a particularly suggestive case in that it documents in detail the much less familiar process of Muslim women's apostasy and introduces the issue of mixed marriage and its impact on family relationships in the Mediterranean. For the Miliot women, the liquid boundaries of the Greek islands were their corridor of escape, and the institutions of marriage and monastery were the bulwarks that prevented their repatriation. The intersection of gender and honor evident in Maria's tale links with the other stories as well. The paternalistic attitudes of male-dominated political institutions deemed women (and children) frail and weak, and therefore much more susceptible to conversion. Religion and honor required that Venice's ruling elites protect what they perceived as the fragile faith of Maria and her daughters (and Catterina Šatorović and Deodata, too), even though doing so carried a high political price. The girls' quick marriages, and Maria's entry into a convent, show the women's intentional use of the burden of honor to influence institutional deliberations and avoid returning to a former husband and home. If societal attitudes and structures subordinated women, they also afforded a certain power to subvert and manipulate gender structures in ways that benefited them.[32]

In the cases of Deodata and Catterina Šatorović—one the Christian daughter of a Zaratine noble family, the other the Muslim daughter of an Ottoman official—both confronted similar circumstances but from opposite sides of the religious and political frontiers of Dalmatia, and each attempted to shape her future in similar fashion. Both girls used the Veneto-Ottoman border as a means to liberate themselves from the threat of unwanted marriages; both ultimately used the walls of the same religious institution, the Casa delle Zitelle, to ward off attempts by their parents to regain control over them, and also as a way to force the hand of their Venetian protectors, who could not honorably expel their wards and expose them to spiritual peril, despite the real political advantages to be gained by doing so. These two cases illustrate the negotiation between the often irreconcilable wishes and aspirations of parents and their children, and suggest ways, admittedly dramatic but not entirely isolated or unique, that both Muslim and Christian girls might, within the structures and strictures of the cultures they inhabited, exercise agency in directing the course of their young lives.

The experiences of all of these women, but particularly of Fatima and the Gozzadini family, also suggest ways in which gender informs Mediterranean religious identity. The view that women are more inherently religious than men, and therefore less susceptible to conversion, is deeply rooted in both sociological and historical literature.[33] Jewish and Coptic women in Egypt have both been found more likely to have resisted conversion to Islam, "in comparison to men."[34] In Spain, it has been argued that both Morisco[35] and Jewish women were more resistant to conversion because of their "maternal role" in perpetuating tradition and "socializing their children."[36] Similar roles have been attributed to women among France's Huguenot and Crete's crypto-Christian communities.[37] However, scholars working in other contexts, from late-classical Rome to the early modern Waldensian valleys, have also shown the opposite, that women were often very open to religious change, in some cases even more so than men.[38] In Reformation France, no set pattern for women's involvement in religious movements has been identified, and several studies have convincingly shown that throughout the Ottoman Mediterranean women's conversion to escape marriage was widespread.[39]

The cases studied here show women both willing to embrace and committed to defying conversion. It seems clear that Fatima decided to convert in order to free herself from a failed second marriage and as a way to benefit herself and her sons. Catterina Šatorović willingly refashioned herself as a Christian to avoid an undesired match arranged by her father; Deodata resisted conversion for the exact same reason. Whereas Margherita converted to free herself from a marriage she no longer wanted, her mother Maria rejected conversion for years, despite being in a mixed relationship that she did not desire. These women's religious choices were voluntary and intentional, not a product of compulsion or the desperation of a slave, which scholars have often emphasized as being characteristic of women's conversions.[40] In other words, Mediterranean women might resist or embrace conversion out of belief, self-interest, fear, or compulsion. There is not a single model of Mediterranean women's conversion. Most converts did not experience "a clear, new religious identity" but rather "ambivalence and tension" as they negotiated the shoals of "adapting to a new faith and preserving an old" one. These were not the archetypal Pauline conversions of Christian tradition; rather, they fit more easily with the conversion that recent studies describe as a contextualized process, "a passage" rather than a single ecstatic event, influenced by a matrix of economic, cultural, social, and political factors that articulate "new forms of relatedness."[41]

This malleability and multivalence of religious identity is also evident in the religious dissimulation Fatima and Maria and her daughters practiced, which was common throughout the region. Although political and religious elites might be distressed by the imprecision and permeability of religious and political identities, for many more people in the early modern Mediterranean this seems not to have been unusual, or even always necessarily troubling. The women studied here found an acceptable place "poised between . . . religions," which just as it unsettled early modern authorities, also challenges our modern proclivity for clear-cut religious homogeneity and orthodoxy.[42] The experiences of these women illustrate the need to approach sweeping generalizations about women's religiosity with caution. Women were probably no more or less inclined to conversion than men; they voluntarily chose, refused, or could occasionally be compelled to convert, and their "apparent greater religiosity" was instead "a social construct," not a product of innate, natural differences.[43]

A central theme of this book is the shared rhythms of the Mediterranean, but in acknowledging this we must not ignore or elide its "infinitely complex" character or its "diversity within unity."[44] Our tales make clear some of these religious, cultural, and political differences. For Fatima, the possibility of obtaining a divorce in the Ottoman Empire only difficultly attainable in Venice factored into her decision to leave. Conversely, the existence of uniquely Christian female religious institutions not present in the Islamic world played an important role in the ability of Catterina Šatorović and Maria Gozzadini to extricate themselves from unwanted family situations. And, too, in inserting these women's experiences into a wider Mediterranean context, we should not assume the existence of an undifferentiated, monolithic Mediterranean woman. The lives of women in this highly diverse region differed according to marital situation, social class, economic condition, vocation, religious affiliation, lay or cloistered status, family configuration, geographic location, and rural or urban setting.[45]

This raises one final point, namely the question of exceptionality and representativity. In a notable critique of Carlo Ginzburg's famous book, *The Cheese and the Worms,* Paola Zambelli posited the question of "*Uno, due, tre, mille Menocchio?*"[46] This is the obvious critique of microhistory—to what degree can we "elaborate a paradigm which hinges on knowledge of the particular"?[47] We might well pose the same question to this book: "One, two, three, a thousand Fatimas?" Historians prefer to buttress and triangulate their arguments through a multiplicity of examples, but the vicissitudes of the past, cultural and institutional attitudes and imperatives, or the fickleness of archival preservation can conspire to limit us to "just one witness."[48] Any historian of the early modern Mediterranean faces these challenges, especially when telling women's stories. Such obstacles do not justify ignoring, nor can they devalue, attempts to tell the stories of scarce, individual lives that would normally be lost to us. Indeed, the narrow focus of microbiographical sketches can reveal facets of a time and place that remain obscured when surveyed from a panoramic societal viewpoint. Both are essential, and when viewed together, the minute details and the broad brushstrokes can paint a compelling and more complete picture.

I would argue that the cases of Fatima, Deodata, Catterina Šatorović, and Maria represent "the exceptional normal."[49] Their experiences reveal a much wider reality than just the slender details of their own admittedly engaging lives. If there is something extraordinary about these women and their stories, it is the level of detail and insight that the sources have permitted us to have into their lives. The motivations and fortunes manifest in their experiences are mirrored in those of many other Mediterranean women about whom we know much less. This is evident in the widespread popularity in the region's literature of tales that contain similar elements, from Cervantes' Zoraida in *Don Quixote* and his play *La gran sultana* to the veritable industry of "Turk" plays produced on European stages of the day.[50] Archives also contain many examples of other renegade women. These range from the wife and children of a janissary who fled Ottoman Chios for Venetian Cerigo in 1626,[51] to the three women who left Tunisia for Venice to become Christians;[52] from early modern Geneva's "walk-away wives," who in the absence of easy divorces ended their marriages by crossing into nearby France or Savoy,[53] to the wife of a Venetian consul who poisoned her husband and with her daughter "sought refuge . . . in a kadi's house where they became Muslims."[54] The growing body of research on catechumens in Italy, Spain, Portugal, and even far-away Goa provides many more examples of similar early modern female border crossers, though not in the same depth of detail that has been possible in these case studies.[55]

Perhaps the most telling indication that the women that we have shadowed in these pages were not exceptional is the archival whispers of similar tales from the same frontier region between the Venetian and Ottoman empires. In all our women's cases, Venetian (and several Ottoman) officials repeatedly emphasized how ordinary such renegade episodes were along the border, and they expressed sincere surprise when these particular instances escalated. When Captain Pietro Mocenigo defended his actions in helping Maria and her daughters flee, he referred to an earlier incident in which another kadi's wife was squired away from Milos by a galley captain for romantic reasons, without, however, the same "exclamations" or "lamentations in the Porte" or from Venetian authorities.[56] On the Dalmatian coast, such cases occurred with even greater frequency. In the early seventeenth century a Muslim woman from Clissa named Sultana fled to Venice, converted, and became a nun.[57] Some years later two young Ottoman girls slipped across the border to Spalato, converted, and were sent to Lissa and then to Venice; two more Ottoman girls intent on conversion followed them not long after.[58] In all of these cases we know nothing about the circumstances or the motivations of the women involved, but it seems reasonable to consider them in the context of the stories developed in these pages.

As the examples at the heart of this book suggest, throughout the Mediterranean—in the Balkans, the Greek islands, Venice, the Ottoman Empire, North Africa, the Iberian peninsula—women faced with constricting cultural attitudes, structures, and institutions often responded in markedly similar ways. Reformulating their identities, embracing new faiths and new rulers, navigating institutions of power, and transgressing and manipulating the regions' intertwined geographical, political, and cultural boundaries, these women on the margins exerted "shaping power" over their own lives. Their actions have parallels in other early modern contexts, and they provide insights into the relationship of gender and boundaries throughout the early modern world, but they also are stories uniquely formed by the Mediterranean stage on which Fatima Hatun, Suor Deodata, Catterina Šatorović, and Maria Gozzadini and her daughters lived and died.

GEOGRAPHIC EQUIVALENTS

Antivari: Bar, Montenegro
Argentiera: Kimolos, Greece
Budua: Budva, Montenegro
Candia: Crete, Greece (also the
 town of Hērákleion, Greece)
Canea: Khaniá, Greece
Cassiope: Kassiopi, Greece
Cerigo: Kythira, Greece
Chios: Khíos, Greece
Clissa: Klis, Croatia
Constantinople: Istanbul, Turkey
Corfu: Kérkira, Greece
Durazzo: Durrës, Albania
Galata: Beyoğlu (Istanbul), Turkey
Kea: Kea, Greece
Lepanto: Nafpaktos, Greece
Lissa: Vis, Croatia

Livno: Livno, Bosnia and
 Herzegovina
Milo: Milos, Greece
Moldavia: Moldova, Romania
Pago: Pag, Croatia
Ragusa: Dubrovnik, Croatia
Rhodes: Ródos, Greece
Rusciuk: Rusciuk, Bulgaria
Scardona: Skradin, Croatia
Sebenico: Šibenik, Croatia
Sifno: Siphnos, Greece
Spalato: Split, Croatia
Thermia: Kythnos, Greece
Trau: Trogir, Croatia
Wallachia: Wallachia, Romania
Zante: Zakynthos, Greece
Zara: Zadar, Croatia

ABBREVIATIONS

Archives

ACDF	Archivio congregatio pro doctrina fidei
ACPF	Archivio della congregazione de propaganda fide
ANK	Genika Archeia tou Kratous, Archeia Nomou Kerkyras
ASFi	Archivio di stato di Firenze
ASPV	Archivio storico del patriarcato di Venezia
ASV	Archivio di stato di Venezia
ASVat	Archivio segreto Vaticano
AZN	Arhiv Zadarske Nadbiskupije
BAV	Biblioteca Vaticana
BL	British Library
BMCV	Biblioteca del Museo Civico Correr di Venezia
BNM	Biblioteca nazionale Marciana
DAZ	Državni Arhiv u Zadru
FHL	Family History Library
IRE	Archivio IRE
PRO	Public Record Office
ZKZ	Znanstvena Knjižnica Zadar

Sources

Albèri	Albèri, E., *Relazioni degli ambasciatori veneti al senato*
APC	Archivi propri degli ambasciatori—Costantinopoli (ASV)
AvCom	Avogaria di comun (ASV)

BAC	Bailo a Costantinopoli (ASV)
Barbaro	Barbaro, M., *Arbori de' patritii veneti* (ASV)
Berchet	Barozzi and Berchet, *Le relazioni degli stati europei . . . Turchia*
CapiXLett	Capi del consiglio di dieci, Letter di ambasciatori (ASV)
CD	Corpus Domini (ASV)
CMarP	Cariche da mar—Processi (ASV)
CollRel	Collegio, Relazioni (ASV)
CRV	Ljubić, ed., *Commissiones et relationes venetae* (tome 1–3); Novak, ed., *Commissiones et relationes venetae* (tome 4–5)
DBI	*Dizionario biografico italiano*
DocTR	Documenti turchi (ASV)
EI²	*Encyclopedia of Islam,* new ed.
EK	Enetokratia (ANK)
FMK	Fonda Matičnih Knjiga Državnog Arhiva Zadru 1500 (DAZ)
Gregolin	Miscellanea Gregolin (ASV)
InqStat	Inquisitori di stato (ASV)
It VI	MS Italiano, classe VI (BNM)
It VII	MS Italiano, classe VII (BNM)
LSTR	Lettere e scritture turchesche (ASV)
NotAtti	Notarile, Atti (ASV)
NotTest	Notarile, Testamenti (ASV)
PSM	Provveditori sopra li monasteri (ASV)
PTM	Provveditori di terra et mar (ASV)
RelXPera	d'Alessio, *Relatione dello stato della cristianità di Pera*
RubriCST	Rubricarii di Costantinopoli (ASV)
SDC	Senato dispacci, Costantinopoli (ASV)
SDCop	Senato dispacci, Copie moderne (ASV)
SDelC	Senato deliberazioni, Costantinopoli (ASV)
SDelR	Senato deliberazioni, Roma (ASV)
SDR	Senato dispacci, Roma (ASV)

SegMiste	Senato segreta, Materie miste notabili (ASV)
SMar	Senato mar (ASV)
SMarMin	Senato mar (minute) (ASV)
SOCG	Scritture originali riferite nelle congregazioni generali (ACPF)
SP	State Papers Foreign, Turkey (PRO)
SRO	Senato Roma ordinaria (ASV)
SSVe	Segreteria di stato, Venezia (ASVat)
VDM	Visite di monache (ASPV)
VSM	V savi alla mercanzia (ASV)
XSeg	Consiglio di dieci—Deliberazioni segrete (ASV)

NOTES

Preface

1. Politi, *Dittionario toscano*, 667; *Le dictionnaire de l'Académie française*, 2: 122; Bailey, *Universal Etymological English Dictionary*, n.p.

Chapter 1: Fatima Hatun née Beatrice Michiel

1. BL, MS 8610, "Relazione of Dalmatia from Giovanni Tiepolo"; "Relazione di Michiel Bon e Gasparo Erizzo," in *CRV*, 3:119; "Itinerario di Giovanni Battista Giustinian," in *CRV*, 2:237.

2. ASV, *Segretario alle voci*, 1593, 3:156.

3. *SMarMin*, b. 1, 19 Sep 1558; Vatin, "L'Empire ottoman et la piraterie," 373.

4. Pedani, "Veneziani a Costantinopoli," 68–69; "Relazione di Girolamo Cappello," in Pedani, *Relazioni*, 417–18; "Selim II," *EI²*, 9:131; Skilliter, "Letters of the Venetian 'Sultana,'" 516–17; Hammer, *Histoire*, 2:199–201.

5. Fetvaci, "Viziers to Eunuchs," 261.

6. Süreyya, *Sicill-i Osmani*, 2:546; Pedani, "Safiye's Household," 14. See the original sources in *CapiXLett*, b. 6, 13 Oct 1582; *SDC*, b. 16, cc. 185r–186r, 29 Sep 1582; and *SDC*, b. 16, c. 199r, 13 Oct 1582.

7. Schmidt, *Pure Water for Thirsty Muslims*, 244.

8. Pedani, "Safiye's Household," 14.

9. Fleischer, *Bureaucrat and Intellectual*, 72–73; "Sokullu," *EI²*, 9:710–11; Danismend, *Osmanli Tarihi Kronolojisi*, 3:2–3.

10. Peirce, *Imperial Harem*, 11; Necipoğlu, *Architecture, Ceremonial, and Power*, 31–183. See also Oberling and Smith, *Food Culture of the Ottoman Palace*, 59; and Darling, "Rethinking Europe and the Islamic World," 237.

11. İnalcık, *Ottoman Empire*, 79–80; "Kapu Aghasi," *EI²*, 4:570–71; Necipoğlu, *Architecture, Ceremonial, and Power*, 88–90.

12. *SDC*, b. 56, cc. 208r–211v, 9 Jan 1602 (MV); *CollRel*, b. 5, c. 18r, "Relazione di Ottaviano Bon"; "Relazione di Girolamo Cappello," in Pedani, *Relazioni*, 417–19; Peachy, *A Year in Selaniki's History*, 241–42.

13. Hammer, *Histoire*, 2:199–201; Kafadar, "Les troubles monétaires," 390–91.

14. *Ganî-zâde Nâdirî*, 3, 81–83, 159; Süreyya, *Sicill-i Osmani*, 2:546; Tanindi, "Bibliophile Aghas," 337, 341; Fetvaci, "Viziers to Eunuchs," 257–96, 351; Le Gall, *A Culture of Sufism*, 148; Artan, "Arts and Architecture," 413.

15. Tietze, *Mustafa Ali's Description of Cairo of 1599*, 25, 28; Schmidt, *Mustafa 'Ali's Künhü'l-Ahbar*, 1–2; Schmidt, "The Egri-Campaign of 1596," 136–37; Fleischer, *Bureaucrat and Intellectual*, 170, 182–83; Hammer, *Histoire*, 2:199–201.

16. Goodwin, *A History of Ottoman Architecture*, 338; Necipoğlu, *The Age of Sinan*, 508–9; Ayverdi, "Gazanfer Ağa Manzümesi," 85; Erdogan, "Mîmar Davud Aga-nin Hayati ve Eserleri," 187, 193; Crane, *Risâle-i mi'māriyye*, 37 n. 25; Eyice, "Gazanfer Ağa Külliyesi," 432–33; Hamadeh, "Splash and Spectacle," 137–38; Fetvaci, "Viziers to Eunuchs," 285.

17. Dursteler, *Venetians in Constantinople*, 121–23.

18. *SDC*, b. 16, cc. 185r–186r, 29 Sep 1582; *SDC*, b. 16, c. 199r, 13 Oct 1582; *CapiXLett*, b. 6, 13 Oct 1582.

19. *SDelC*, b. 6, 29 Dec 1584; *SDelC*, b. 8, 9 Sep 1585.

20. *BAC*, b. 279, reg. 401, cc. 7v–8v, 13 Apr 1615; *BAC*, b. 279, reg. 401, cc. 13r–15r, 17 Jun 1615; Dolcetti, *Il libro d'argento*, 1:26–27; Cicogna, *Delle iscrizioni veneziane*, 5:201; *It VII 27* (7761), c. 84v.

21. Zannini, *Burocrazia e burocrati*. See also Grubb, "Elite Citizens," 339–56.

22. "Relazione di Giovanni Moro," in *Albèri*, 9:361; *SDC*, b. 52, cc. 368r–373r, 31 Jan 1600 (MV); *SDC*, b. 18, c. 426r, 24 Jan 1583 (MV); *CollRel*, b. 4, 32r–v. See also "Relazione di Lorenzo Bernardo," in *Albèri*, 6:361–62; and "Relazione di Matteo Zane," in *Albèri*, 9:437–38.

23. ASPV, *Parocchia San Giacomo dall'Orio, Battesimi*, r. 2, 9 Oct 1584.

24. *SDC*, b. 39, cc. 40v–45v, 24 Mar 1594 (MV).

25. ASV, *Provveditori alla sanità, necrologi*, r. 819, 31 Jan 1587 (MV).

26. Baernstein, "In Widow's Habit," 788–90; Davis, *Women on the Margins*, 71; King, *Women of the Renaissance*, 58.

27. Klapisch-Zuber, *Women, Family, and Ritual,* 124–31, 261–82; Calvi, "Reconstructing the Family," 278–79; Ruggiero, *Boundaries of Eros,* 167; Bell, *How to Do It,* 272.

28. Chojnacka, "Singlewomen in Early Modern Venice," 215–21; Ambrosini, "Toward a Social History of Women in Venice," 429.

29. Chojnacki, *Men and Women in Renaissance Venice,* 100–101; Chabot, "Lineage Strategies and the Control of Widows," 140; Bellavitis, *Identité, mariage, mobilité sociale,* 210.

30. *SDC,* b. 33, c. 366v, 5 Jan 1590 (MV); Dolcetti, *Il libro d'argento,* 3:115–18.

31. *SDelC,* b. 8, 4 Feb 1591 (MV).

32. *BAC,* b. 317, cc. 15r–16v, 1 Jul 1598; *Gregolin,* b. 12 II, 10 Jan 1593 (MV), Zuane Zaghis to Tullio Fabri; *SDelC,* b. 7, 15 Feb 1590 (MV); *SDC,* b. 33, c. 366v, 5 Jan 1590 (MV); *SDC,* b. 33, c. 199r, 26 May 1591; *SDC,* b. 32, cc. 132v–133r, 29 Sep 1590.

33. *SDelC,* b. 8, 1 Jul 1592; *SDelC,* b. 8, 27 Jul 1592; *SDelC,* b. 8, 9 Sep 1585.

34. Lane, *Venice,* 333–34; Pullan, "Wage-Earners and the Venetian Economy," 157–58, 173.

35. Cowan, "Rich and Poor among the Patriciate," 152–53, 157; Cowan, *The Urban Patriciate,* 165–67.

36. Queller and Madden, "Father of the Bride," 695–97; Ferraro, *Marriage Wars,* 136–37, 153–54; Bellavitis, "Dot et richesse des femmes à Venise," 91, 96–97; Bellavitis, "La famiglia «cittadina» veneziana," 52, 57, 64.

37. Cox, "The Single Self," 527; Ferraro, *Marriage Wars,* 8, 124–29, 135–37; Chojnacki, "Dowries and Kinsmen," 587.

38. Ferraro, "The Power to Decide," 492–95, 500–11; Ferraro, *Marriage Wars,* 8–9, 22, 121, 137; Rigo, "Giudici del Procurator," 247–63; Guzzetti, "Separations and Separated Couples," 252–54, 266; Menchi and Quaglioni, *Coniugi nemici.*

39. Zannini, "Un censimento inedito," 88.

40. Bellavitis, "La famiglia «cittadina» veneziana," 58; Hacke, *Women, Sex, and Marriage,* 14, 36–52.

41. *SDC,* b. 51, c. 372r, 29 Jul 1600.

42. *SDCop,* r. 8, c. 38, 27 Dec 1591; *SDC,* b. 34, cc. 285r–v, 289r–v, 28 Dec 1591; Pedani, "Safiye's Household," 25.

43. Ginio, "Childhood, Mental Capacity, and Conversion to Islam," 96–97; Faroqhi, *Subjects of the Sultan*, 102; Aslan, *No god but God*, 43–45.

44. Krstić, "Illuminated by the Light of Islam," 59. Examples of conversion ceremonies abound. See, for example, Naima, *Annals*, 1:191; Wratislaw, *Adventures of Baron Wenceslas Wratislaw*, 10–18; and Selânikî, *Tarih-i Selânikî*, 2:854–56.

45. Pedani, "Veneziani a Costantinopoli," 75. This position is moderated somewhat in Pedani, "Safiye's Household," 25–26.

46. On this, see *SDC*, b. 33, c. 336v, 22 Dec 1590; *SDC*, b. 33, cc. 234r–236r, 1 Jun 1591; and Pedani, "Veneziani a Costantinopoli," 75.

47. *SDelC*, b. 8, 1 Jul 1592; "Relazione di Lorenzo Bernardo," in *Albèri*, 6:361–62.

48. *SDC*, b. 32, c. 336v, 22 Dec 1590; *SDC*, b. 33, c. 199r, 26 May 1591; *SDC*, b. 33, cc. 220r–221v, 234r–236r, 1 Jun 1591; *SDC*, b. 35, cc. 388r–v, 10 Jul 1592.

49. *SDC*, b. 32, cc. 167v–168r, 13 Oct 1590; *SDC*, b. 32, c. 336v, 22 Dec 1590; *SDC*, b. 33, c. 199r, 26 May 1591, Letter from Kapı Ağası; *SDC*, b. 33, cc. 220r–221v, 234r–236r, 1 Jun 1591.

50. *SDCop*, r. 8, c. 38, 27 Dec 1591; *SDC*, b. 34, cc. 289r–v, 28 Dec 1591; *SDelC*, b. 8, Copy of 4 Feb 1591 (MV).

51. Dursteler, *Venetians in Constantinople*, 112–14.

52. Gerber, "Social and Economic Position of Women in an Ottoman City," 231; McGinty, *Becoming Muslim*, 4.

53. Zilfi, "Introduction," 5; Meriwether and Tucker, "Introduction," 10–11. On this comparison generally, see Hunt, "Women in Ottoman and Western European Law Courts."

54. Keddie, *Women in the Middle East*, 58.

55. Gerber, "Social and Economic Position of Women in an Ottoman City," 231–33; Faroqhi, "Crisis and Change," 2:598–99; Zilfi, "We Don't Get Along," 269–72; Nashat, "Women in the Middle East: 8000 B.C.E.–C.E. 1800," 71; Tucker, "Rescued from Obscurity," 399.

56. Masters, *Christians and Jews in the Ottoman Arab World*, 27, 34–35; Greene, *A Shared World*, 93–94; Jennings, *Christians and Muslims in Ottoman Cyprus*, 139–41; Goodblatt, *Jewish Life in Turkey*, 104; Cassia, "Religion, Politics, and Ethnicity in Cyprus," 22–24.

57. Veinstein, "Sur les conversions à l'Islam," 164; Ginio, "Childhood, Mental Capacity, and Conversion to Islam," 94–95.

58. Safley, "Marital Litigation in the Diocese of Constance," 71–73; Watt, "Divorce in Early Modern Neuchâtel," 137–55; Bonfield, "Developments in European Family Law," 108–13; Wiesner-Hanks, *Women and Gender in Early Modern Europe*, 72–73; Wiesner-Hanks, *Christianity and Sexuality in the Early Modern World*, 78–80.

59. Porter, *English Society in the Eighteenth Century*, 31; Muir, *Ritual in Early Modern Europe*, 48–50; Karant-Nunn, "Continuity and Change," 29; Hacke, *Women, Sex, and Marriage*, 231.

60. Kissling, "Türkenfurcht und Türkenhoffnung," 1–18; Ricci, *Ossessione turca*, 389–90; Dursteler, "Power and Information," 601.

61. Blanks, "Western Views of Islam in the Premodern Period," 35; Setton, "Lutheranism and the Turkish Peril," 137, 141; Wilson, "Reflecting on the Turk," 42.

62. Ventura, "Scrittori politici e scritture di governo," 3:553–54; Valensi, *The Birth of the Despot*, 13; Infelise, *Prima dei giornali*, v–x, 10, 154; Burke, "Early Modern Venice as a Center of Information and Communication," 392, 397, 403–4; Sforza, "Un libro sfortunato contro i Turchi," 207–13; Allegri, "Venezia e il Veneto dopo Lepanto," 2:953–54.

63. "Khurrem," *EI²*, 5:66–67; Sokolnicki, "La sultane Ruthène," 229–39; Rouillard, *The Turk in French History, Thought, and Literature*, 421–66; Chew, *The Crescent and the Rose*, 497–503.

64. Bassano, *Costumi et i modi particolari*, 8v.

65. Peirce, *Imperial Harem*; "Nūr Bānū," *EI²*, 8:124; Skilliter, "Letters of the Venetian 'Sultana,'" 519–27; "Baffo, Cecilia," *DBI*, 5:161–63; Arbel, "Nūr Bānū."

66. Attar, "Dangerous Liaisons," 170–71, 190–95.

67. Baer, *Honored by the Glory of Islam*.

68. Davis, *Christian Slaves, Muslim Masters*, 21; Kologlu, "Renegades and the Case Uluç/Kiliç Ali," 513–14, 525; Clissold, "Christian Renegades and Barbary Corsairs," 509–10.

69. Minkov, *Conversion to Islam in the Balkans*, 64–109; Zhelyazkova, "Islamization in the Balkans," 233–66; Baer, *Honored by the Glory of Islam*, 192–94; Strauss, "Ottoman Rule Experienced and Remembered," 203–8; Derengil, "There Is No Compulsion in Religion," 549–53.

70. Derengil, "There Is No Compulsion in Religion," 547–71; Davis, *Christian Slaves, Muslim Masters,* 21, 44.

71. "Relazione di Matteo Zane," in *Albèri,* 9:437–38; Iorga, *Geschichte des osmanischen Reiches,* 3:184.

72. *SDelC,* b. 8, 4 Feb 1591 (MV).

73. al-Misri, *Reliance of the Traveller,* 532, 595–96; Shatzmiller, "Marriage, Family, and the Faith," 242–43.

74. *SDelC,* b. 8, 1 Jul 1592, letter from Baldassare and Giacomo Michiel; *SDelC,* b. 8, 1 Jul 1591, letter from Zuane Zaghis. On canonical law and conversion, see Kedar, "Muslim Conversion in Canon Law," 321–29.

75. *SDelC,* b. 8, 18 Mar 1592; *SDelC,* b. 7, 15 Feb 1590 (MV); *SDC,* b. 33, c. 129r, 19 Apr 1591.

76. *SDC,* b. 37, cc. 278r–v, 7 Jun 1593; "Relazione di Matteo Zane," in *Albèri,* 9:437–38; *SDC,* b. 39, cc. 8v–10v, 12 Mar 1594; *SDC,* b. 51, cc. 87r–89r, 7 Apr 1600; "Relazione di Girolamo Cappello," in Pedani, *Relazioni,* 417–19.

77. Martin, *Venice's Hidden Enemies,* 123–46; Zagorin, *Ways of Lying;* Snyder, *Dissimulation and the Culture of Secrecy,* 1–26.

78. Eire, "Calvin and Nicodemism," 44–46, 67–69; Biondi, "La giustificazione della simulazione," 59; Burns, "The Politics of Conversion," 10; Martin, "*Renovatio* and Reform in Early Modern Italy," 12–13; Martin, "Salvation and Society," 28.

79. Scaraffia, *Rinnegati,* 115–20; Rostagno, *Mi faccio turco,* 52; Bennassar, "Conversions, esclavage, et commerce des femmes," 102–3. Muslim women often presented a similar facade of conversion, while secretly raising their children as Muslims. Perry, "Contested Identities," 179; Perry, *The Handless Maiden,* 34.

80. Rostagno, *Mi faccio turco,* 19, 23, 34–35; Scaraffia, *Rinnegati,* 103, 105–9; Audisio, "Renégats marseillais," 50–51; Wickersham, "Results of the Reformation," 279.

81. "Takiyya," *EI²,* 10:134–36; Zagorin, *Ways of Lying,* 4–5; Perry, "Behind the Veil," 42; Perry, "Moriscas and the Limits of Assimilation," 279.

82. Zagorin, *Ways of Lying,* 38–62; Graizbord, *Souls in Dispute,* 172; Elukin, "From Jew to Christian," 170–72; Siebenhüner, "Conversion, Mobility, and the Roman Inquisition," 7–10.

83. Hoerder, *Cultures in Contact,* 15–16.

84. *SDelC,* b. 8, 27 Jul 1592; *SDC,* b. 33, cc. 234r–236r, 1 Jun 1591;

SDC, b. 33, c. 336v, 22 Dec 1590. On the marriage market and its impact on Venetian women of this era, see Cox, "The Single Self."

85. Hathaway, *The Politics of Households in Ottoman Egypt*, 109–24; Molho, *Marriage Alliance*; Kunt, *The Sultan's Servants*, 45–46.

86. *SDC*, b. 37, cc. 30r–v, 14 Mar 1593; Pedani, "Safiye's Household," 25–26; Pedani, "Veneziani a Costantinopoli," 74.

87. *SDC*, b. 39, cc. 8v–10v, 12 Mar 1594; Peirce, "Seniority, Sexuality, and Social Order," 181; Imber, "Women, Marriage, and Property," 86.

88. Esposito, *Women in Muslim Family Law*, 14; Reindl-Kiel, "A Woman Timar Holder," 223; Shatzmiller, "Marriage, Family, and the Faith," 249; Zilfi, "Muslim Women in the Early Modern Era," 242–43.

89. *SDC*, b. 37, c. 128v, 24 Apr 1593; *SDC*, b. 37, cc. 278r–v, 7 Jun 1593; "Relazione di Matteo Zane," in *Albèri*, 9:437–38; Süreyya, *Sicill-i Osmani*, 1:234; *SDelC*, b. 10, 9 May 1602, letter from Ali Ağa.

90. *SDC*, b. 39, cc. 279v–280r, 19 May 1594.

91. ASFi, *Mediceo del principato*, b. 4277, c. 347r.

92. Selânikî, *Tarih-i Selânikî*, 2:672, 774; Süreyya, *Sicill-i Osmani*, 1:234; Tanindi, "Transformation of Words to Images," 144–45; İnalcık, *Ottoman Empire*, 81.

93. Naima, *Annals*, 1:212–14; *SDelC*, b. 10, 9 May 1602, letter from Ali Ağa; "Relazione di Girolamo Cappello," in Pedani, *Relazioni*, 418; Gibb and Bowen, *Islamic Society and the West*, 1:61, 66; Sertoğlu, *Osmanlı tarih lügatı*, 366–67.

94. *Ganî-zâde Nâdirî*, 191, 247–49; Tanindi, "Transformation of Words to Images," 144.

95. "Relazione di Girolamo Cappello," in Pedani, *Relazioni*, 417–19; "Relazione di Matteo Zane," in *Albèri*, 9:437–38.

96. "Relazione di Matteo Zane," in *Albèri*, 9:437–38; BAC, b. 269, "Protocollo," cc. 21v–22r, 10 Jan 1594.

97. Peirce, *Imperial Harem*, 3; Hunt, "Women in Ottoman and Western European Law Courts," 177; Zilfi, "Muslim Women in the Early Modern Era," 228–31; Malieckal, "Slavery, Sex, and the Seraglio," 58–73. See, for example, Coco, *Secrets of the Harem*.

98. Peirce, *Imperial Harem*, 219–28; Tucker, "Rescued from Obscurity," 395; Nashat, "Women in the Middle East: 8,000 B.C.E.–C.E. 1800," 70–71; Meriwether and Tucker, "Introduction," 3–4; Thys-Şenocak, *Ottoman Women Builders*, 55–65.

99. *BAC*, b. 269, "Protocollo," cc. 21v–22r, 10 Jan 1594.

100. "Relazione di Girolamo Cappello," in Pedani, *Relazioni*, 417–19.

101. Göçek and Baer, "Social Boundaries of Ottoman Women's Experience," 63; Peirce, "Seniority, Sexuality, and Social Order," 183; Zilfi, "We Don't Get Along," 280.

102. Peirce, "Beyond Harem Walls," 44.

103. *SDC*, b. 39, cc. 282r–v, 20 May 1594, Fatima Hatun to Marco Venier.

104. *SDCop*, r. 11, cc. 174–85, 1 Nov, 5 Dec 1596; Pedani, "Safiye's Household," 27. On Malchi, see Lamdan, "Malchi, Esperanza," 13:430; Bornstein-Makovetsky, "Kiera," 12:147–48.

105. "Relazione di Gianfrancesco Morosini," in Albèri, 9:298–99; *SDC*, b. 20, cc. 16r–19r, 4 Sep 1584; *CollRel*, b. 4, cc. 32r–v, "Relazione di Lorenzo Bernardo."

106. *SDC*, b. 39, cc. 282r–v, 20 May 1594, Fatima Hatun to Marco Venier; *SDC*, b. 39, cc. 8v–10v, 12 Mar 1594.

107. *SDC*, b. 35, c. 311v, 12 Jun 1592; *SDC*, b. 37, cc. 211r–v, 17 May 1593; *SDC*, b. 50, cc. 67v–68r, 2 Oct 1599; *SDC*, b. 55, c. 1r, 11 Mar 1602; *SDC*, b. 50, cc. 238r–246r, 10 Jan 1599 (MV); *SDC*, b. 39, cc. 40v–42v, 24 Mar 1594; *SDC*, b. 51, cc. 120r–v, 20 Apr 1600; "Relazione di Girolamo Cappello," in Pedani, *Relazioni*, 408, 417–19; *SDC*, b. 40, cc. 481r–482v, 31 Jan 1594 (MV); *SDC*, b. 47, cc. 302r–303r, 25 Jul 1598.

108. *SDC*, b. 39, cc. 8v–10v, 12 Mar 1594; *SDCop*, r. 11, cc. 274–76, 15 Feb 1596 (MV); *SDC*, b. 52, cc. 296r–297r, 6 Jan 1600 (MV); *SDC*, b. 56, c. 169v, 5 Jan 1602 (MV); Pedani, "Veneziani a Costantinopoli," 76.

109. *SDC*, b. 40, c. 142r, note from Kapı Ağası; *SDC*, b. 33, cc. 42v–42r, 16 Mar 1591; *SDC*, b. 52, cc. 296r–297r, 6 Jan 1600 (MV); Dursteler, "A Continual Tavern in My House."

110. Bellavitis, *Famille, genre, transmission*, 80–85; Bellavitis, *Identité, mariage, mobilité sociale*, 217–20; Kirshner, "Introduction," 2–3; Calvi, "Widows, the State, and the Guardianship of Children," 210–13; Chojnacki, *Men and Women in Renaissance Venice*, 100, 273 n. 42.

111. *SDC*, b. 37, c. 1r, 12 Mar 1593; *SDC*, b. 37, cc. 30r–v, 14 Mar 1593; *SDCop*, reg. 10, c. 18, 16 Oct 1593; *SDCop*, reg. 10, cc. 97–98, 13 Feb 1593; *SDelC*, b. 8, 4 Feb 1591; *SDC*, b. 47, cc. 139v–140r, 15 May 1598; *BAC*, b. 269, "Protocollo," cc. 21v–22r, 10 Jan 1594; *SDC*, b. 35,

c. 33r, 7 Mar 1592; *BAC*, b. 317, cc.15r–17r, 1 and 11 Jul 1598; *SDCop*, r. 9, c. 8, n.d.; *SDC*, b. 38, cc. 443v–444r, 13 Feb 1593 (MV); *SDC*, b. 38, cc. 11v–14r, 6 Sep 1593; *SDC*, b. 39, c. 244v, 4 May 1594; *NotAtti*, b. 3383–84, cc. 193r–196r, 11 May 1607.

112. "Relazione di Girolamo Cappello," in Pedani, *Relazioni*, 417–19.

113. *BAC*, b. 339, 11 Apr 1595; *SDC*, b. 53, c. 14r, 3 Mar 1601; *SDC*, b. 52, cc. 69v–70v, 23 Oct 1600; *BAC*, b. 269, reg. 382, c. 182v, 26 Mar 1596. See *BAC*, b. 368, #68, #75–76, #78–80.

114. *SDC*, b. 52, cc. 318r–319v, 14 Jan 1600 (MV); *SDC*, b. 52, cc. 326r–328v, 20 Jan 1600 (MV); *SDC*, b. 52, cc. 368r–373r, 31 Jan 1600 (MV); *SDC*, b. 52, cc. 42r–v, 5 Oct 1600; *SDelC*, b. 10, 7 Sep 1600; *BAC*, b. 270, reg. 385, c. 137v, 13 Jun 1600; *BAC*, b. 317, cc. 16v–17r, 11 Jul 1598; *SDC*, b. 51, cc. 87r–89r, 7 Apr 1600; *BAC*, b. 269, "Protocollo," cc. 21v–22r, 10 Jan 1594; *BAC*, b. 270, reg. 385, c. 140r, 15 Jun 1600; *VSM*, I, reg. 139, c. 20r, 9 Sep 1593; *SDC*, b. 53, cc. 332r–336v, 12 Jul 1601; *SDC*, b. 51, cc. 400r–v, 12 Aug 1600; *SDC*, b. 41, cc. 162r–v, 22 Apr 1595; *SDC*, b. 52, cc. 304r–v, 7 Jan 1600 (MV); Tenenti, *Naufrages, corsairs, et assurances maritimes*, 252; *SDC*, b. 51, cc. 400r–v, 12 Aug 1600; *SDelC*, b. 10, 9 May 1602, letter from Ali Ağa; *SDC*, b. 53, c. 232v, 30 May 1601.

115. *SDC*, b. 57, cc. 63r–64r, 21 Mar 1603; *SDC*, b. 57, cc. 264v–265r, 31 May 1603; *SDC*, b. 57, cc. 291r–292r, 13 Jun 1603; *SDC*, b. 56, cc. 234r–235v, 19 Jan 1602 (MV); "Relazione di Girolamo Cappello," in Pedani, *Relazioni*, 417–19.

116. *BAC*, b. 276, reg. 395, cc. 55r–56r, 22 Dec 1610; *It VII* 341 (8623), cc. 94r–96r; Pedani, "Veneziani a Costantinopoli," 75.

117. *SDelC*, b. 10, 4 Feb 1591 (MV); *CapiXLett*, b. 7, #3–5, 21 Apr–6 May 1600; ASPV, *Visite parochiali*, b. 2, 26 Aug 1604; ASPV, *Visite parochiali*, b. 4, cc. 13r–v.

118. *SDC*, b. 37, cc. 328r–331v, 21 Jun 1593; *SDC*, b. 37, cc. 278r–v, 7 Jun 1593; *SDC*, b. 37, c. 385v, 4 Jul 1593; "Relazione di Matteo Zane," in *Albèri*, 9:437–38; *LSTR*, b. 5, cc. 132r–v, 27 Mar 1593, Paşa of Bosnia to Senate; *SDC*, b. 51, cc. 87r–89r, 7 Apr 1600.

119. ASV, *Senato terra*, b. 182, Baldissare Bianchi to Senate. For the details of the plot, see *CapiXLett*, b. 7, #3–5, 21 Apr–6 May 1600.

120. *BAC*, b. 276, reg. 395, cc. 79r–v, 23 Mar 1611; *SDC*, b. 51, cc. 120v–121r, 20 Apr 1600; Vercellin, "Mercanti turchi e sensali a Venezia,"

243–76; *SMar,* r. 45, c. 148r, 22 Sep 1582; *NotAtti,* b. 3371–72, cc. 290r–291r, 18 Jun 1600; BAV, *Urb. Lat.,* 1739. On the Bustrone of Cyprus, see Rudt de Collenberg, "Les «custodi» de la Marciana," 41–46.

121. *SDC,* b. 51, c. 105r, 8 Apr 1600; *SDC,* b. 51, cc. 183v–186v, 19 May 1600; *SDC,* b. 51, c. 167r, 6 May 1600; *SDC,* b. 51, cc. 242r–245v, 16 Jun 1600; *SDC,* b. 51, cc. 340v–341v, 15 Jul 1600; *SDC,* b. 51, c. 372r, 29 Jul 1600; *SDC,* b. 51, cc. 412r–413r, 26 Aug 1600; *SDC,* b. 52, cc. 2v–3r, 12 Sep 1600; *BAC,* b. 279, reg. 401, cc. 7v–8v, 13 Apr 1615.

122. Sagredo, *Memorie istoriche,* 613; "Relazione di Girolamo Cappello," in Pedani, *Relazioni,* 418–19; *SDC,* b. 51, cc. 87r–89r, 7 Apr 1600.

123. *SDC,* b. 56, c. 316r, 9 Feb 1602 (MV); *SDC,* b. 57, cc. 156v–157r, 19 Apr 1603; *SDC,* b. 56, cc. 259v–260r, 20 Jan 1602 (MV); *BAC,* b. 279, reg. 401, cc. 55r–v, 20 Apr 1616. See also *SDC,* b. 78, cc. 210r–211v, 21 Jan 1614 (MV).

124. *BAC,* b. 279, reg. 401, cc. 7v–8v, 13 Apr 1615.

125. Danismend, *Osmanli Tarihi Kronolojisi,* 3:384–85; Dorigo-Ceccato, "Su Bekrī Muṣṭafā," 89; Pedani, "Safiye's Household," 27; Hammer, *Histoire,* 2:497. On Murad's final days, see *It VII* 1087 (8524), cc. 432r–v, 1 Feb 1639 (MV); *It VII* 1087 (8524), cc. 438r–v, 9 Feb 1639 (MV); also Vatin and Veinstein, *Le sérail ébranlé,* 47–48, 194–96.

126. Dorigo-Ceccato, "Su Bekrī Muṣṭafā," 85–96.

127. ASPV, Parocchia San Barnabà, *Matrimoni,* r. 1.

128. Neff, "Chancellery Secretaries," 192; *It VII* 341 (8623), cc. 17r–22v; *It VII* 27 (7761), c. 87v; *AvCom,* b. 157, cc. 94v–96r, 5 Jan 1609; *AvCom,* b. 371, #45, 17 May 1619; *NotTest,* b. 172.46, 25 Jun 1642; Pedani, "Safiye's Household," 26.

129. *SMar,* r. 45, cc. 99v–100r, 10 Mar 1582; *SDC,* b. 51, cc. 254r–266v, 10 Jan 1599 (MV); *SDC,* b. 33, c. 199r, 26 May 1591; *NotAtti,* b. 8423, t. III, cc. 343r–348v, 9 Dec 1617; *AvCom,* b. 157, cc. 94v–96r, 5 Jan 1609; *AvCom,* b. 366, #3, 11 Sep 1629.

130. *BAC,* b. 279, reg. 401, cc. 7v–8v, 13 Apr 1615; *NotTest,* b. 172.46, 25 Jun 1642.

131. Imber, *The Ottoman Empire,* 66–76; Parker and Smith, *The General Crisis of the Sixteenth Century,* 1–33; Shaw, *History of the Ottoman Empire,* 1:170–75; İnalcık, *Ottoman Empire,* 41–52; Faroqhi, "Crisis and Change"; Barkey, *Bandits and Bureaucrats,* 141–228; Kafadar, "The Ottomans and Europe," 1:613.

132. Boyar and Fleet, *A Social History of Ottoman Istanbul*, 190–93.

133. Galanté, "Esther Kyra," 8–16; Mordtmann, "Die jüdischen Kira im Serai der Sultane," 15–17; Pedani, "Veneziani a Costantinopoli," 80. For a horrifyingly detailed description of the murder, see Sanderson, *The Travels of John Sanderson*, 85.

134. Naima, *Annals*, 1:212–14. On the revolt, see Shaw, *History of the Ottoman Empire*, 1:186; İnalcık, *Ottoman Empire*, 47.

135. Naima, *Naîmâ Târihi*, 1:317; Sanderson, *The Travels of John Sanderson*, 216 n. 1; Burian, *The Report of Lello*, 12–13; Hammer, *Histoire*, 2:303–4; SDC, b. 56, cc. 208r–211v, 9 Jan 1602 (MV).

136. ASFi, *Mediceo del principato*, b. 4277, cc. 368r–369v, 9 Jan 1600; SP, b. 97/4, cc. 199r–200r, 201r–v, 10 Jan 1602 (MV); SSVe, b. 37, cc. 64v–65r, 8 Mar 1603. See also Kortepeter, *Ottoman Imperialism during the Reformation*, 223.

137. Peçevi, *Peçevi Târihi*, 2:239–40; Naima, *Naîmâ Târihi*, 1:317. See also Carli, *Cronologia historica*, 156.

138. SDC, b. 56, c. 222r, 9 Jan 1602 (MV); SDC, b. 56, cc. 259v–260r, 20 Jan 1602 (MV); SDC, b. 56, cc. 277r–v, 1 Feb 1602 (MV); SDC, b. 56, c. 316r, 9 Feb 1602 (MV); SDC, b. 57, c. 29r, 7 Mar 1603; ASFi, *Mediceo del principato*, b. 4277, c. 398r, 9 Mar 1603; SSVe, b. 37, c. 95r, 12 Apr 1603; Orhonlu, *Telhîsler*, #39, #41, #91; Kunt, *The Sultan's Servants*, 55.

139. SSVe, b. 37, c. 95r, 12 Apr 1603.

140. Kunt, *The Sultan's Servants*, 55; Meriwether, *The Kin Who Count*, 153–77; Zilfi, "Muslim Women in the Early Modern Era," 253.

141. SDC, b. 56, cc. 259v–260r, 20 Jan 1602 (MV); SDC, b. 57, cc. 156v–157r, 19 Apr 1603.

142. *NotAtti*, b. 3383–84, cc. 193r–196r, 11 May 1607; BAC, b. 276, reg. 395, cc. 7r–v, 26 Mar 1609.

143. BAC, b. 279, reg. 401, cc. 7v–8v, 13 Apr 1615; BAC, b. 317, cc. 15r–16v, 1 Jul 1598; *NotAtti*, b. 8422, t. I, cc. 39v–49v, 19 May 1616; *NotAtti*, b. 8423, t. III, cc. 343r–348v, 9 Dec 1617.

144. Corner, *Notizie storiche delle chiese e monasteri di Venezia*, 162–64, 380–83; Pullan, *Rich and Poor in Renaissance Venice*, 207, 259–63, 368–69, 413; Evangelisti, "Wives, Widows, and Brides of Christ," 246.

145. On the Convertite, see McGough, "Women, Private Property, and the Limitations of State Authority," 33–34; Pullan, *Rich and Poor in Renaissance Venice*, 258, 377–80, 416–17.

Chapter 2: *Elena Civalelli / Suor Deodata and Mihale/Catterina Šatorović*

1. Praga, *History of Dalmatia,* 178; Bracewell, *The Uskoks of Senj,* 156; Braudel, *Mediterranean,* 2:845–47.

2. Braudel, *Mediterranean,* 2:759, 889; Colley, *Captives,* 121.

3. Solitro, *Documenti sull'Istria e la Dalmazia,* 257–68; Pedani, "Beyond the Frontier," 174; Pedani, "Dalla frontiera al confine," 39–55; Traljić, "Tursko-mletačke granice u Dalmaciji."

4. Dursteler, *Venetians in Constantinople,* 16–17. For a comparative context, see Sahlins, *Boundaries,* 12, 275.

5. ASV, *Commemoriali,* r. 25; *LSTR,* b. 5; *SDelC,* b. 5, 24 Feb 1581 (MV).

6. Fabijanec, "Le développement commercial de Zadar et de Split," 77; Paci, *La scala di Spalato,* 45.

7. "Relazione di Antonio Pasqualigo," in *CRV,* 3:187; *CollRel,* b. 72, c. 4v, "Relazione di Giulio Contarini." Officials also acknowledged exaggerating the problems on the frontier for diplomatic effect, *APC,* b. 20/II, c. 107v, 3 Feb 1626 (MV).

8. "Relazione di Alvise Barbaro," in *CRV,* 4:312; BMCV, PD 567c, #48, 3 Feb 1582.

9. Benvenuto, *Storia di Zara,* 131. On the Uskoks, see Minucci, *Historia degli Uscochi.*

10. Rothenberg, "Christian Insurrections in Turkish Dalmatia."

11. *SDelC,* b. 12, 21 Nov 1612; Benvenuto, *Storia di Zara,* 133. See other examples in *PTM,* b. 929, 11 May 1622; *APC,* b. 18/11, cc. 50v–51r, 11 Jun 1622; *APC,* b. 18/13, cc. 43r–v, 1 Oct 1622; Kunt, *The Sultan's Servants,* 123.

12. BMCV, PD 567c, #48, 3 Feb 1582; also BL, MS 8604, "Correspondence of Sultan Murad," passim.

13. Kužić, "Prilog biografiji nekih Kačićevih," 223–24; *It VII* 1217 (9448), #18, c. 249r, "Relatione di Dalmatia"; Luca, "The Vlachs/Morlaks in the Hinterlands," 315–21; BL, MS 8613, cc. 81r–88r, "Relatione sopra i Morlacchi."

14. Vitezić, *La prima visita apostolica postridentina in Dalmazia,* 19, 31, 34.

15. "Relazione di Marco Barbarigo," in *CRV,* 4:342; BL, MS 8605, cc. 9r–v, "Relazione di Nicolo Donado"; "Relazione di Andrea Rhenier," in

CRV, 6:67; "Relazione di Marino Mudazzo," in CRV, 6:202–3; ASV, Collegio, Risposte di fuori, b. 352, 12 Jul 1599; Bracewell, The Uskoks of Senj, 35–36; Pedani, "Beyond the Frontier," 46.

16. Paci, La scala di Spalato, 14, 101; BL, MS 8610, c. 14r, "Relazione di Giovanni Tiepolo"; Novak, "Poljoprivreda na dalmatinskom," 75; PTM, b. 422, 18 Oct 1628.

17. Pedani, "Beyond the Frontier," 46.

18. Traljić, "Zadar i turska pozadina," 226; Marani, Atti pastorali di Minuccio Minucci, 60–61.

19. Lithgow, The Totall Discourse of the Rare Adventures, 44–45; "Relazione di Alvise Dolfin," in CRV, 4:223; Bracewell, The Uskoks of Senj, 35–36.

20. Fleischer, Bureaucrat and Intellectual, 63.

21. Marani, Atti pastorali di Minuccio Minucci, 50, 52–53; Horvat, "Glagolaši u Dalmaciji početkom," 557–59.

22. Bracewell, The Uskoks of Senj, 32, 34; Vitezić, La prima visita apostolica postridentina in Dalmazia, 19, 31, 34.

23. BMCV, Cicogna 1881, cc. 305r–v.

24. Fondra, Istoria della insigne reliquia di San Simeone, 279; Raukar, Zadar u XV stoljeću, 114–20; Krekić, "Developed Autonomy," 195; Semi and Tacconi, Istria e Dalmazia, 652.

25. CollRel, b. 72, "Relazione de Sindici de Dalmatia et di Levante del Clmo G. Andrea Giustiniano"; BL, MS 29444, c. 396r, "Relatione de Sindici de Dalmatia et di Levante del Clmo G. Andrea Giustiniano"; Benvenuto, Storia di Zara, 128.

26. "Relazione di Victoris Barbadico," in CRV, 2:44; Wilkinson, Dalmatia and Montenegro, 81–84; Fortis, Travels into Dalmatia, 14; Bernardy, Zara e i monumenti italiani della Dalmazia, 45–50; Lane, Venice, 24, 37, 63–64.

27. Beauvau, Relation journalière du voyage du Levant, 3; Lithgow, The Totall Discourse of the Rare Adventures, 44–45; Evliya Çelebi, Seyahatnamesi.

28. Vilfan, "Towns and States," 49; Benvenuto, Storia di Zara, 127; Luxardo de Franchi, Le fortificazioni venete, 67; BL, MS 8605, c. 7r, "Sommario della relatione dell'Illmo Sr Nicolo Donado."

29. Graovac, "Populacijski razvoj Zadra," 54–55; CollRel, b. 72, "Relatione de Lunardo Zulian"; also BMCV, Cicogna 2854, cc. 107r–v, 123r–125r,

"La discretion delle anime nella Città de Zara et suo Territorio, fatta li 24 Dec 1579."

30. Benvenuto, *Storia di Zara*, 128–29; *PTM*, b. 418, 2 Jun 1603; "Relazione di Victoris Barbadico," in *CRV*, 2:46. On the debate over Venice's responsibility for Zara's woes, see Toth, "Per una storia della Dalmazia," 362.

31. Hocquet, *Le sel et la fortune de Venise*, 85, 193–94; Raukar, "Venezia, il sale e la struttura economica e sociale della Dalmazia," 155–56; Raukar, "Le città della Dalmazia," 37.

32. "Relazione di Pauli Justiniani," in *CRV*, 3:52–53; Juran, "Kad i u kojim povijesnim," 139; Kolumbić, "Grbovi zadarskih plemićkih obitelji," 56–57; "Civalelli," in *Hrvatski biografski leksikon*, 2:689–90.

33. Gliubich, *Dizionario biografico*, 85–86.

34. Hocquet, *Le sel et la fortune de Venise*, 85, 193–94, 289–99; Hocquet, "Commercio e navigazione in Adriatico," 225–32; Raukar, "Venezia, il sale e la struttura economica e sociale della Dalmazia," 155–56.

35. Krekić, "Developed Autonomy," 193, 205; "Relazione di Victoris Barbadico," in *CRV*, 2:45; *VSM*, I, reg. 137, c. 122v, 17 Sep 1584.

36. "Relazione di Antonio Diedo," in *CRV*, 3:27.

37. *CollRel*, b. 72, "Relatione di Polo Giustiniano"; "Relazione di Pauli Justiniani," in *CRV*, 3:52–53.

38. ZKZ, MS 306, c. 231; "Relazione di Zacharie Vallaresso," in *CRV*, 1:204.

39. *FMK*, c. 298.

40. AZN, *Kršteni*, r. 3, c. 132r; AZN, *Kršteni*, r. 4, cc. 39v, 77v; *FMK*, cc. 216, 246, 252.

41. *Collegio, Risposte di fuori*, b. 352, 5 Sep 1599.

42. BL, MS 8605, c. 13v, "Relazione di Giovanni Tiepolo"; *SDC*, b. 33, c. 91v, 30 Mar 1591; *SDC*, b. 33, c. 360r, 24 Aug 1591; *SMar*, f. 135, ca. 28 Apr 1597. On Venice's artillerymen generally, see Hale and Mallett, *Military Organization of a Renaissance State*, 395–408.

43. "Relazione di Vicenzo Moresini," in *CRV*, 4:440; *SMar*, f. 135, 13 Aug 1597; "Relazione di Lorenzo Cocco," in *CRV*, 4:297; BL, MS 8605, cc. 86v–87v, 91r–v, "Relazione from an anonymous Provveditore Generale in Dalmatia."

44. ZKZ, MS 824.

45. *FMK*, cc. 234–51; Kertzer, *Sacrificed for Honor*, 72–73.

46. Setton, *The Papacy and the Levant*, 4:953 n. 133; Braudel, *Mediterranean*, 2:1100.

47. Graovac, "Populacijski razvoj Zadra," 54–55.

48. Selânikî, *Tarih-i Selânikî*, 1:387; İpşirli, "Mustafa Selânikî and His History," 452–53; SDC, b. 28, cc. 442r–v, 28 Jan 1588 (MV); SDC, b. 33, c. 360r, 24 Aug 1591; SDC, b. 52, cc. 296r–297r, 6 Jan 1600 (MV); "Relazione di Matteo Zane," in *Albèri*, 9:438; "Relazione di Girolamo Cappello," in Pedani, *Relazioni*, 420.

49. Sertoğlu, *Osmanlı tarih lügatı*, 303.

50. *SDCop*, r. 13, c. 12, 31 Dec 1598; SDC, b. 50, cc. 238r–246r, 10 Jan 1599 (MV); Gibb and Bowen, *Islamic Society and the West*, 1:332.

51. Selânikî, *Tarih-i Selânikî*, 2:854–56; Pedani, "Safiye's Household," 20–21; Pedani, "Veneziani a Costantinopoli," 73, 80; Luca, "Miscellanea italo-romena," 335–36; SDelC, b. 10, 9 Mar 1604.

52. SDC, b. 28, cc. 442r–v, 28 Jan 1588 (MV); SDC, b. 32, cc. 167v–168r, 13 Oct 1590; SDC, b. 30, c. 329r, 6 Jan 1589 (MV); SDC, b. 32, cc. 26r–v, 12 Sep 1590.

53. Povolo, *L'intrigo dell'onore*, 165, 269; BL, MS 8605, c. 4r, "Sommario della relatione dell'Illmo Sr Nicolo Donado."

54. ASV, *Capi del consiglio di dieci, lettere di rettori*, b. 283, 16 Jul 1561; SDC, b. 32, c. 132v, 29 Sep 1590; Pedani, "Safiye's Household," 20–21.

55. SDC, b. 32, cc. 26r–v, 12 Sep 1590; SDC, b. 32, cc. 72v–73v, 15 Sep 1590; SDC, b. 32, cc. 235v–236r, 10 Nov 1590.

56. SDC, b. 32, cc. 26r–v, 12 Sep 1590.

57. SDC, b. 32, cc. 26r–v, 12 Sep 1590; SDC, b. 32, cc. 72v–73v, 15 Sep 1590; SDC, b. 32, c. 132v, 29 Sep 1590; SDC, b. 33, c. 91v, 30 Mar 1591.

58. SDC, b. 33, c. 360r, 24 Aug 1591; SDC, b. 32, cc. 235v–236r, 10 Nov 1590.

59. al-Misri, *Reliance of the Traveller*, 529, 532, 595–96.

60. SDC, b. 33, c. 360r, 24 Aug 1591; SDelC, b. 10, copy 9 Mar 1604; SDelC, b. 8, 3 Oct 1591; SDC, b. 32, cc. 235v–236r, 10 Nov 1590; "Relazione di Matteo Zane," in *Albèri*, 9:438; Pedani, "Veneziani a Costantinopoli," 72–73.

61. Praga, *History of Dalmatia*, 180; O'Connell, *Men of Empire*, 47–48.

62. *SDC*, b. 32, cc. 235v–236r, 10 Nov 1590; *SDC*, b. 32, cc. 26r–v, 12 Sep 1590; *SDelC*, b. 8, 3 Oct 1591; *FMK*, c. 306; *PSM*, b. 264, n.d. [May–19 Jun 1600]; also Dal Borgo, "Nuovi documenti," 161–63; *SMar-Min*, b. 113, 7 Oct 1591; *Barbaro*, 5:13. On the Martinengo, see Freschot, *La nobiltà veneta*, 364–65; Schröeder, *Repertorio genealogico*, 1:500–1.

63. *SDelC*, b. 8, 3 Oct 1591.

64. *PSM*, b. 264, n.d. [May–19 Jun, 1600]; also Dal Borgo, "Nuovi documenti," 161–63; "Relazione di Matteo Zane," in *Albèri*, 9:438.

65. Marani, *Atti pastorali di Minuccio Minucci*, 42, 46–47; Maschek, *Manuale del regno di Dalmazia*, 170–71. See also *SSVe*, b. 33, cc. 454r–455v.

66. Corner, *Notizie storiche delle chiese e monasteri di Venezia*, 552; Cohen, "Asylums for Women in Counter-Reformation Italy," 169; Cohen, "Convertite e Malmaritate."

67. Ellero, "Vergini christiane," 74; Chojnacka, "Women, Charity, and Community," 68–69, 79–84; Pullan, *Rich and Poor*, 388–89; Lunardon, "Le Zitelle alla Giudecca," 15–16, 28–29.

68. Chojnacka, "Women, Charity, and Community," 79, 85; Lunardon, "Le Zitelle alla Giudecca," 26–27; Ellero, "Vergini christiane," 74; Chojnacka, "Singlewomen in Early Modern Venice," 226–29; Pullan, *Rich and Poor*, 388–89, 415.

69. Mazza, "Governare i 'luoghi pii'," 295; Chojnacka, "Women, Charity, and Community," 81–85.

70. *BAC*, b. 268, reg. 380, cc.1r–v, 21 Feb 1591 (MV).

71. *SDelC*, b. 9, 31 Oct 1597; *SDCop*, r. 11, cc. 274–76, 15 Feb 1596 (MV); Luca, "Miscellanea italo-romena," 335–36.

72. IRE, *Zitelle*, b. G1, "Carte diverse," 2 Nov 1597.

73. *SDelC*, b. 9, 30 Dec 1597; *SDelC*, b. 9, 25 Dec 1599.

74. Molho, *Marriage Alliance*; Kafadar, "The Ottomans and Europe," 593; Peirce, "Seniority, Sexuality, and Social Order," 173; Peirce, *Imperial Harem*, 12, 29; Weinstein, *Marriage Rituals Italian Style*, 52–112; Goitein, *A Mediterranean Society*, 3:55–61.

75. Jennings, "Women in Early-17th-Century Ottoman Judicial Records," 162–65; Lombardi, "Fidanzamenti e matrimoni dal concilio di Trento," 215, 219, 224–25.

76. *SDC*, b. 47, c. 8v, 11 Mar 1598; *SDC*, b. 47, c. 177r, 30 May 1598; *SDelC*, b. 9, 18 Apr 1598. Canon law allowed parents to invalidate a

daughter's vows if they were taken before she reached age twelve, and if they acted within a year and a day of her taking them. Reid, *Power over the Body*, 94–95.

77. *SDC*, b. 50, cc. 216r–217v, 26 Dec 1599; Panaite, "Power Relationships in the Ottoman Empire," 52–54.

78. Iorga, *Pretendenţi domnesci*, 59–60; Tappe, *Documents Concerning Rumanian History*, 52; Barbaro, 7:331; *SDC*, b. 39, cc. 1r–v, 12 Mar 1594; Iorga, "Venezia ed i paesi romeni," 307–8.

79. *Prospect of Hungary, and Transylvania*, 44–45; Maxim, "I principati romeni e l'impero ottomano," 173–74.

80. Maxim and Panaite, "Pax ottomanica," 35:13; 36:94; Platon, "Tra gli Imperi Ottomano, Austriaco e Russo," 195–96; Panaite, "The Voivodes of the Danubian Principalities," 59–76; Panaite, "Power Relationships in the Ottoman Empire," 47–57; Cernovodeanu, "An English Diplomat at War," 430; "Boghdan," *EI*², 1:1252–53; Lewis, *The Crisis of Islam*, 42; Olteanu, *Les pays roumains à l'époque de Michel le Brave*, 78. See, for example, *SP*, b. 97/4, c. 22r, 21 Mar 1598.

81. Mehmed, "La crise ottomane dans la vision de Hasan Kiafi Akhisari," 399; Panaite, "Power Relationships in the Ottoman Empire," 61; Sugar, *Southeastern Europe under Ottoman Rule*, 120–22; Iorga, *Histoire des Roumains*, 305, 319.

82. *SDCop*, r. 11, cc. 56–62, n.d.; *SDC*, b. 50, cc. 216r–217v, 26 Dec 1599; Doglioni, *L'Ungheria spiegata*, 9; Iorga, "Venezia ed i paesi romeni," 307.

83. Maxim, *Noi documente turceşti privind*, 242–43; "Ferhād Pasha," *EI*², 2:880; Panaite, "The Voivodes of the Danubian Principalities," 60–61.

84. Doglioni, *L'Ungheria spiegata*, 206–7; Atanasiu, *Mihai Viteazul: Campanii*, 130–38; Neagoe, *Mihai Viteazul*, 78–80; Iorga, *Pretendenţi domnesci*, 61; Iorga, "Contribuţiunĭ la istoria Munteniei," 103–4.

85. *SDCop*, r. 11, cc. 56–62, n.d.; *SDC*, b. 50, cc. 216r–217v, 26 Dec 1599; Tappe, *Documents Concerning Rumanian History*, 117.

86. *SDC*, b. 50, cc. 219r–v, 15 Oct 1599, Bogdan to Omer Ağa.

87. *SDC*, b. 50, cc. 219r–v, 15 Oct 1599, Bogdan to Omer Ağa; *PSM*, b. 264, n.d. [May–19 Jun 1600]; also Dal Borgo, "Nuovi documenti," 161–63.

88. *SDC*, b. 50, cc. 219r–v, 15 Oct 1599, Bogdan to Omer Ağa.

89. *SDelR*, b. 21, 26 Oct 1599.

90. Niero, *I patriarchi di Venezia*, 103–5; Sperling, *Convents*, 143.

91. *SDelR*, b. 21, 30 Oct 1599; *SRO*, reg. 12, c. 143v, 30 Oct 1599.

92. Martin, "*Renovatio* and Reform in Early Modern Italy," 15; Sperling, *Convents*, 281 n. 54; Laven, *Virgins of Venice*, 28; Dinan, *Women and Poor Relief in Seventeenth-Century France*, 18; Diefendorf, "Give Us Back Our Children," 286.

93. *SRO*, reg. 12, c. 143v, 30 Oct 1599.

94. ASVat, *Sacra congregazione, Episcoporum & Regularium, Positiones*, lett. S–V, anno 1599, 8 Jun 1599. On the relationship between Venice's patriarchs and its rulers, see Prodi, "The Structure and Organization of the Church in Renaissance Venice," 415–16.

95. *SDR*, b. 44, cc. 105r–106r, 6 Nov 1599.

96. *SRO*, reg. 12, c. 151v, 27 Nov 1599; *SRO*, reg. 12, c. 147r, 13 Nov 1599; *SDR*, b. 44, cc. 144v–145r, 149v, 155r, 20 Nov 1599; ASV, *Commemoriali*, r. 26, cc. 58r–v, 20 Nov 1599.

97. Luca, "Veneziani, levantini e romeni," 251.

98. *SDelC*, b. 9, 30 Dec 1597; *SDelC*, b. 9, 18 Apr 1598.

99. Maynes, "Age as a Category of Historical Analysis," 116–18; Marshall, "Childhood in Early Modern Europe," 65.

100. Davis, "Boundaries and the Sense of Self," 59–62.

101. Orme, *Medieval Children*, 337; Ago, "Young Nobles in the Age of Absolutism," 311–12; Ferraro, *Marriage Wars*, 38–39.

102. Rapley, "Women and Religious Vocation," 625–26, 630; Diefendorf, "Give Us Back Our Children," 266–71; Baernstein, *A Convent Tale*, 16–17; Wiesner-Hanks, "Women's Response to the Reformation," 152; Hacke, *Women, Sex, and Marriage*, 110. See also Bynum, *Holy Fast and Holy Feast*, 113–86, 220–27.

103. Bornstein, "Introduction," 1–2; Canosa, *Il velo e il cappuccio*; LaBalme, "Venetian Women on Women," 99–100. There is still debate among scholars on this. See Schutte, "The Permeable Cloister," 20–23; Schutte, "Legal Remedies for Forced Monachization in Early Modern Italy," 231–47.

104. Baernstein, *A Convent Tale*, 14–15; Ago, "Young Nobles in the Age of Absolutism," 308.

105. Baernstein, "In Widow's Habit," 787; Rapley, "Women and Religious Vocation," 626, 629. Also, Chojnacka, "Women, Charity, and Community," 69.

106. Ambrosini, "Toward a Social History of Women in Venice," 423.

107. *PSM*, b. 264, n.d. [May–19 Jun 1600]; also Dal Borgo, "Nuovi documenti," 161–63; *SDelC*, b. 10, 9 Mar 1604; *SDelC*, b. 9, 25 Dec 1599; *SDelC*, b. 9, 19 Feb 1599 (MV).

108. *PSM*, b. 264, 1 May 1600; *PSM*, b. 264, n.d. [May–19 Jun 1600]; also Dal Borgo, "Nuovi documenti," 161–63. There are other examples of nobles disregarding Corpus Domini's cloistered status; see *PSM*, b. 260, 6 Feb 1628, 29 Oct 1626.

109. *SDC*, b. 51, cc. 246r–v, 16 Jun 1600.

110. *PSM*, b. 264, n.d. [May–19 Jun 1600]; also Dal Borgo, "Nuovi documenti," 161–63; *PSM*, b. 264, 19 Jun 1600.

111. *SDC*, b. 55, cc. 215v–216r, 7 Jul 1602.

112. Sanderson, *The Travels of John Sanderson*, xxxv, 269 n. 2; Brown, *Calendar of State Papers*, 11:xvii–xviii, 413–14, 427.

113. Iorga, *Pretendenți domnesci*, 61–67; Iorga, *Studiĭ și documente cu privire la Istoria romînilor*, 107–8; Luca, "Miscellanea italo-romena," 335–36; Luca, "Călători și pribegi din țările romăne," 51.

114. Corner, *Notizie storiche delle chiese e monasteri di Venezia*, 320; Bornstein, "Introduction," 4–5; Sperling, *Convents*, 258; Bassi, *Tracce di chiese veneziane distrutte*, 260–61; Franzoi and di Stefano, *Le chiese di Venezia*, 103; Mazzarotto, *Le feste veneziane*, 164–69.

115. *VDM*, b. 4, #13, 31 Aug 1620; Corner, *Notizie storiche delle chiese e monasteri di Venezia*, 320.

116. *VDM*, b. 3, cc. 557r–562r, 27 Nov 1596; *VDM*, b. 4, #13, 31 Aug 1620; Evangelisti, "Wives, Widows, and Brides of Christ," 241.

117. *VDM*, b. 4, 17 Oct 1620; Evangelisti, "Wives, Widows, and Brides of Christ," 241; Baernstein, "In Widow's Habit," 794.

118. Schutte, "The Permeable Cloister," 24; Sperling, *Convents*, 158–63.

119. *VDM*, b. 3, cc. 557r–562r, 27 Nov 1596; *VDM*, b. 4. #13, 31 Aug 1620; *VDM*, b. 5, #21, 6 Nov 1613; *VDM*, b. 1, #12, 20 Jun 1651 to 9 Apr 1652; ASPV, *Monalium*, b. 1, f. 4, 17 Jul 1634.

120. Pedani, *In nome del Gran Signore*, 66, 208.

121. *SDelC*, b. 10, 9 Mar 1604.

122. *SDelC*, b. 10, 9 Mar 1604.

123. *CD*, b. 6, 7 Feb 1609 (MV); *CD*, Catastico, b. 1, "Catastico," 5 Feb 1623 (MV); *CD*, b. 11, #16, 7 Sep 1638; *CD*, b. 4, 16 Dec 1647.

124. *VDM*, b. 3, cc. 557r–562r, 27 Nov 1596.

125. *VDM*, b. 1, #12, 27 Jun 1651.

126. *CollRel*, b. 72, "Relazione di Giacomo Michiel"; *PTM*, b. 929, 11 May 1622. On the office of count of Spalato, see O'Connell, *Men of Empire*, 3–7.

127. *SDelC*, b. 15, 12 Jan 1621 (MV).

128. *Barbaro*, 5:116; Maschietto, *Elena Lucrezia Cornaro Piscopia*, 6 n. 10.

129. Fabijanec, "Le développement commercial de Zadar et de Split," 37; Paci, *La scala di Spalato*, 18, 45, 53, 128–29; *CollRel*, b. 72, "Relazione di Bartolomeo Pisani"; "Relazione di Alvise Loredan," in *CRV*, 4:229; "Relazione di Nicolo Correr," in *CRV*, 4:332.

130. ASV, *Collegio, risposte di dentro*, b. 10, #131, 11 Jul 1597; Frejdenberg, "Venetian Jews and Ottoman Authorities on the Balkans," 56.

131. Lane, *Venice*, 303; Arbel, "Jews in International Trade," 90–91; Kafadar, "The Ottomans and Europe," 617; Paci, *La scala di Spalato*, 17, 71, 92–93; Kafadar, "A Death in Venice," 205.

132. BL, MS 8605, c. 7v, "Relazione di Nicolo Donado."

133. *It VI* 105 (5728), c. 5r; "Itinerario di Giovanni Battista Giustinian," in *CRV*, 2:211; Evliya Çelebi, *Putopis*, 152–53.

134. De Benvenuti, "Fortezze e castelli di Dalmazia," 16:28, 37–39, 17:16; "Dalmatia," *EI²*, 12:184–85; Singleton, *A Short History of the Yugoslav Peoples*, 5, 60–61; BMCV, *Cicogna* 3098, "Compendio di varie revolutioni della famosa fortezza di Clissa."

135. "Relazione di Nicolo Correr," in *CRV*, 4:338; "Revisti Dalmati confini del dragoman Salvago," in *CRV*, 7:32; "Relazione di Pietro Basadonna," in *CRV*, 8:224–25.

136. "Bosna," *EI²*, 1:1261–75; "Livno," *EI²*, 5:774; Malcolm, *Bosnia: A Short History*, 90–91; Rački, "Prilozi za geografsko-statistički opis bosanskoga pašalika," 179. Also, BL, MS 8655, cc. 3v–11v.

137. FHL, *Matičnih Knjiga*, r. 1, c. 148r, 23 Jan 1622; *PTM*, b. 929, 15 Mar 1622; *SDelC*, b. 15, 18 Feb 1621 (MV); *PTM*, b. 929, 18 Mar 1622, letter from Ibrahim Paşa; Vanzan, "In Search of Another Identity," 331.

138. Kužić, "Osmanlijski zapovjedni kadar," 188, 203, 205; *SDelC*, b. 20, Mar 1627, translation of letter from Sultan.

139. Kužić, "Osmanlijski zapovjedni kadar," 197, 202–3; Tomić, *Grada za istoriju pokreta*, 1, 35, 38; Horvat, *Monumenta Uscocchorum*, 1:102.

140. Cesco, "Il rapimento a fine di matrimonio," 393–95; Lopasic, "The Turks of Bosnia," 15; Wolff, *Venice and the Slavs*, 163–65; Sugar, *Southeastern Europe under Ottoman Rule*, 106–7.

141. *SDelC*, b. 15, 18 Feb 1621 (MV); *PTM*, b. 929, 15 Mar 1622; "Relazione di Alvise Barbaro," in *CRV*, 4:312; Marani, *Atti pastorali di Minuccio Minucci*, 52–53, 59–60.

142. *SDelC*, b. 15, 18 Feb 1621 (MV); *SDelC*, b. 15, 12 Jan 1621 (MV); *BAC*, b. 108, Feb 1622.

143. Novak, "Poljoprivreda na dalmatinskom," 98; "Relazione di Catherino Corner," in *CRV*, 7:259; BL, MS 8623, cc. 21r–v.

144. *PTM*, b. 929, 2 Apr 1622; *SDelC*, b. 16, 12 Apr 1622; "Itinerario di Giovanni Battista Giustinian," in *CRV*, 2:221.

145. *PTM*, b. 929, 15 Mar 1622; *SDelC*, b. 15, 18 Feb 1621 (MV); *APC*, b. 18/10, c. 2v, 16 Apr 1622.

146. ASVat, *Congregazioni romane, Concilio, Relationes dioecesium*, b. 759A, "Relatione del Procuratore del Arcivescovo di Spalato Francesco Crasso"; ASVat, *Congregazioni romane, Concilio, Relationes dioecesium*, b. 759A, "Relatio status Ecclesiae Spalatensis pro Anno 1609"; ACPF, *Visite e collegi*, b. 2, cc. 823–35, 19–21 Jan 1623.

147. *PTM*, b. 929, 4 Mar 1622; *PTM*, b. 929, 15 Mar 1622; *SDelC*, b. 15, 18 Feb 1621 (MV); *SDelC*, r. 18, c. 43r, 7 Jun 1627.

148. *SDelC*, b. 15, 18 Feb 1621 (MV).

149. *PTM*, b. 929, 15 Mar 1622; *APC*, b. 18/10, cc. 1c, 2v, 6 Apr 1622; *BAC*, b. 108, Feb 1622.

150. *SDelC*, b. 15, 18 Feb 1621 (MV); FHL, *Matičnih Knjiga*, r. 1, c. 148r, 23 Jan 1622; *PSM*, b. 114, 19 Sep 1622; Gauchat, *Hierarchia catholica medii et recentioris aevi*, 4:320.

151. *SDelC*, b. 15, 12 Jan 1621 (MV); *PTM*, b. 929, 15 Mar 1622; *PSM*, b. 114, 19 Sep 1622; Wratislaw, *Adventures of Baron Wenceslas Wratislaw*, 17–18; Matar, *Turks, Moors, and Englishmen*, 37; Lopasic, "Islamization of the Balkans," 175–76; Kaplan, *Divided by Faith*, 269–70.

152. *SDelC*, b. 15, 12 Jan 1621 (MV).

153. *SDelC*, b. 15, 18 Feb 1621 (MV).

154. Novak, *Povijest Splita*, 2:1139.

155. BL, MS 8610, cc. 21v–22r, "Relazione di Giovanni Tiepolo"; "Relazione di Marino Mudazzo," in *CRV*, 6: 286. On the state of Spalato's

defenses, see BL, MS 8610, cc. 43v–46r, "Relatione di Dalmatia Alvise Mocenigo."

156. *SDelC,* b. 15, 12 Jan 1621 (MV); *SDelC,* b. 15, 18 Feb 1621 (MV); *SDelC,* b. 16, 12 Mar 1622; *PTM,* b. 929, 15 Mar 1622; "Leonardo Foscolo," *DBI,* 49:455.

157. Hardwick, "Did Gender Have a Renaissance," 344.

158. *SDelC,* b. 15, 12 Jan 1621 (MV).

159. *APC,* b. 18/10, cc. 33r–36v, 1 Apr 1622.

160. Milan, Politi, and Vianello, *Guida alle magistrature,* 142; Mocenigo, *Storia della marina veneziana,* 22. On Belegno, see "Giusto Antonio Belegno," *DBI,* 7:560–61.

161. *SDelC,* b. 15, 12 Jan 1621 (MV).

162. *PTM,* b. 929, 3 Mar 1622; *PTM,* b. 929, 4 Mar 1622; *PTM,* b. 929, 15 Mar 1622.

163. *PTM,* b. 929, 18 Mar 1622, letter from Ibrahim Paşa; *PTM,* b. 929, 19 Mar 1622.

164. *SDelC,* b. 15, 18 Feb 1621 (MV); *PTM,* b. 929, 15 Mar 1622; *PTM,* b. 929, 25 Mar 1622; *PTM,* b. 929, 20 Mar 1622, letter from Ibrahim Paşa; *PTM,* b. 929, 21 Mar 1622, letter from Ibrahim Paşa; *BAC,* b. 108, May 1622, hüccet from kadi of Clissa; Fabijanec, "Le développement commercial de Zadar et de Split," 67, 78.

165. DAZ, *Atti del provveditore generale,* r. 2, cc. 417r–418r; *SMar,* r. 34, c. 11v, 2 Apr 1558; *SDelC,* b. 22, 9 Mar 1630.

166. *APC,* b. 18/9, cc. 33r–36v, 1 Apr 1622; *APC,* b. 18/10, c. 2v, 16 Apr 1622; *APC,* b. 18/12, cc. 4r–v, 25 Jun 1622; Kramer, "Mustafā I," 7:759–60.

167. *PTM,* b. 929, 2 Apr 1622; *SDelC,* b. 16, 12 Apr 1622; *SDelC,* b. 16, 12 Mar 1622.

168. Gregory, *Salvation at Stake,* 15; Gregory, "To the Point of Shedding Your Blood," 77–82; Wickersham, "Results of the Reformation," 269–83. For the Ottoman context, see Krstić, "Illuminated by the Light of Islam," 36.

169. Veinstein, "Sur les conversions à l'Islam," 165; Fiorani, "Verso la nuova città," 172; Rambo, "Theories of Conversion," 264.

170. *SDelC,* b. 20, 11 Jun 1627; *SDelC,* b. 20, 3 Jun 1627; Ellero, "Vergini christiane," 74.

171. *SDelC,* b. 20, Mar 1627, translation of letter from Sultan; *SDelC,* b. 20, 3 Jun 1627; *SDelC,* b. 20, 11 Jun 1627.

172. al-Misri, *Reliance of the Traveller,* 595–96; Derengil, "There Is No Compulsion in Religion," 550; Félix, "Children on the Frontiers of Islam," 64–65.

173. *SDelC,* b. 20, 11 Jun 1627; *SDelC,* b. 20, 3 Jun 1627; *SDelC,* b. 20, 4 Jun 1627; Vanzan, "In Search of Another Identity," 331.

174. *SDelC,* r. 18, cc. 39v–41v, 5 Jun 1627.

175. *SDelC,* r. 18, cc. 41v–44r, 7 Jun 1627.

176. Rothman, "Between Venice and Istanbul," 381–82.

177. *SDelC,* r. 18, cc. 41v–44r, 7 Jun 1627.

178. *SDelC,* b. 20, 2 Jun 1627; also Vanzan, "In Search of Another Identity," 331.

179. *SDelC,* b. 20, 11 Jun 1627; *SDelC,* b. 9, 19 Feb 1599 (MV); *SDelC,* b. 9, 26 Mar 1598; *SDelC,* b. 9, 31 Oct 1597.

180. Davis, "Boundaries and the Sense of Self," 59.

181. *SDelC,* b. 20, 3 Jun 1627; Kužić, "Osmanlijski zapovjedni kadar," 195, 211.

Chapter 3: Maria Gozzadini and Her Daughters — Aissè, Eminè, Catigè

1. *Barbaro,* 5:189; Mocenigo, *Storia della marina veneziana,* 23.

2. *SDC,* b. 118, cc. 474r–476v, 1 Aug 1637; *BAC,* b. 364, Sep 1637; *PTM,* b. 1375, 20 Jul 1637; *CMarP,* b. 5, cc. 35–36.

3. *Turcograeciae,* 207; Randolph, *The Present State of the Islands in the Archipelago,* 32–34; Dankoff and Leslie, *Evliya Çelebi in Albania,* 143; Lithgow, *The Totall Discourse of the Rare Adventures,* 84; Miller, *The Latins in the Levant,* 616.

4. ACPF, *Visite e collegi,* b. 17, cc. 72v–73r; Tournefort, *Relation d'un voyage,* 61; Borromeo, *Voyageurs occidenteaux dans l'empire ottoman,* 1:145; Armao, *In giro per il mar Egeo,* 259–61.

5. Bruce, *Journal of a Voyage into the Mediterranean,* 53; Piacenza, *L'egeo redivio,* 273–74; Frazee, *The Island Princes of Greece,* 43; Borromeo, "Les Cyclades à l'époque ottomane," 128.

6. Vacalopoulos, *The Greek Nation,* 85–90; Randolph, *The Present State of the Islands in the Archipelago,* 32–34; Boschini, *L'Arcipelago,* 1–2, 28–29; Zachariadou, "The Sandjak of Naxos," 331, 332; Slot, *Archipelagus Turbatus,* 1:24–25, 122.

7. Lamansky, *Secrets d'état de Venise*, 2:72; *SDC*, b. 107, Jul 1628, command from Sultan to Kadi of Milos; Frazee, *The Island Princes of Greece*, 11–42, 63, 86–89; "Djazāir-i Bahr-i Safīd," *EI²*, 2:521.

8. Bruce, *Journal of a Voyage into the Mediterranean*, 54.

9. Vatin, "Îles grecques," 72–73, 86–87; Slot, *Archipelagus Turbatus*, 1:14, 24–25, 91–92, 100–101, 286–87; Zachariadou, "The Sandjak of Naxos," 329–30, 337; Roth, *The Duke of Naxos*, 75–89; Borromeo, "Les Cyclades à l'époque ottomane," 133–34; Randolph, *The Present State of the Islands in the Archipelago*, 32–34. For a comparative context, see İnalcık, "Ottoman Methods of Conquest," 104–29.

10. Armao, *In giro per il mar Egeo*, 258; Slot, *Archipelagus Turbatus*, 1:25; Hasluck, "Depopulation in the Aegean Islands," 156–60, 172–75; Lendaki, *E katastrophe tes Melou*, 29; Sphyroeras, "Metanasteuseis kai epoikismoi Kykladiton," 172.

11. Borromeo, *Voyageurs occidenteaux dans l'empire ottoman*, 1:144; Balta, "The Ottoman Surveys of Siphnos," 54; Carayon, *Relations inédites des missions de la Compagnie de Jésus*, 126; Kasdagli, *Land and Marriage Settlements in the Aegean*, 27.

12. Bruce, *Journal of a Voyage into the Mediterranean*, 53–54; Evliya Çelebi, *Seyahatnamesi*, 9:260.

13. *Turcograeciae*, 207; Armao, *In giro per il mar Egeo*, 259–60; Frazee, *The Island Princes of Greece*, 43, 89; Vacalopoulos, *The Greek Nation*, 278.

14. Thévenot, *Voyage du Levant*, 174–75; du Fresne-Canaye, *Le voyage du Levant*, 171–72; Randolph, *The Present State of the Islands in the Archipelago*, 32–34; Slot, *Archipelagus Turbatus*, 1:22.

15. Vingopoulou, *Le monde grec vu par les voyageurs*, 232; Slot, *Archipelagus Turbatus*, 1:25; Vacalopoulos, *The Greek Nation*, 89, 276; Angelomatis-Tsougarakis, "Greek Women," 340–48. For another example, see Piacenza, *L'egeo redivio*, 277.

16. *SOCG*, b. 184, c. 45v.

17. *CMarP*, b. 5, cc. 2, 15, 29–30, 35–36.

18. Slot, *Archipelagus Turbatus*, 1:25, 115, 134, 261, 2:381 n.73; Miller, *The Latins in the Levant*, 587–606.

19. *CMarP*, b. 5, cc. 1–2, 10, 15; *BAC*, b. 364, 15 Jul 1637.

20. Peirce, "Seniority, Sexuality, and Social Order," 185; Semerdjian, *Off the Straight Path*, 38–39; Lopasic, "The Turks of Bosnia," 15.

21. Viscuso, *Sexuality, Marriage, and Celibacy*, 112–14; Viscuso, "Mar-

riage between Christians and Non-Christians," 271; Viscuso, "An Orthodox Perspective on Marriage," 313; Levin, *Sex and Society,* 101–5; *SOCG,* b. 184, cc. 300r–v.

22. Bassano, *Costumi et i modi particolari,* 52; Faroqhi, *Subjects of the Sultan,* 102.

23. Vryonis, "Byzantine and Turkish Societies and their Sources of Manpower," #3, 143; Cassia, "Religion, Politics, and Ethnicity in Cyprus," 22–23; Derengil, "There Is No Compulsion in Religion," 548.

24. Kasdagli, "Gender Differentiation and Social Practice," 72.

25. Kasdagli, *Land and Marriage Settlements in the Aegean,* 214, 236–37; Angelomatis-Tsougarakis, "Women in the Society of the Despotate of Epirus," 474.

26. *CMarP,* b. 5, cc. 2–3, 7, 12–13, 17, 32, 37; *BAC,* b. 364, 15 Jul 1637; Faroqhi, *Subjects of the Sultan,* 102; "Saghīr," *EI²,* 8:821–27.

27. Morris, "Mediterraneanization," 30–31.

28. Lopasic, "The Bulgarian Moslems, or Pomaks," 123–24; Lopasic, "The Turks of Bosnia," 17–21; Tóth, "Between Islam and Christianity," 241; Minkov, *Conversion to Islam in the Balkans,* 102–5; Zachariadou, "Co-Existence and Religion," 120.

29. Perry, "Contested Identities," 182; Kamen, "Strategies of Survival," 217; Faroqhi, *Subjects of the Sultan,* 183; Burke, "Civilizations and Frontiers," 138. See also Hasluck, *Christianity and Islam under the Sultans.*

30. *It VII* 882 (8505), cc. 34r–v, "Descritione dell'Imperio Turchesco"; Vacalopoulos, *The Greek Nation,* 33.

31. *SOCG,* b. 206, cc. 326r, 328r–329v, 540v–41r.

32. Skendi, "Crypto-Christianity in the Balkan Area," 227–46; Cassia, "Religion, Politics, and Ethnicity in Cyprus," 21–22.

33. *CMarP,* b. 5, cc. 12, 15.

34. *CMarP,* b. 5, c. 40; *PTM,* b. 1375, 20 Jul 1637.

35. Tucker, *In the House of the Law,* 124–43; Tucker, "The Fullness of Affection," 232–38; Faroqhi, "Crime, Women, and Wealth," 9.

36. Kasdagli, *Land and Marriage Settlements in the Aegean,* 231–32.

37. Akyilmaz, "Woman According to the Ottoman Law of Family," 628; Esposito, *Women in Muslim Family Law,* 15; Tucker, *In the House of the Law,* 155–56; Lewis, *Everyday Life in Ottoman Turkey,* 100.

38. *CMarP,* b. 5, c. 10.

39. Iskowitz, *The Ottoman Empire and Islamic Tradition,* 43; İnalcık,

"Decision Making in the Ottoman State," 14–15; Gerber, *State, Society, and Law in Islam,* 15–18, 76, 173.

40. ASV, *Commemoriali,* r. 28, c. 133v, Sep 1637; *SDC,* b. 118, cc. 333r–334r, 29 May 1637.

41. *SDC,* b. 118, cc. 333r–334r, 29 May 1637; *It VII* 1085 (8522), cc. 61v–65r, 28 May 1637.

42. İnalcık, "Decision Making in the Ottoman State," 14–15; Jennings, "Kadi, Court, and Legal Procedure," 136–38.

43. *SDC,* b. 118, cc. 511r–519v, 14 Aug 1637; *SDC,* b. 118, cc. 474r–476v, 1 Aug 1637; *CMarP,* b. 5, cc. 10–11; *BAC,* b. 364, 15 Jul 1637.

44. Gerber, *State, Society, and Law in Islam,* 148; Peirce, "Seniority, Sexuality, and Social Order," 190; Zilfi, "Muslim Women in the Early Modern Era," 244–45.

45. Esposito, *Women in Muslim Family Law,* 32–33; Tucker, *In the House of the Law,* 79; Zilfi, "We Don't Get Along," 274–75.

46. *CMarP,* b. 5, c. 11.

47. *CMarP,* b. 5, cc. 2, 15, 29–30, 35–36; Mocenigo, *Storia della marina veneziana,* 32.

48. *PTM,* b. 1192, 28 Sep 1637; *SDC,* b. 118, cc. 511r–519v, 14 Aug 1637; *SDelC,* b. 29, 4 Nov 1637; *SDelC,* r. 24, c. 80v, 31 Oct 1637; *SDelC,* b. 30, 3 Apr 1638.

49. *SDC,* b. 118, cc. 474r–476v, 1 Aug 1637; *CMarP,* b. 5, cc. 4, 8, 13, 15, 17, 32, 36.

50. *CMarP,* b. 5, c. 40.

51. *SDC,* b. 118, cc. 474r–476v, 1 Aug 1637; *BAC,* b. 364, hüccet of Hassan Efendi Kadi of Milos.

52. Pagratis, "Tracce della presenza francescana in Levante," 102; Miller, "The Ionian Islands under Venetian Rule," 217, 229; Lane, *Venice,* 198, 362; Pagratis, "Trade and Shipping in Corfu," 172–73.

53. Sherley, "Discours of the Turkes," 19; *It VII* 1217 (9448), cc. 213r–v, "Relazione dell'Isola di Corfu."

54. *CMarP,* b. 5, cc. 5, 38.

55. *CMarP,* b. 5, cc. 5, 14, 33–34.

56. Bade, *Migration in European History,* 1–2; Moch, *Moving Europeans,* 22–59; Forbes, "Early Modern Greece," 111–12.

57. Isaacs, "Introduction," xi; Braudel, *Mediterranean,* 1:47–49, 85–102; Horden and Purcell, *The Corrupting Sea,* 377–400.

58. Sutton, "Liquid Landscapes," 85, 103; Galasso, "La mobilità delle persone nel mediterraneo," 209; Purcell, "Fixity," 78.

59. Dursteler, *Venetians in Constantinople*, 61–102; McGowan, "The Age of the Ayans," 646–52; Adanır, "The Ottoman Peasantries," 291.

60. Forsén, "Regionalism and Mobility in Early Modern Greece," 238–40; Malliaris, "Population Exchange and Integration of Immigrant Communities in the Venetian Morea," 98–104; Sphyroeras, "Metanasteuseis kai epoikismoi Kykladiton," 172.

61. Sutton, "Liquid Landscapes," 88–89; Oris and Ochiai, "Family Crisis in the Context of Different Family Systems," 58–60.

62. *PTM*, b. 1375, 20 Jul 1637; *PTM*, b. 1192, 30 Aug 1637; Karsten, "Die Gleichschaltung der Eminenzen," 242.

63. *BAC*, b. 364, 15 Jul 1637.

64. Miller, "The Ionian Islands under Venetian Rule," 218–19; Hofmann, "La chiesa cattolica in Grecia," 165; Pagratis, *Ekklesia kai krato sta venetika nesia tou Ioniou Pelagous*, 72; Gerouki, *Les excommunications à Corfou*, 46–52.

65. Pagratis, "Tracce della presenza francescana in Levante," 102; Pagratis, *Ekklesia kai krato sta venetika nesia tou Ioniou Pelagous*, 66–67; Tsitsas, *Venetokratoumene Kerkyra*, 38.

66. Faroqhi, *Subjects of the Sultan*, 102; Zachariadou, "Co-Existence and Religion," 123–24.

67. Laiou, "Christian Women in an Ottoman World," 246–47; Wickersham, "Results of the Reformation," 273.

68. Elsie, *Early Albania*, 79, 96.

69. Kaplan, *Divided by Faith*, 268, 278–93.

70. *SOCG*, b. 206, cc. 328r–329v; Pagratis, *Ekklesia kai krato sta venetika nesia tou Ioniou Pelagous*, 64; Hofmann, "La chiesa cattolica in Grecia," 167.

71. Pagratis, *Ekklesia kai krato sta venetika nesia tou Ioniou Pelagous*, 51, 64–71; Arbel, "Roman Catholics and Greek Orthodox," 80–85; Peri, "L'«incredibile risguardo» e l'«incredibile destrezza»," 599–625.

72. Karapidakis, *Civis fidelis*, 121–22.

73. Baernstein, "In Widow's Habit," 787; King, *Women of the Renaissance*, 57–58.

74. *PTM*, b. 1375, 20 Jul 1637; *PTM*, b. 1192, 30 Aug 1637; *CMarP*, b. 5, c. 14; Sturdza, *Grandes familles de Grèce*, 243–45.

75. Rangabé, *Livre d'or*, 253–57; Marmora, *Della historia di Corfu*, 312–13; Sturdza, *Grandes familles de Grèce*, 439–40.

76. Pagratis, *Hoi ektheseis ton Veneton,* 378; *PTM,* b. 1375, 20 Jul 1637; *PTM,* b. 1192, 30 Aug 1637; Karapidakis, *Civis fidelis,* 225; *CMarP,* b. 5, c. 26.

77. ANK, *Grandi protopapa,* b. 2, c. 236r, 16 Feb 1640.

78. *PTM,* b. 1375, 20 Jul 1637; *PTM,* b. 1192, 30 Aug 1637; ANK, *Grandi protopapa,* b. 2, c. 202r, 17 Jul 1637.

79. *EK,* b. 13, c. 270r; *EK,* b. 5, c. 281r; Pagratis, "Sources for the Maritime History of Greece," 139.

80. Karapidakis, *Civis fidelis,* 224; Rangabé, *Livre d'or,* 14.

81. *EK,* b. 9, f. 1, c. 5r; *EK,* f. 5, c. 115r; *EK,* f. 6, c. 17r; *EK,* b. 13, cc. 144r, 153v, 173r–v, 192r–v.

82. *EK,* b. 15, cc. 15r, 35r; *EK,* b. 16, f. 6, c. 17v; *EK,* b. 16, f. 8, cc. 2v–3r; *EK,* b. 17, f. 6, c. 43r; *EK,* b. 17, f. 9, c. 15r; ANK, *Grandi protopapa,* b. 2, c. 202r, 17 Jul 1637.

83. Giotopoulou-Sisilianou, *Presveies tes Venetokratoumenes Kerkyras,* 602–4; *EK,* b. 16, f. 7, c. 7r; *EK,* b. 17, f. 3, c. 20v.

84. Evangelisti, "Wives, Widows, and Brides of Christ," 245–46.

85. *SDelC,* r. 24, c. 39v, 18 Aug 1637.

86. *SDC,* b. 118, cc. 474r–476v, 1 Aug 1637; *CMarP,* b. 5, cc. 4, 14; *PTM,* b. 1375, 20 Jul 1637.

87. *PTM,* b. 1375, 20 Jul 1637; BMCV, *Donà delle Rose,* b. 153, c. 2r, "Relazion di Giovanni Contarini."

88. Sarti, *Europe at Home,* 63; Laiou, "Christian Women in an Ottoman World," 247; Kasdagli, "Gender Differentiation and Social Practice," 74–85; Hartnup, *On the Beliefs of the Greeks,* 133.

89. *CMarP,* b. 5, cc. 25–26, 39.

90. *It VII* 1085 (8522), cc. 119r–123v, 14 Aug 1637.

91. *SDelC,* b. 24, c. 60v, 19 Sep 1637; *PTM,* b. 1192, 30 Aug 1637.

92. *SSVe,* b. 60A, c. 219v, 31 Oct 1637; Dursteler, "Power and Information," 605–6.

93. *SDelC,* r. 24, cc. 23r–v, 27 Jun 1637; *It VII* 1085 (8522), c. 65v, 13 Jun 1637.

94. Lollino, *Vita del cavaliere Ottaviano Bon,* 8–9; Dursteler "The *Bailo* in Constantinople," 2–5.

95. *It VII* 1085 (8522), c. 45v, 23 May 1637; "Alvise Contarini," *DBI,* 28:82–91; "Relazione di Alvise Contarini," in *Berchet,* 1:330.

96. *SDC,* b. 118, cc. 329r–332r, 29 Mar 1637.

97. *SDC*, b. 118, cc. 333r–334r, 29 May 1637. On the social reforms under Murad IV, see Zilfi, "The Kadizadelis," 256–58; Baer, "Honored by the Glory of Islam," 99–149.

98. Fischer and Villani, "People of Every Mixture," 97.

99. *SDC*, b. 118, cc. 577r–579v, 19 Sep 1628.

100. *SDC*, b. 118, cc. 333r–334r, 29 May 1637; *SDC*, b. 118, cc. 511r–519v, 14 Aug 1637.

101. *SDC*, b. 118, cc. 333r–334r, 29 May 1637; *SDC*, b. 118, cc. 511r–519v, 14 Aug 1637; *It VII* 1085 (8522), cc. 106v–110r, 1 Aug 1637.

102. Cassia, "Navigating an Anthropology of the Mediterranean," 88. On the anthropological debates, see, among many works, Peristiany, *Honour and Shame;* Herzfeld, "The Horns of the Mediterraneanist Dilemma"; Herzfeld, "Honour and Shame"; Gilmore, *Honor and Shame and the Unity of the Mediterranean;* Pina-Cabral, "The Mediterranean as a Category of Regional Comparison," 399–404; Lever, "Honour as a Red Herring."

103. Strocchia, "Gender and Rites of Honour," 39; Kollmann, *By Honor Bound,* 20–24; Burke, "Civilizations and Frontiers," 133; Horodowich, *Language and Statecraft in Early Modern Venice,* 212; Bryson, *The Point of Honor in Sixteenth Century Italy,* 1–14; Muir, *Mad Blood Stirring,* 247; Burke, *Historical Anthropology of Early Modern Italy,* 13–14; Povolo, *L'intrigo dell'onore,* 265.

104. Povolo, *L'intrigo dell'onore,* 358–61; Dean, "Gender and Insult in an Italian City," 218–24; Strocchia, "Gender and Rites of Honour," 54; Cohen, "Honor and Gender in the Streets of Early Modern Rome," 598–600.

105. *SDC*, b. 32, cc. 167v–168r, 13 Oct 1590.

106. Kollmann, *By Honor Bound,* 26; Ruggiero, "Più che la vita caro," 755–56; Roper, *Oedipus and the Devil,* 65, 107–9; Nye, *Masculinity and Male Codes of Honor,* 9–10; Cavallo and Cerutti, "Female Honor and the Social Control of Reproduction," 81, 89; Weinstein, *The Captain's Concubine,* 149; Bryson, *The Point of Honor in Sixteenth Century Italy,* 12.

107. Romei, *The Courtiers Academie,* 126–27.

108. Peirce, *Imperial Harem,* 271; Peirce, *Morality Tales,* 354; Peirce, "Seniority, Sexuality, and Social Order," 18, 185–87.

109. Horodowich, *Language and Statecraft in Early Modern Venice,* 118; Muir, *Mad Blood Stirring,* 165–66; McLean, *The Art of the Network,* 59–60; Horodowich, *Language and Statecraft in Early Modern Venice,* 117–18.

110. BL, MS 8604, cc. 66r–71v.

111. Adams, "The Rule of the Father," 238–39; Hanley, "Engendering the State," 8–9; Brewer, *By Birth or Consent*, 19–20; Adams, *The Familial State*, 3–4, 29.

112. Horodowich, *Language and Statecraft in Early Modern Venice*, 2–12, 57–58, 95–118.

113. Ruggiero, *Boundaries of Eros*, 17–22, 47, 72, 92.

114. Sperling, *Convents*, 69.

115. Chojnacka, "Women, Charity, and Community," 70; Pullan, "La nuova filantropia," 10–34; Bock, "Women's History and Gender History," 9; Ferrante, "Honor Regained," 47–64; Cohen, "Convertite e Malmaritate."

116. Baer, "Islamic Conversion Narratives of Women," 428.

117. Skilliter, "Catherine de' Medici's Turkish Ladies-in-Waiting"; Setton, *The Papacy and the Levant*, 4:836–41. See also Weiss, "Commerce, Conversion, and French Religious Identity," 285–86.

118. Series of Ottoman documents with translations, in *BAC*, b. 364, ca. 10–28 May 1637.

119. Slot, *Archipelagus Turbatus*, 1:156; Paspati, "Life of the Patriarch Cyril," 482; Adler, *Jewish Travellers*, 331–33.

120. Slot, *Archipelagus Turbatus*, 1:156, 172, 213; Fodor, "The Organisation of Defence," 91.

121. *It VII* 1085 (8522), cc. 106v–110r, 1 Aug 1637; series of Ottoman documents with translations, in *BAC*, b. 364, ca. 10–28 May 1637.

122. *SOCG*, b. 184, c. 45v.

123. Hammer, *Histoire*, 9:156.

124. *SDC*, b. 118, cc. 474r–476v, 1 Aug 1637.

125. *It VII* 1085 (8522), cc. 106v–110r, 1 Aug 1637; *PTM*, b. 1192, 28 Sep 1637.

126. *It VII* 1085 (8522), cc. 66v–67v, 13 Jun 1637; *It VII* 1085 (8522), cc. 126v–128v, 29 Aug 1637; *SDC*, b. 118, cc. 535r–537v, 29 Aug 1637.

127. *PTM*, b. 1215, 24 Jul 1637.

128. *PTM*, b. 1375, 20 Jul 1637; *PTM*, b. 1375, 28 Mar 1637; *PTM*, b. 1215, 24 Jul 1637.

129. *SMar*, r. 312, 15 Jun 1637; *PTM*, b. 1191, 5 Jan 1637 (MV); *Barbaro*, 5:189.

130. *CMarP*, b. 5, cc. 19–26; *It VII* 1085 (8522), cc. 119r–123v, 14 Aug 1637.

131. *PTM*, b. 1215, 3 Aug 1637; *PTM*, b. 1215, 24 Jul 1637; *CMarP*, b. 5, cc. 4–5, 8, 13–18, 37.

132. *PTM*, b. 1215, 3 Aug 1637; *PTM*, b. 1215, 24 Jul 1637; *PTM*, b. 1192, 30 Aug 1637; *CMarP*, b. 5, cc. 27–28.

133. *PTM*, b. 1192, 30 Aug 1637; *PTM*, b. 1192, 17 Mar 1638; *PTM*, b. 1215, 25 Aug 1637; *PTM*, b. 1192, 6 Nov 1637.

134. *CollRel*, b. 74, "Relatione degli Inquisitori in Levante Cappello, Correr, Contarini 1638."

135. *SDelC*, r. 24, cc. 26r–v, 27 Jun 1637.

136. *SDC*, b. 118, cc. 511r–519v, 14 Aug 1637; *It VII* 1085 (8522), cc. 119r–123v, 14 Aug 1637.

137. *PTM*, b. 1192, 28 Sep 1637; *PTM*, b. 1192, 12 Aug 1637; *PTM*, b. 1192, 30 Aug 1637.

138. *SDC*, b. 118, cc. 511r–519v, 14 Aug 1637; *It VII* 1085 (8522), cc. 119r–123v, 14 Aug 1637.

139. Zorattini, "Battesimi," 172–73.

140. *SDC*, b. 118, cc. 511r–519v, 14 Aug 1637; *It VII* 1085 (8522), cc. 119r–123v, 14 Aug 1637.

141. Félix, "Children on the Frontiers of Islam," 65; "Saghīr," *EI²*, 8:825–26; Giladi, *Children of Islam*, 23, 52–53, 116; Ginio, "Childhood, Mental Capacity, and Conversion to Islam," 98–104. The age of consent for baptism in France was also seven; Luria, *Sacred Boundaries*, 188–89.

142. Siebenhüner, "Conversion, Mobility, and the Roman Inquisition," 19; Heyberger, "Se convertir à l'Islam," 140; Shatzmiller, "Marriage, Family, and the Faith."

143. Kaplan, *Divided by Faith*, 278–79; Angelomatis-Tsougarakis, "Greek Women," 392–93.

144. Reid, *Power over the Body*, 147–48; Kedar, "Muslim Conversion in Canon Law," 321–25.

145. Pearl, *Muslim Personal Law*, 209–11; Esposito, *Women in Muslim Family Law*, 34.

146. *SDC*, b. 118, cc. 511r–519v, 14 Aug 1637; *It VII* 1085 (8522), cc. 119r–123v, 14 Aug 1637.

147. Belin, "Relations diplomatiques," 416–17; Theunissen, "Ottoman-Venetian Diplomatics," 514–17; *SDC*, b. 118, cc. 577r–579v, 19 Sep 1628.

148. *SDC*, b. 118, cc. 648r–649v, 14 Nov 1637.

149. *SDC*, b. 118, cc. 511r–519v, 14 Aug 1637; *It VII* 1085 (8522), cc. 119r–123v, 14 Aug 1637.

150. *SDC*, b. 118, cc. 577r–579v, 19 Sep 1628.

151. Peters, *Patterns of Piety*, 7, 154; Wiesner-Hanks, "Women's Response to the Reformation," 148–51; Weber, *Teresa of Avila and the Rhetoric of Femininity*, 19–25.

152. Davis, "Women on Top," 147–48; Davis, *Society and Culture in Early Modern France*, 65; Lewis, "The 'Weakness' of Women," 84; Wiesner-Hanks, *Gender, Church, and State*, 85.

153. Dursteler, *Venetians in Constantinople*, 93–94; Topping, "Patriarchal Prejudice and Pride in Greek Christianity," 9–11; Mantran, *Istanbul au siècle de Soliman le Magnifique*; 168; Clissold, "Christian Renegades and Barbary Corsairs," 509–10.

154. Lewis, *Islam and the West*, 49–50; "Takiyya," *EI²*, 10:134–36; Perry, "Behind the Veil," 42; Perry, "Moriscas and the Limits of Assimilation," 279.

155. Vitkus, "Trafficking with the Turk," 45–48; Stanivukovic, "Cruising the Mediterranean," 65–68; Vitkus, "Early Modern Orientalism," 223–24; Matar, *Turks, Moors, and Englishmen*, 112–27; Davis, *Christian Slaves, Muslim Masters*, 125–27; Clissold, *The Barbary Slaves*, 42–47; Colley, *Captives*, 128–30; Schick, "Christian Maidens, Turkish Ravishers," 279. For the medieval roots of these views, see Daniel, *Islam and the West*, 158–85.

156. Nicolay, *The Navigations*, 8r; *CollRel*, b. 4, cc. 81v–84v, "Relazione di Lorenzo Bernardo." See also *SDC*, b. 70, c. 214r, 13 Nov 1610.

157. Bennassar and Bennassar, *Les chrétiens d'Allah*, 235; Mantran, *Istanbul au siècle de Soliman le Magnifique*, 168; Weiss, "Commerce, Conversion, and French Religious Identity," 276.

158. al-Misri, *Reliance of the Traveller*, 532, 595–96; Ginio, "Childhood, Mental Capacity, and Conversion to Islam," 98; Warrraq, *Leaving Islam*, 17–23; Derengil, "There Is No Compulsion in Religion," 550; Lewis, *The Crisis of Islam*, 55, 141.

159. *SDC*, b. 118, cc. 535r–537v, 29 Aug 1637; *It VII* 1085 (8522), cc. 126v–128v, 29 Aug 1637; *SDC*, b. 118, cc. 577r–579v, 19 Sep 1628.

160. ASV, *Commemoriali*, r. 28, c. 133v, Sep 1637; also *SDC*, b. 118, cc. 583r–584r, 19 Sep 1637; *BAC*, b. 364, "Tradottione di Scrittura di quietanza che fa un Kadi da Milos."

161. *It* VII 1085 (8522), cc. 191v–192r, 12 Dec 1637; *It* VII 1085 (8522), cc. 198r–v, 9 Jan 1637 (MV); *SDC*, b. 118, c. 709v, 12 Dec 1637; *PTM*, b. 1192, 17 Mar 1638; *PTM*, b. 1192, 5 Apr 1638; *PTM*, b. 792, 12 Jan 1637 (MV); *SDelC*, r. 24, c. 99v, 29 Dec 1637; *SDelC*, r. 24, cc. 61v–62r, 23 Sep 1637.

162. *SDC*, b. 118, cc. 648r–649v, 14 Nov 1637; *PTM*, b. 1192, 6 Nov 1637.

163. *CMarP*, b. 5, c. 11.

Conclusion

1. Burke, "History of Events and the Revival of Narrative," 240–42.

2. Abulafia, "What Is the Mediterranean," 9–13; Abulafia, "Mediterraneans," 64; Kamen, "Strategies of Survival," 206.

3. Burke, "Civilizations and Frontiers," 136; Burke, "Passing through Three Crises," 99.

4. Davis, "Women's History," 83.

5. Colley, *The Ordeal of Elizabeth Marsh*, 291; Scott, "The Problem of Invisibility," 5.

6. See Twinam, "Women and Gender in Colonial Latin America," 187–237; Benjamin, *The Atlantic World*, 420–64.

7. Hurlburt, "Columbus' Sister." The only attempt to approach gender in a fully Mediterranean context is Sperling and Wray, *Across the Religious Divide: Women, Property, and Law in the Wider Mediterranean (ca. 1300–1800)*, which is a recent, innovative collected volume that examines one small aspect of women's experiences—dowries and inheritance.

8. Braudel, *Mediterranean*, 1:276–77.

9. Horden and Purcell, *The Corrupting Sea*, 5; Horden and Purcell, "The Mediterranean," 733–39; Horden and Purcell, "Four Years of Corruption," 356–64; Morris, "Mediterraneanization," 32, 37–38; Brummett, "Visions of the Mediterranean," 35, 38.

10. Subrahmanyam, *Mughals and Franks*, 213; Molho, "Review of *The Corrupting Sea*," 490; Purcell, "The Boundless Sea," 20–21.

11. Morris, "Mediterraneanization," 37–38.

12. Edwards, *Families and Frontiers*, 4–5; Power, "Frontiers," 2–3, 20.

13. Purcell, "The Boundless Sea," 20–22; Faroqhi, *Subjects of the Sultan*, 279–80.

14. Krstić, "Illuminated by the Light of Islam," 38–39; Burke, "Civilizations and Frontiers," 137; Bulliet, *The Case for Islamo-Christian Civilization,* 32; Ortega, "Pleading for Help," 333.

15. Ginzburg, *The Cheese and the Worms,* 49–51; Schwartz, *All Can Be Saved,* 1–9; Ibarra, "Reflexiones sobre la conversión al Islam," 195; Martin, *Venice's Hidden Enemies,* 28.

16. Bulliett, *Islam: The View from the Edge;* Bulliet, *The Case for Islamo-Christian Civilization,* 138–46.

17. Kamen, "Strategies of Survival," 214–20.

18. Abulafia, "What Is the Mediterranean," 26.

19. Greenblatt, *Renaissance Self-Fashioning,* 256.

20. Dayton, "Rethinking Agency, Recovering Voices," 827 n.1, 842–43; Johnson, "On Agency," 113–16; Scully, "Marriage or a Career," 857.

21. The literature on agency is truly immense. As a starting point, see Hurlburt, "Columbus' Sister," and Seeff and Hartman, *Structures and Subjectivities.*

22. Zilfi, "Introduction," 5; Scully, "Marriage or a Career," 857.

23. Politi, *Dittionario toscano,* 667; *Le dictionnaire de l'Académie françoise,* 2:122; Bailey, *Universal Etymological English Dictionary,* n.p.

24. Rostagno, *Mi faccio turco,* 27; Scaraffia, *Rinnegati,* 8; Bennassar, "Conversion ou reniement," 1349–50.

25. Vitkus, "Early Modern Orientalism," 215; Shatzmiller, "Marriage, Family, and the Faith," 235, 260.

26. See, for example, the classic work of Bennassar and Bennassar, *Les chrétiens d'Allah;* also Rostagno, *Mi faccio turco;* Scaraffia, *Rinnegati;* and Clissold, "Christian Renegades and Barbary Corsairs."

27. Wiesner-Hanks, "Women's Response to the Reformation," 166–67; Bennassar, "Conversions, esclavage, et commerce des femmes," 102.

28. Baer, *Honored by the Glory of Islam,* 189–92; Woodberry, "Conversion in Islam," 22.

29. Scaraffia, *Rinnegati,* 4–5; Bennassar and Bennassar, *Les chrétiens d'Allah,* 228–50; Bennassar, "Conversion ou reniement," 1363–64.

30. For comparisons, see Shatzmiller, "Marriage, Family, and the Faith," 255; Greene, *A Shared World,* 93–94; Baer, "Islamic Conversion Narratives of Women," 426–27; Povero, *Missioni in terra di frontiera,* 161–62, 303–4; Siebenhüner, "Conversion, Mobility, and the Roman Inquisition."

31. Wiesner-Hanks, *Gender, Church, and State,* 3, 6; Kessler-Harris, "What Is Gender History Now," 101–2.

32. Scott, "Gender," 1072–73; Restall, "He Wished It in Vain," 578–80, 586.

33. De Vaus and McAllister, "Gender Differences in Religion," 472; Miller and Hoffman, "Risk and Religion," 63–64; Walter and Davie, "The Religiosity of Women in the Modern West," 640–41.

34. Shatzmiller, "Marriage, Family, and the Faith," 236–37.

35. Perry, "Contested Identities," 179, 181; Perry, "Behind the Veil," 39–44; Perry, "Moriscas and the Limits of Assimilation," 274–75. See also Fournel-Guérin, "La femme morisque en Aragon," 528, 533–34.

36. Meyerson, "Aragonese and Catalan Jewish Converts," 138; Melammed, "Crypto-Jewish Women," 199–200, 208–9. See also Foa, "The Marrano's Kitchen," 14–15.

37. Bernos, "Conversion ou apostasie," 41; Skendi, "Crypto-Christianity in the Balkan Area," 232.

38. Stark, *The Rise of Christianity,* 95–128; Povero, *Missioni in terra di frontiera,* 304, 323.

39. Roelker, "The Appeal of Calvinism," 402; Davis, *Society and Culture in Early Modern France,* 81; Karant-Nunn, "The Reformation of Women," 180.

40. Bennassar, "Conversions, esclavage, et commerce des femmes," 101–2; Veinstein, "Sur les conversions à l'Islam," 165.

41. Mills and Grafton, "Introduction," ix–xii; Rambo, *Understanding Religious Conversion,* 5, 7; Coleman, "Continuous Conversion," 17–18; Austin-Broos, "The Anthropology of Conversion," 2, 9; Hefner, "Introduction," 4, 17.

42. Siebenhüner, "Conversion, Mobility, and the Roman Inquisition," 7, 27–29.

43. Crawford, *Women and Religion in England,* 73–97; Eales, *Women in Early Modern England,* 87.

44. Molho, "Review of *The Corrupting Sea,*" 488; Abulafia, "What Is the Mediterranean," 18–19, 26; Sperling and Wray, "Introduction," 19.

45. Wiesner-Hanks, *Gender, Church, and State,* 7; Chojnacki, "Comment: Blurring Genders," 747; Bock, "Women's History and Gender History," 8.

46. Zambelli, "Uno, due, tre, mille Menocchio."

47. Levi, "On Microhistory," 109.

48. Ginzburg, "Just One Witness," 85.

49. Levi, "On Microhistory," 109.

50. Dalla Porta, *La turca;* Andreini, *La sultana commedia;* Andreini, *La turca commedia boscareccia et maritima;* Loredano, *La turca.* See also Donizetti's opera, *La rinegata.*

51. *APC,* b. 20/I, cc. 46v–47r, 14 Jun 1626.

52. *SDelC,* b. 13, 14 Jan 1614 (MV).

53. Monter, "Women in Calvinist Geneva," 195–96; Wiesner-Hanks, "Women's Response to the Reformation," 166–67.

54. Vanzan, "In Search of Another Identity," 332.

55. See for example, Rothman, "Becoming Venetian"; Zorattini, *I nomi degli altri;* Allegra, "L'ospizio dei catecumeni di Torino"; Caffiero, *Battesimi forzati;* Lopes, "A problemática da conversão"; Campanini, "L'identità coatta"; and Lattes, "Gli ebrei di Ferrara e le imposte per i catecumeni."

56. *PTM,* b. 1375, 20 Jul 1637.

57. Rothman, "Between Venice and Istanbul," 377.

58. *SDelC,* b. 17, 14 Sep 1624; *SDelC,* b. 21, 2 Nov 1628.

GLOSSARY

Writing Mediterranean history inevitably means making linguistic decisions. In general I have chosen to leave many technical terms in their original language, even when a more commonly used version exists. My reason is that the English equivalent runs the risk of imprecision. In most instances I have opted for the Turkish spelling of Ottoman titles, except where a commonly used English version exists, such as kadi. For place names, I have generally defaulted to the terms most commonly used in contemporary documents, with some exceptions where modern Anglicized versions are in common usage, such as Venice or Istanbul.

ağa. Signor, lord; honorary title usually applied to military commanders and imperial palace personnel.

ahidname. Written pledge of privilege granted by the sultan.

akça. Ottoman silver coin, the empire's standard monetary unit; *asper*, in English.

bailo. Venetian consul and ambassador in Istanbul; plural, *baili.*

baş defterdar. Chief comptroller; head of Ottoman finances.

beglerbegi. Governor-general of an Ottoman province (*beglerbegilik*).

bey/beg. Title of commander or military-administrative head of a *sancak.*

buyuk mirahur. Head of the imperial stables.

capitano del golfo. Venetian captain of the gulf, charged with protecting shipping in the Adriatic Sea.

çavuş. Official Ottoman messenger; member of corps of couriers.

cittadino originario. Original citizen of Venice; a member of a privileged, non-noble minority that monopolized the republic's chief bureaucratic offices.

Collegio. Powerful Venetian administrative council comprising many of the highest state officials.

Council of Ten. The highest government body in Venice, made up of ten patricians, joined by the doge and his six councilors.

dar al-harb. Literally "abode of war"; lands not under Muslim rule.

devşirme. Levy of boys from the Christian subject population of the Ottoman Empire for military service.

divan. Sultan's imperial council; the Ottoman government.

doge. Titular elected head of the Venetian Republic.

dragoman. Interpreter.

efendi. Master; an Ottoman honorific title for educated men.

emin. A trusted person, usually an official of the sultan.

epitropi. Greek leaders, heads of community.

eyalet. Ottoman province, also *beglerbeglik.*

galleass. Large, heavily armed Venetian galley; also known as a *galia grossa.*

harac. Tax required of all non-Muslim Ottoman subjects.

haraçgüzar. Non-Muslim Ottoman subject, required to pay *harac.*

haseki. Favorite, principal concubine of the sultan.

has oda başı. Head of the imperial privy chamber.

hidana. The right of a mother, under Islamic law, to care for her young children; boys until age seven, girls until nine.

hüccet. Ottoman legal document.

inquisitori di Levante. State auditors charged with a range of administrative duties in the Venetian *stato da mar.*

kadi. An Ottoman judge who also fulfilled some administrative and military duties.

kahya. An Ottoman steward or deputy.

ka'immakam. Deputy, usually the official left to administer Istanbul when the grand vizier was away.

kanun. Ottoman imperial law, supplements sharia religious law.

kapı ağası. Head of the white eunuchs and chief of the imperial palace and its staff.

kapudan paşa. Admiral of the Ottoman fleet.

khul. A form of divorce permitted by Islamic law; it could be initiated by a woman but had to be accepted by her husband, usually in return for some form of compensation.

kira. Lady; usually refers to a non-Muslim attendant of the *valide sultan.*

madrasa. Muslim school of higher learning that taught theology, Koranic exegesis, Arabic language, and jurisprudence.

megas protopapas. Archpriest of the Greek Orthodox rite.

more veneto. Refers to the Venetian calendar year, which began on March 1; abbreviated MV.

müteferrika. Member of the sultan's elite personal escort.

paşa. Honorific title reserved for the highest Ottoman dignitaries.

podestà. Venetian governor and military official.

Pomaks. Bulgarian Muslims who inhabit the Rhodope Mountains.

popolani. Venetian commoners.

provveditore. Commissioner or superintendent, a senior Venetian patrician official charged with the oversight of military, civil or commercial activities.

provveditore dell'armata. Senior official charged with supervising all Venetian land and sea forces in the Levant.

provveditore general da mar. Head of all Venetian land and sea forces in the Levant and of the Ionian islands.

provveditore generale in Dalmazia e Albania. Second-most important peacetime Venetian naval official; the governor-general of Dalmatia with supreme administrative and military powers.

provveditori sopra li monasteri. Venetian officials charged with the oversight of the city's monasteries.

sancak. An administrative subdivision of a *beglerbegilik,* administered by a *sancak beg.*

saray ağası. *Ağa* of the palace, responsible for the safety and order of the inner palace.

seraglio. Italian rendering of *saray,* palace, usually used to refer to the imperial Topkapi Palace.

sharia. Islamic holy law.

Signoria. The core council of the Venetian government, composed of ten men—the doge, the six ducal councillors, and the three heads of the *Quarantia Criminal,* the supreme appeals court of Venice.

sipahi. Member of Ottoman cavalry; plural, *sipāhī.*

stato da mar. The Venetian maritime empire in the eastern Mediterranean.

taqiyya. Muslim practice of outward conformity in a non-Muslim religious setting while preserving internal faith in Islam.

terraferma. The Venetian landed empire, located in northeastern Italy.

timar. Military fief given to a sipahi in return for military service.

ulema. Chief religious and judicial hierarchy of the Ottoman Empire.

Uskoks. Christian freebooters and Habsburg subjects who operated along the northern and central Adriatic coast.

valide sultan. Royal mother; mother of the reigning sultan.

Vlachs. A pre-Slavic ethnic group descended from the Dacians who inhabit mountainous areas of the Balkans and are often shepherds and herders.

voivode. Slavic title for a prince, especially the puppet rulers of the Ottoman tributaries of Wallachia and Moldavia.

BIBLIOGRAPHY

Unpublished Primary Sources

Archivio congregatio pro doctrina fidei (ACDF), Vatican City
  Dubia diversa ab anno 1570 ad annum 1668
Archivio della congregazione de propagand fide (ACPF), Vatican City
  Scritture originali riferite nelle congregazioni generali
  Visite e collegi
Archivio di stato di Firenze (ASFi), Florence, Italy
  Mediceo del principato
Archivio di stato di Venezia (ASV), Venice, Italy
  Archivi propri degli ambasciatori—Costantinopoli
  Avogaria di comun
  Avogaria di comun, Nascite, libro d'oro
  Bailo a Costantinopoli
  Barbaro, M., *Arbori de' patritii veneti*
  Capi del consiglio di dieci, Lettere di ambasciatori
  Capi del consiglio di dieci, Lettere di rettori
  Cariche da mar, Processi
  Collegio, Relazioni
  Collegio, Risposte di dentro
  Collegio, Risposte di fuori
  Commemoriali
  Consiglio di dieci, Deliberazioni segrete
  Corpus Domini
  Dieci savi alle decime in Rialto
  Documenti turchi
  Giudici di petizion
  Inquisitori di stato
  Lettere e scritture turchesche
  Maggior consiglio, Deliberazioni

Miscellanea Gregolin
Notarile, Atti
Notarile, Testamenti
Provveditori alla sanità, Necrologi
Provveditori di terra e da mar
Provveditori sopra li monasteri
Provveditori sopra ospedali e luoghi pii
Rubricarii di Costantinopoli
Segretario alle voci, Maggior consiglio
Senato deliberazioni, Costantinopoli
Senato deliberazioni, Roma
Senato dispacci, Copie moderne
Senato dispacci, Costantinopoli
Senato dispacci, Roma
Senato mar
Senato mar (minute)
Senato Roma ordinaria
Senato segreta, Materie miste notabili
Senato terra
Sopraconsoli dei mercanti
V savi alla mercanzia
Archivio Istituzioni di Ricovero e di Educazione (IRE), Venice, Italy
Zitelle carte diverse in oggetti vari, sec XVI–XVII
Archivio segreto Vaticano (ASVat), Vatican City
Congregazioni romane, Concilio, Relationes dioecesium
Sacra congregazione, Episcoporum & regularium, Positiones
Segreteria di stato, Venezia
Archivio storico del patriarcato di Venezia (ASPV), Venice, Italy
Monalium, Documenti diversi, Carte varie riguardanti monasteri
feminili
Parocchia San Barnabà, Matrimoni
Parocchia San Giacomo dall'Orio, Battesimi
Visite de monache
Visite parocchiali
Arhiv Zadarske Nadbiskupije (Archive of the Archbishop of Zadar) (AZN),
Zadar, Croatia
Kršteni

Biblioteca del Museo Civico Correr di Venezia (BMCV), Venice, Italy

Cod Cicogna 1881, "Istoria delle Reliquie del Glorioso S. Simeone Profeta detto il Giusto esistenti nella Città di Zara"

Cod Cicogna 2854, "Miscellanea"

Cod Cicogna 3098, "Fortezze"

Donà delle Rose 153, "Corfu Armata"

MS Cicogna 1971, "Memorie Turche"

MS PD 567c, "Documenti istorici, manoscritti antichi dal 1560 al 1771"

Biblioteca nazionale Marciana (BNM), Venice, Italy

MS Italiano, classe VI

It VI 105 (5728), "Viaggio da Venezia a Costantinopoli"

MS Italiano, classe VII

It VII 27 (7761), "Cronaca di famiglie cittadine originarie venete"

It VII 341 (8623), "Cronaca delle famiglie cittadinesche venete"

It VII 882 (8505), "Relazioni di Turchia"

It VII 1084–88 (8521–25), "Alvise Contarini, lettere al senato"

It VII 1217 (9448), "Miscellanea"

Biblioteca Vaticana (BAV), Vatican City

Urb. Lat. 1739, "Successi della guerra fra Sultan Amurat imperator di Turchi, et del Mehmet Chotavent Re di Persiani, et di Giorgiani Cristiani dal 1571 fatto l'anno MDLXXXI"

British Library (BL), London, U.K.

MS 8604, "Correspondence of Sultan Murad III and Bosnian Officials Relating to the Borders of Dalmatia, 1575–1591"

MS 8605, "Relazioni to the Venetian Senate Relating to Dalmatia, Candia, Albania, Corfu, Zante, and Cephalonia; Late 16th cent.–17th cent."

MS 8610, "Relazioni of Dalmatia from Provveditori Generali; 1591–1687"

MS 8613, "Relazioni, Letters and Papers Relating to Dalmatia; 1633–1707"

MS 8623, "Description of the Island of Lissa (Vis); 1803"

MS 8655, "Ayn-i Ali Makalesi: Two Tracts Relating to the Administrative and Military Structure of the Ottoman Empire; circa 1609"

MS 29444, "Copies of Relations of Different Countries"

Državni Arhiv Zadar (Zadar State Archive) (DAZ), Zadar, Croatia
  Atti del provveditore generale in Dalmazia ed Albania Giustinian Bellegno, 1617–1622
  Fonda Matičnih Knjiga Državnog Arhiva Zadru 1500
Family History Library (FHL), Salt Lake City, Utah, U.S.A.
  Matičnih Knjiga [Births], 1615–31. *Roman Catholic Church, Split (Croatia), St. Doimus Parish Registers, 1615–1653.* Microfilmed by the Genealogical Society of Utah, 1994. FHL Intl. film 2009238, it. 1
Genika Archeia tou Kratous, Archeia Nomou Kerkyras (Archives of the Prefecture of Corfu) (ANK), Corfu, Greece
  Enetokratia
  Grandi protopapa
Public Record Office, London (PRO), London, U.K.
  State Papers Foreign, Turkey
Znanstvena Knjižnica Zadar (Research Library of Zadar) (ZKZ), Zadar, Croatia
  MS 306, "Documenti delle famiglie Andreis, Cega, Cippico di Trau, Civalelli di Zara, e Paladini di Lesina"
  MS 824, "Cronache di Zara"

Published Primary Sources

Adler, Elkan Nathan. *Jewish Travellers.* Abingdon, U.K.: Routledge, 2004.

Albèri, Eugenio. *Relazioni degli ambasciatori veneti al senato durante il secolo decimosesto.* Series 3. Vols. 1–3. Florence: Società editrice fiorentina, 1840–55.

Andreini, Giovanni Battista. *La sultana commedia.* Paris: Nicolas Della Vigna, 1622.

———. *La turca commedia boscareccia et maritima.* Casale: Pantaleone Goffi, 1611.

Bailey, Nathan. *An Universal Etymological English Dictionary* . . . London: N. Bailey, 1675.

Barozzi, Niccolò, and Guglielmo Berchet, eds. *Le relazioni degli stati europei lette al senato dagli ambasciatori veneziani nel secolo decimosettimo. Turchia: Parte I–II.* Venice: P. Nartovich, 1871–72.

Bassano, Luigi. *Costumi et i modi particolari della vita de' Turchi.* Rome:

Antonio Blando Asolano, 1545. Reprint, Munich: Casa editrice Max Hueber, 1963.

Beauvau, Henry de. *Relation journalière du voyage du Levant*. Toul: François du Bois, 1608.

Belin, M. "Relations diplomatiques de la république de Venise avec la Turquie (Fragment)." *Journal Asiatique* 8 (1876): 381–424.

Boschini, Marco. *L'Arcipelago*. Venice: Francesco Nicolini, 1657.

Brown, Horatio, ed. *Calendar of State Papers and Manuscripts Relating to English Affairs Existing in the Archives and Collections of Venice and in Other Libraries of Northern Italy*. Vol. 11. London: His Majesty's Stationery Office, 1904.

Bruce, John, ed. *Journal of a Voyage into the Mediterranean by Sir Kenelm Digby, A.D. 1628*. N.p.: The Camden Society, 1868.

Burian, Orhan, ed. *The Report of Lello Third English Ambassador to the Sublime Porte*. Ankara: Türk Tarih Kurumu Basimevi, 1952.

Carayon, Auguste, ed. *Relations inédites des missions de la Compagnie de Jésus a Constantinople et dans le Levant au XVIIe siècle*. Poitiers: Henri Oudain, 1864.

Carli, Giovanni Rinaldo. *Cronologia historica scritta in lingua Turca, Persiana, et Araba da Hazi Halifé Mustafá*. Venice: Andrea Poletti, 1697.

Cervantes, Miguel de. *The First Part of the Delightful History of the Most Ingenious Knight Don Quixote of the Mancha*. Translated by Thomas Shelton. New York: P. F. Collier and Son, 1938.

Corner, Flaminio. *Notizie storiche delle chiese e monasteri di Venezia, e di Torcello*. Padua: Stamperia del Seminario, 1758. Reprint, Bologna: Arnaldo Forni Editore, 1990.

Crane, Howard. *Risāle-i mi'māriyye: An Early-Seventeenth-Century Ottoman Treatise on Architecture*. Leiden: Brill, 1987.

d'Alessio, E. Dalleggio. *Relatione dello stato della cristianità di Pera e Costantinopoli obediente al sommo pontefice romano*. Constantinopole: Edizioni Rizzo and Son, 1925.

Dalla Porta, Gio Battista. *La turca. Comedia nuova*. Venice: Pietro Ciera, 1606.

Dankoff, Robert, and Robert Leslie, eds. *Evliya Çelebi in Albania and Adjacent Regions (Kosovo, Montenegro, Ohrid)*. Leiden: Brill, 2000.

Le dictionnaire de l'Académie françoise, dédié au Roy. Paris: Veuve de Jean Baptiste Coignard, 1694.

Doglioni, Gio Nicolo. *L'Ungheria spiegata.* Venice: Damian Zenaro, 1595.

Donizetti, Gaetano, and Antonio Monticini. *La rinegata. Dramma lirico in tre atti da rappresentarsi nel Regio Teatro il carnovale del 1846–47 alla presenza delle LL. SS. RR. MM.* Turin: Tipografia dei fratelli Favale, n.d.

Elsie, Robert, ed. *Early Albania: A Reader of Historical Texts, 11th–17th Centuries.* Wiesbaden: Harrassowitz Verlag, 2003.

Evliya Çelebi. *Putopis: Odlomci o júgoslavenskim zemljama.* Edited by Hazim Šabanović. Sarajevo: Svjetlost, 1967.

———. *Seyahatnamesi.* Vol. 9. Istanbul: Devlet Matbaasi, 1935.

Fortis, Alberto. *Travels into Dalmatia.* London: J. Robson, 1778. Reprint, New York: Arno, 1971.

Foster, Charles Thornton, and F. H. Blackburne Daniell, eds. *The Life and Letters of Ogier Ghiselin de Busbecq.* 2 vols. London: C. Kegan Paul, 1881.

Freschot, D. Casmiro. *La nobiltà veneta.* Venice: G. Hertz, 1707. Reprint, Bologna: Arnaldo Forni Editore, 1970.

Fresne-Canaye, Philippe du. *Le voyage du Levant.* Edited by M. H. Hauser. Paris: Ernest Leroux, 1897.

Fuscus, Palladius. *Palladii Fvsci Patavini de sitv orae Illyrici.* Rome: Antonius Bladus, 1540.

Külekçi, Numan, ed. *Ganî-zâde Nâdirî ve dîvânından seçmeler.* Ankara: Kültür Bakanlığı, 1989.

Horvat, Carolus. *Monumenta Uscocchorum.* Part I. In *Monumenta spectantia historiam Slavorum meridionalium,* vol. 32. Zagreb: Academiae Scientiarum et Artium Slavorum Meridionalium, 1910.

Iorga [Jorga], Nicolae. *Studiǐ și documente cu privire la Istoria romînilor.* Vol. 11. Bucharest: Editura Ministeriuluǐ de Instrucție, 1906.

Lamansky, Vladimir. *Secrets d'état de Venise.* 2 vols. Saint Petersburg: Impr. de l'Académie Impériale des Sciences, 1884. Reprint, New York: Burt Franklin, 1968.

Lithgow, William. *The Totall Discourse of the Rare Adventures and Painefull Peregrinations ... to the most famous Kingdomes in Europe, Asia, and Affrica.* London: Okes, 1632. Reprint, Glasgow: James MacLehose and Sons, 1906.

Ljubić, Simeon, ed. *Commissiones et relationes venetae.* Tome 1 (1433–1527). In *Monumenta spectantia historiam Slavorum meridionalium,* vol. 6. Zagreb: Academia Scientiarum et Artium Slavorum Meridionalium, 1876.

―――. *Commissiones et relationes venetae.* Tome 2 (1525–53). In *Monumenta spectantia historiam Slavorum meridionalium,* vol. 8. Zagreb: Academia Scientiarum et Artium Slavorum Meridionalium, 1877.

―――. *Commissiones et relationes venetae.* Tome 3 (1553–71). In *Monumenta spectantia historiam Slavorum meridionalium,* vol. 11. Zagreb: Academia Scientiarum et Artium Slavorum Meridionalium, 1880.

Loredano, Gio Francesco. *La turca. Comedia del S. Gio. Francesco Loredano, Di nuovo posta in luce.* Venice: Libreria della Speranza, 1597.

Marani, Alberto, ed. *Atti pastorali di Minuccio Minucci arcivescovo di Zara (1596–1604).* Rome: Edizioni di Storia e Letteratura, 1970.

Marmora, Andrea. *Della historia di Corfu.* Venice: Curti, 1672.

Maschek, Luigi. *Manuale del regno di Dalmazia per l'anno 1872.* Anno II. Zadar: Tipografia Fratelli Battara, 1872.

Mastraca, Stefano. *Descrizione dell'Isola di Corfu fatta nel 1630.* Venice: Pietro Naratovich, 1869.

Maxim, Mihai. *Noi documente turceşti privind Ţările Române şi Înalta Poartă (1526–1602).* Brăila: Editura Istros, 2008.

Merlo, Giovanni. *Vero e real disegno della inclita cita di Venezia.* Venice: N.p., 1696.

Minucci, Minuccio. *Historia degli Uscochi.* N.p., n.d. [after 1602].

al-Misri, Ahmad ibn Naqib. *Reliance of the Traveller.* Edited and translated by Nuh Ha Mim Keller. Evanston, Ill.: Sunna Books, 1994.

Naima, Mustafa. *Annals of the Turkish Empire from 1591 to 1659 of the Christian Era.* Translated by Charles Fraser. London: Oriental Translation Fund of Great Britain and Ireland, 1832.

―――. *Naîmâ Târihi.* Istanbul: Z. Danisman Yayinevi, 1967–69.

Nicolay, Nicholas de. *The Navigations into Turkie.* London: Thomas Dawson, 1585. Reprint, Amsterdam: Theatrum Orbis Terrarum, 1968.

Novak, Grga, ed. *Commissiones et relationes venetae.* Tome 4 (1572–90). In *Monumenta spectantia historiam Slavorum meridionalium,* vol. 47. Zagreb: Academia Scientiarum et Artium Slavorum Meridionalium, 1964.

―――, ed. *Commissiones et relationes venetae.* Tome 6 (1588–1620). In *Monumenta spectantia historiam Slavorum meridionalium,* vol. 49. Zagreb: Academia Scientiarum et Artium Slavorum Meridionalium, 1970.

―――. "Poljoprivreda na dalmatinskom primorju i otocima u XVIII stoljeću." *Starine* 51 (1962): 61–111.

Orhonlu, Cengiz, ed. *Osmanlı Tarihine Âid Belgeler—Telhîsler (1597–1607)*. Istanbul: İstanbul Üniversitesi Edebiyat Fakültesi Basımevi, 1970.

Pagratis, Gerassimos D., ed. *Hoi ektheseis ton Veneton vailon kai pronoeton tes Kerkyras (160s aionas)*. Athens: Ethniko Hidryma Ereunon, 2008.

Peachy, William Samuel. "A Year in Selaniki's History: 1593–4." Ph.D. diss., Indiana University, 1984.

Peçevi, Ibrahim. *Peçevi Tarihi*. 2 vols. Edited and translated by Bekir Sıtkı Baykal. Ankara: Kültür Bakanlığı, 1982.

Pedani, Maria Pia. *Relazioni di ambasciatori veneti al senato*. Vol. 14, *Costantinopoli: Relazioni inedite (1512–1789)*. Padua: Bottega d'Erasmo, 1996.

Piacenza, Francesco. *L'egeo redivio, o' sia chorographia dell'arcipelago*. Modena: Solani, 1688.

Politi, Adriano. *Dittionario toscano: Compendio del vocabolario della Crusca*. Rome: Gio. Angelo Ruffinelli, 1614.

A Prospect of Hungary, and Transylvania: With a Catalogue of the Kings of the one, and the Princes of the other . . . London: William Miller, 1664.

Randolph, Ber. *The Present State of the Islands in the Archipelago, or Arches, Sea of Constantinople and Gulph [sic] of Smyrna; With the Islands of Candia and Rhodes*. Oxford: N.p., 1687.

Romei, Annibale. *The Courtiers Academie*. [London]: Valentine Sims, [1598].

Sagredo, Giovanni. *Memorie istoriche de monarchi ottomani*. Bologna: Gio Ricaldini, 1674.

Sanderson, John. *The Travels of John Sanderson in the Levant, 1584–1602*. Edited by William Foster. London: Hakluyt Society, 1931. Reprint, Nendeln: Kraus Reprint, 1967.

Sansovino, Francesco, and Giustiniano Martinioni. *Venetia, città nobilissima, et singolare: Descritta in XIIII. libri*. Venice: Curti, 1663.

Schmidt, Jan. ed. and trans. *Mustafa 'Ali's "Künhü'l-Ahbar" and Its Preface According to the Leiden Manuscript*. Leiden: Nederlands Historisch-Archaeologisch Instituut Te Istanbul, 1987.

Selânikî, Mustafa Efendi. *Tarih-i Selânikî*. Edited by Mehmet Ipsirli. 2 vols. Istanbul: Edebiyat Fakültesi Basimevi, 1989.

Sherley, Thomas. "Discours of the Turkes." *Camden Miscellany* 16 (1936): 1–38.

Solitro, V. *Documenti sull'Istria e la Dalmazia*. Venice: G. Gattei, 1844.

Tappe, E. D., ed. *Documents Concerning Rumanian History (1427–1601) Collected from British Archives.* London: Mouton, 1964.

Thévenot, Jean. *Voyage du Levant.* Edited by Stéphane Yerasimos. Paris: François Maspero, 1980.

Tietze, Andreas, ed. and trans. *Mustafa Ali's Counsel for Sultans of 1581.* Vienna: Verlag der Österreichischen Akademie der Wissenschaften, 1979.

————, ed. and trans. *Mustafa Ali's Description of Cairo of 1599.* Vienna: Verlag der Österreichischen Akademie der Wissenschaften, 1975.

Tomić, Jovan N. *Grada za istoriju pokreta na Balkanu protiv Turaka krajem XVI i početkom VII veka.* Belgrade: Srpska kraljevska akademija, 1933.

Tournefort, M. Pitton de. *Relation d'un voyage du Levant.* Amsterdam: Aux Dépens de la Compagnie, 1718.

Turcograeciae libri octo a Martino Crusio, in Academia Tybingensi Graeco & Latino Professore, utraque lingua edita. Quibus Graecorum status sub imperio Turcico, in politia & ecclesia, oeconomia & scholis, iam inde ab amissa Constantinopoli, ad haec usque tempora, luculenter describitur . . . Basel: Leonhard Ostein für Verlag Sebastian Henricpetris, 1584.

Urechi, Grégoire. *Chronique de Moldavie depuis le milieu du XIVe siècle jusqu'à l'an 1594.* Translated by Émile Picot. Paris: Ernest Leroux, 1878.

Vecellio, Cesare. *De gli habiti antichi, et moderni.* Venice: Damian Zenaro, 1590.

Wilkinson, J. Gardner. *Dalmatia and Montenegro.* Vol. 1. London: John Murray, 1848.

Wratislaw, A.H., trans. *Adventures of Baron Wenceslas Wratislaw of Mitrowitz.* London: Bell and Daldy, 1862.

Published Secondary Sources

Abulafia, David. "Mediterraneans." In *Rethinking the Mediterranean,* edited by W. V. Harris. Oxford: Oxford University Press, 2005.

————. "What Is the Mediterranean?" In *The Mediterranean in History,* edited by David Abulafia. Los Angeles: J. Paul Getty Museum, 2003.

Adams, Julia. *The Familial State: Ruling Families and Merchant Capitalism in Early Modern Europe.* Ithaca, N.Y.: Cornell University Press, 2005.

————. "The Rule of the Father: Patriarchy and Patrimonialism in Early

Modern Europe." In *Max Weber's "Economy and Society": A Critical Companion,* edited by Charles Camic, Philip S. Gorski, and David M. Trubek. Stanford: Stanford University Press, 2005.

Adanır, Fikret. "The Ottoman Peasantries, c. 1360–c. 1860." In *The Peasantries of Europe: From the Fourteenth to the Eighteenth Centuries,* edited by Tom Scott. London: Longman, 1998.

Ago, Renata. "Young Nobles in the Age of Absolutism: Paternal Authority and Freedom of Choice in Seventeenth Century Italy." In *A History of Young People in the West,* edited by Giovanni Levi and Jean-Claude Schmitt, vol. 2. Cambridge, Mass.: Harvard University Press, 1997.

Akyilmaz, Gul. "Woman According to the Ottoman Law of Family." In *The Turks,* vol. 3, *The Ottomans,* edited by Hasan Celâl Güzel, C. Cem Oguz, and Osman Karatay. Ankara: Yeni Türkiye, 2002.

Allegra, Luciano. "Conversioni dal ghetto di Torino." *Dimensioni e problemi della ricerca storica* 2 (1996): 187–202.

———. "L'ospizio dei catecumeni di Torino." *Bollettino storico-bibliografico subalpino* 88 (1990): 513–73.

Allegri, Mario. "Venezia e il Veneto dopo Lepanto." In *Letteratura italiana, storia e geografia,* vol. 2, *L'età moderna,* edited by Alberto Asor Rosa. Turin: Einaudi, 1987.

Ambrosini, Federica. "Toward a Social History of Women in Venice: From the Renaissance to the Enlightenment." In *Venice Reconsidered: The History and Civilization of an Italian City-State, 1297–1797,* edited by John Jeffries Martin and Dennis Romano. Baltimore: Johns Hopkins University Press, 2000.

Angelomatis-Tsougarakis, Helen. "Greek Women, 16th–19th Century: The Travellers' View." *Mesaionika kai nea Ellinika* 4 (1992): 321–403.

———. "Women in the Society of the Despotate of Epirus." *Jahrbuch der Österreichischen Byzantinistik* 32 (1982): 473–80.

Arbel, Benjamin. "Jews in International Trade: The Emergence of the Levantines and Ponentines." In *The Jews of Early Modern Venice,* edited by Robert C. Davis and Benjamin Ravid. Baltimore: Johns Hopkins University Press, 2001.

———. "Nūr Bānū (c. 1530–1583): A Venetian Sultana?" *Turcica* 24 (1992): 241–59.

———. "Roman Catholics and Greek Orthodox in the Early Modern Venetian State." In *The Three Religions,* edited by Nili Cohen and Andreas Heldrich. Munich: Utz, 2002.

Armao, Ermanno. *In giro per il mar Egeo con Vincenzo Coronelli: Note di topologia, toponomastica e storia medievali. Dinasti e famiglie italiane in Levante.* Florence: Olschki Editore, 1951.

Artan, Tülay. "Arts and Architecture." In *The Cambridge History of Turkey,* vol. 3, *The Later Ottoman Empire, 1603–1839,* edited by Suraiya N. Faroqhi. Cambridge: Cambridge University Press, 2006.

Aslan, Reza. *No god but God: The Origins, Evolution, and Future of Islam.* New York: Random House, 2005.

Atanasiu, Victor. *Mihai Viteazul: Campanii.* Bucharest: Editura militară, 1972.

Attar, Karina. "Dangerous Liaisons: Jews, Christians, and Muslims in the Renaissance Italian Novella." Ph.D. diss., Columbia University, 2005.

Audisio, Gabriel. "Renégats marseillais (1591–1595)." *Renaissance and Reformation* 28, no. 3 (1992): 31–58.

Austin-Broos, Diane. "The Anthropology of Conversion: An Introduction." In *The Anthropology of Religious Conversion,* edited by Andrew Buckser and Stephen D. Glazier. Lanham, Md.: Rowman and Littlefield, 2003.

Ayverdi, Ekrem Hakki. "Gazanfer Ağa Manzümesi." *Istanbul Enstitüsü Dergisi* 3 (1957): 85–97.

Bade, Klaus J. *Migration in European History.* Translated by Allison Brown. Oxford: Blackwell, 2003.

Baer, Marc. *Honored by the Glory of Islam: Conversion and Conquest in Ottoman Europe.* Oxford: Oxford University Press, 2008.

———. "Honored by the Glory of Islam: The Ottoman State, Non-Muslims, and Conversion to Islam in Late Seventeenth-Century Istanbul and Rumelia." Ph.D. diss., University of Chicago, 2001.

———. "Islamic Conversion Narratives of Women: Social Change and Gendered Religious Hierarchy in Early Modern Ottoman Istanbul." *Gender & History* 16 (2004): 425–58.

Baernstein, P. Renée. *A Convent Tale: A Century of Sisterhood in Spanish Milan.* New York: Routledge, 2002.

———. "In Widow's Habit: Women between Convent and Family in Sixteenth-Century Milan." *Sixteenth Century Journal* 25 (1994): 787–807.

Balta, Evangelia. "The Ottoman Surveys of Siphnos (17th–18th Centuries)." *Osmanlı Tarihi Araştırma ve Uygulama Merkezi Dergisi* 18 (2005): 51–69.

Barkey, Karen. *Bandits and Bureaucrats: The Ottoman Route to State Centralization.* Ithaca, N.Y.: Cornell University Press, 1997.

Bashir, Shahzad. "Islamic Tradition and Celibacy." In *Celibacy and Religious Traditions,* edited by Carl Olson. Oxford: Oxford University Press, 2007.

Bassi, Elena. *Tracce di chiese veneziane distrutte: Ricostruzioni dai disegni di Antonio Visentini.* Venice: Istituto Veneto di Scienze, Lettere ed Arti, 1997.

Bayerle, Gustav. *Pashas, Begs, and Effendis: A Historical Dictionary of Titles and Terms in the Ottoman Empire.* Istanbul: Isis Press, 1997.

Bell, Rudolph M. *How to Do It: Guides to Good Living for Renaissance Italians.* Chicago: University of Chicago Press, 2000.

Bellavitis, Anna. "Dot et richesse des femmes à Venise au XVIe siècle." *Clio* 7 (1998): 91–100.

———. "La famiglia «cittadina» veneziana nel XVI secolo: dote e successione. Le leggi e le fonti." *Studi veneziani* 30 (1996): 55–68.

———. *Famille, genre, transmission à Venise au XVIe siècle.* Rome: École française de Rome, 2008.

———. *Identité, mariage, mobilité sociale: Citoyennes et citoyens à Venise au XVI siècle.* Rome: École française de Rome, 2001.

Benjamin, Thomas. *The Atlantic World: Europeans, Africans, Indians, and Their Shared History, 1400–1900.* Cambridge: Cambridge University Press, 2009.

Bennassar, Bartolomé. "Les chrétiens convertis à l'Islam: «Renégats» et leur intégration aux XVI–XVII siècles." *Cahiers de Tunisie* 44 (1991): 45–53.

———. "Conversion ou reniement? Modalités d'une adhésion ambiguë des chrétiens à l'Islam (XVIe–XVIIe siècles)." *Annales: ESC* 6 (1988): 1349–66.

———. "Conversions, esclavage, et commerce des femmes dans les peninsules iberique, italienne, ou balkanique aux XVIe et XVIIe siècles." *Dimensioni e problemi della ricerca storica* 2 (1996): 101–9.

———. "Frontières religieuses entre islam et chrétienité: L'expérience vécue par les 'Renégats.'" In *Les frontières religieuses en Europe du XVe au*

XVIIe siècle: Actes du XXXIe colloque international d'études human-istes, edited by Alain Ducellier et al. Paris: J. Vrin, 1992.

Bennassar, Bartolomé, and Lucile Bennassar. *Les chrétiens d'Allah: L'histoire extraordinaire des renégats, XVIe–XVIIe siècles.* Paris: Perrin, 1989.

Benvenuto, Angelo de. *Storia di Zara dal 1409 al 1797.* Milan: Fratelli Bocca, 1944.

Bernardy, Amy A. *Zara e i monumenti italiani della Dalmazia.* Bergamo: Istituto italiano d'arti grafiche, 1928.

Bernos, Marcel. "Conversion ou apostasie? Comment les chrétiens voyaient ceux qui quittaient leur église pour l'église adverse.'" *Seventeenth-Century French Studies* 18 (1996): 33–48.

Biondi, Albano. "La giustificazione della simulazione nel Cinquecento." In *Eresia e riforma nell'Italia del Cinquecento. Miscellanea I.* Florence: Sansoni, 1974.

Blanks, David R. "Western Views of Islam in the Premodern Period: A Brief History of Past Approaches." In *Western Views of Islam in Medieval and Early Modern Europe: Perception of Other,* edited by David R. Blanks and Michael Frassetto. New York: St. Martin's, 1999.

Blili, Leîla. "Course e captivité des femmes dans la régence de Tunis aux XVIe et XVIIe siècles." In *Captius i esclaus a l'antiguitat i al món mod-ern,* edited by María Luisa Sánchez León and Gonçal López Nadal. Naples: Jovene Editore, 1996.

Bock, Gisela. "Women's History and Gender History: Aspects of an International Debate." *Gender & History* 1 (1989): 7–30.

Bonfield, Lloyd. "Developments in European Family Law." In *The History of the European Family: Family Life in Early Modern Times (1500–1789),* edited by David I. Kertzer and Marzio Barbagli. New Haven: Yale University Press, 2001.

Bornstein, Daniel. "Introduction." In *Life and Death in a Venetian Convent: The Chronicle and Necrology of Corpus Domini, 1395–1436,* edited and translated by Daniel Bornstein. Chicago: University of Chicago Press, 2000.

Bornstein-Makovetsky, Leah. "Kiera." In *Encyclopaedia Judaica,* 2nd ed., vol. 12. Detroit: Macmillan Reference, 2007.

Borromeo, Elisabetta. "Les Cyclades à l'époque ottomane. L'insularité vue par les missionaires jésuites." In *Insularités ottomanes,* edited by Nicolas Vatin and Gilles Veinstein. Paris: Maisonneuve et Larose, 2004.

———. *Voyageurs occidentaux dans l'empire ottoman (1600–1644)*. 2 vols. Paris: Masionneuve et Larose, 2007.

Boyar, Ebru, and Kate Fleet. *A Social History of Ottoman Istanbul*. Cambridge: Cambridge University Press, 2010.

Bracewell, Catherine Wendy. *The Uskoks of Senj: Piracy, Banditry, and Holy War in the Sixteenth-Century Adriatic*. Ithaca, N.Y.: Cornell University Press, 1992.

Braudel, Fernand. *The Mediterranean and the Mediterranean World in the Age of Philip II*. 2 vols. New York: Harper and Row, 1972.

Brewer, Holly. *By Birth or Consent: Children, Law, and the Anglo-American Revolution in Authority*. Chapel Hill: University of North Carolina Press, 2005.

Brummett, Palmira. "'Turks' and 'Christians': The Iconography of Possession in the Depiction of the Ottoman-Venetian-Hapsburg Frontiers, 1550–1689." In *The Religions of the Book: Christian Perceptions, 1400–1660*, edited by Matthew Dimmock and Andrew Hadfield. New York: Palgrave Macmillan, 2008.

———. "Visions of the Mediterranean: A Classification." *Journal of Medieval and Early Modern Studies* 1 (2007): 9–55.

Bryson, Frederick Robertson. *The Point of Honor in Sixteenth Century Italy: An Aspect of the Life of the Gentleman*. New York: Institute of French Studies, 1935.

Buckser, Andrew, and Stephen D. Glazier, eds. *The Anthropology of Religious Conversion*. Lanham, Md.: Rowman and Littlefield, 2003.

Bulliet, Richard W. *The Case for Islamo-Christian Civilization*. New York: Columbia University Press, 2004.

———. *Islam: The View from the Edge*. New York: Columbia University Press, 1995.

Burke, Peter. "Civilizations and Frontiers: Anthropology of the Early Modern Mediterranean." In *Early Modern History and the Social Sciences: Testing the Limits of Braudel's Mediterranean*, edited by John A. Marino. Kirksville, Mo.: Truman State University Press, 2002.

———. "Early Modern Venice as a Center of Information and Communication." In *Venice Reconsidered: The History and Civilization of an Italian City-State, 1297–1797*, edited by John Jeffries Martin and Dennis Romano. Baltimore: Johns Hopkins University Press, 2000.

———. *The Historical Anthropology of Early Modern Italy: Essays on*

Perception and Communication. Cambridge: Cambridge University Press, 1987.

——. "History of Events and the Revival of Narrative." In *New Perspectives on Historical Writing*, edited by Peter Burke. University Park: Pennsylvania State University Press, 1992.

——. "Passing through Three Crises." In *L'anthropologie de la Méditerranée*, edited by Dionigi Albera, Anton Blok, and Christian Bromberger. Paris: Maisonneuve et Larose, 2001.

Burns, Loretta T. Johnson. "The Politics of Conversion: John Calvin and the Bishop of Troyes." *Sixteenth Century Journal* 25 (1994): 809–22.

Bynum, Caroline Walker. *Holy Fast and Holy Feast: The Religious Significance of Food to Medieval Women*. Berkeley: University of California Press, 1987.

Caffiero, Marina. *Battesimi forzati: Storie di ebrei, cristiani e convertiti nella Roma dei papi*. Rome: Viella, 2004.

Calvi, Giulia. "Reconstructing the Family: Widowhood and Remarriage in Tuscany in the Early Modern Period." In *Marriage in Italy, 1300–1650*, edited by Trevor Dean and K.J.P. Lowe. Cambridge: Cambridge University Press, 1998.

——. "Widows, the State, and the Guardianship of Children in Early Modern Tuscany." In *Widowhood in Medieval and Early Modern Europe*, edited by Sandra Cavallo and Lyndan Warner. London: Longman, 1999.

Campanini, Antonella. "L'identità coatta: La Casa dei catecumeni a Bologna." In *Verso l'epilogo di una convivenza: gli ebrei a Bologna nel XVI secolo*, edited by Maria Giuseppina Muzzarelli. Florence: Giuntina, 1996.

Canosa, Romano. *Il velo e il cappuccio: Monacazioni forzate e sessualità nei conventi femminili in Italia tra quattrocento e settecento*. Rome: Sapere, 1991.

Casanova, Cesarina. "Il buon matrimonio di Anna Maria alias Cremesina, neofita lughese." In *Le donne delle minoranze: Le ebree e le protesanti d' Italia*, edited by Claire E. Honess and Verina R. Jones. Turin: Claudiana, 1999.

Cassia, Paul Sant. "Navigating an Anthropology of the Mediterranean: Recent Developments in France." *History and Anthropology* 14 (2003): 87–94.

——. "Religion, Politics, and Ethnicity in Cyprus during the Turkocratia (1571–1878)." *Archives européennes de sociologie* 27 (1986): 3–28.

Cavallo, Sandra, and Simona Cerutti. "Female Honor and the Social Control of Reproduction in Piedmont between 1600 and 1800." In *Sex and Gender in Historical Perspective,* edited by Edward Muir and Guido Ruggiero. Baltimore: Johns Hopkins University Press, 1990.

Cernovodeanu, Paul. "An English Diplomat at War: Edward Barton's Attendance of the Ottoman Campaign in Central Europe (1596)." *Revue roumaine d'histoire* 28 (1989): 429–49.

Cesco, Valentina. "Il rapimento a fine di matrimonio. Una pratica sociale in età moderna tra retorica e cultura." In *L'amministrazione della giustizia penale nella Repubblica di Venezia (secoli XVI–XVIII),* vol. 2, *Retoriche, stereotipi, prassi,* edited by G. Chiodi and C. Povolo. Verona: Cierre, 2004.

Chabot, Isabelle. "Lineage Strategies and the Control of Widows in Renaissance Florence." In *Widowhood in Medieval and Early Modern Europe,* edited by Sandra Cavallo and Lyndan Warner. London: Longman, 1999.

Chew, Samuel C. *The Crescent and the Rose: Islam and England during the Renaissance.* Oxford: Oxford University Press, 1937.

Chojnacka, Monica. "Singlewomen in Early Modern Venice: Communities and Opportunities." In *Singlewomen in the European Past, 1250–1800,* edited by Judith M. Bennett and Amy M. Froide. Philadelphia: University of Pennsylvania Press, 1998.

———. "Women, Charity, and Community in Early Modern Venice: The Casa delle Zitelle." *Renaissance Quarterly* 51 (1998): 68–91.

Chojnacki, Stanley. "Comment: Blurring Genders." *Renaissance Quarterly* 40 (1987): 743–51.

———. "Dowries and Kinsmen in Early Renaissance Venice." *Journal of Interdisciplinary History* 4 (1975): 571–600.

———. *Men and Women in Renaissance Venice.* Baltimore: Johns Hopkins University Press, 2000.

Cicogna, Emanuele. *Delle iscrizioni veneziane raccolte ed illustrate.* 6 vols. Venice: Antonelli, 1824–53.

Clissold, Stephen. *The Barbary Slaves.* New York: Harper Collins, 1977.

———. "Christian Renegades and Barbary Corsairs." *History Today* 26 (1976): 508–15.

Coco, Carla. *Secrets of the Harem.* New York: Vendome, 1997.

Cohen, Elizabeth S. "Honor and Gender in the Streets of Early Modern Rome." *Journal of Interdisciplinary History* 22 (1992): 597–625.

Cohen, Sherrill. "Asylums for Women in Counter-Reformation Italy." In *Women in Reformation and Counter-Reformation Europe: Public and Private Worlds,* edited by Sherrin Marshall. Bloomington: Indiana University Press, 1989.

———. "Convertite e Malmaritate: Donne «irregolari» e ordini religiosi nella Firenze rinascimentale." *Memoria* 5 (1982): 46–63.

Coleman, Simon. "Continuous Conversion? The Rhetoric, Practice, and Rhetorical Practice of Charismatic Protestant Conversion." In *The Anthropology of Religious Conversion,* edited by Andrew Buckser and Stephen D. Glazier. Lanham, Md.: Rowman and Littlefield, 2003.

Colley, Linda. *Captives: Britain, Empire, and the World, 1600–1850.* New York: Pantheon, 2002.

———. *The Ordeal of Elizabeth Marsh: A Woman in World History.* New York: Random House, 2008.

Cowan, Alexander. "Rich and Poor Among the Patriciate in Early Modern Venice." *Studi veneziani* 6 (1982): 147–60.

———. *The Urban Patriciate: Lübeck and Venice, 1580–1700.* Cologne: Böhlau, 1986.

Cox, Virginia. "The Single Self: Feminist Thought and the Marriage Market in Early Modern Venice." *Renaissance Quarterly* 48 (1995): 530–76.

Crawford, Patricia. *Women and Religion in England, 1500–1720.* 2nd ed. London: Routledge, 1996.

Dal Borgo, Michela. "Nuovi documenti sul mancato matrimonio tra il pretendente principesco moldavo Stefano Bogdan ed Elena Cievalelli, Suor Deodata al monastero Corpus Domini di Venezia (1600)." In *L'Italia e l'Europa Centro-Orientale attraverso i secoli,* edited by Cristian Luca, Gianluca Masi, and Andrea Piccardi. Brăila: Istros Editrice, 2004.

Daniel, Norman. *Islam and the West: The Making of an Image.* Revised ed. Oxford: Oneworld, 1993.

Danismend, Ismail Hami. *Osmanli Tarihi Kronolojisi.* Vol. 3. Istanbul: Türkiye Yayinevi, 1961.

Darling, Linda. "Rethinking Europe and the Islamic World in the Age of Exploration." *Journal of Early Modern History* 2 (1998): 221–46.

Davis, Natalie Zemon. "Boundaries and the Sense of Self in Sixteenth-Century France." In *Reconstructing Individualism: Autonomy, Individuality, and the Self in Western Thought,* edited by Thomas C. Heller et al. Stanford: Stanford University Press, 1986.

————. *Society and Culture in Early Modern France.* Stanford: Stanford University Press, 1975.

————. *Women on the Margins: Three Seventeenth-Century Lives.* Cambridge, Mass.: Harvard University Press, 1995.

————. "Women on Top: Symbolic Sexual Inversion and Political Disorder in Early Modern Europe." In *The Reversible World: Symbolic Inversion in Art and Society.* Ithaca, N.Y.: Cornell University Press, 1978.

————. " 'Women's History' in Transition: The European Case." *Feminist Studies* 3 (spring–summer 1976): 83–103.

Davis, Robert C. *Christian Slaves, Muslim Masters: White Slavery in the Mediterranean, the Barbary Coast, and Italy, 1500–1800.* New York: Palgrave Macmillan, 2003.

————. "The Geography of Gender in the Renaissance." In *Gender and Society in Renaissance Italy,* edited by Judith C. Brown and Robert C. Davis. London: Longman, 1998.

————. "Slave Redemption in Venice, 1585–1797." In *Venice Reconsidered: The History and Civilization of an Italian City-State, 1297–1797,* edited by John Jeffries Martin and Dennis Romano. Baltimore: Johns Hopkins University Press, 2000.

Dayton, Cornelia Hughes. "Rethinking Agency, Recovering Voices." *American Historical Review* 109 (2004): 827–43.

Dean, Trevor. "Gender and Insult in an Italian City: Bologna in the Later Middle Ages." *Social History* 29 (2004): 217–31.

De Benvenuti, Angelo. "Fortezze e castelli di Dalmazia: La fortezza di Clissa." *La rivista dalmatica* 16, no. 4 (1935): 28–40; 17, no. 1 (1936): 16–27.

Derengil, Selim. " 'There Is No Compulsion in Religion': On Conversion and Apostasy in the Late Ottoman Empire, 1839–1856." *Comparative Study of Society and History* 42 (2000): 547–71.

De Vaus, David, and Ian McAllister. "Gender Differences in Religion: A Test of the Structural Location Theory." *American Sociological Review* 52 (1987): 472–81.

Diefendorf, Barbara. "Give Us Back Our Children: Patriarchal Authority and Parental Consent to Religious Vocations in Early Counter-Reformation France." *Journal of Modern History* 68 (1996): 263–307.

Dinan, Susan E. *Women and Poor Relief in Seventeenth-Century France: The Early History of the Daughters of Charity.* Aldershot, U.K.: Ashgate, 2006.

Dizionario biografico degli italiani. 73 vols. Rome: Istituto della enciclo-
pedia italiana, 1960–.

Dolcetti, Giovanni. *Il libro d'argento delle famiglie venete.* Venice: n.p.,
1922–28. Reprint, Bologna: Arnaldo Forni Editore, 1983.

Dorigo-Ceccato, Rosella. "Su Bekrī Muşţafā personaggio del teatro d'ombre
turco e arabo." *Quaderni di studi arabi* 15, supplement (1997): 85–96.

Dursteler, Eric. "The *Bailo* in Constantinople: Crisis and Career in Venice's
Early Modern Diplomatic Corps." *Mediterranean Historical Review* 16
(2001): 1–25.

———. " 'A Continual Tavern in My House': Food and Diplomacy in Early
Modern Constantinople." In *Renaissance Studies in Honor of Joseph
Connors,* edited by Louis A. Waldman and Machtelt Israëls. Florence:
Olschki, forthcoming 2012.

———. "Power and Information: The Venetian Postal System in the Mediterranean, 1573–1645." In *From Florence to the Mediterranean: Essays
in Honor of Anthony Molho,* edited by Diogo Ramado Curto et al.,
vol. 2. Florence: Olschki, 2009.

———. *Venetians in Constantinople: Nation, Identity, and Coexistence in
the Early Modern Mediterranean.* Baltimore: Johns Hopkins University
Press, 2006.

Eales, Jacqueline. *Women in Early Modern England, 1500–1700: Intro-
ductions to History.* London: UCL Press, 1998.

Edwards, Kathryn A. *Families and Frontiers: Re-creating Communities and
Boundaries in the Early Modern Burgundies.* Leiden: Brill, 2002.

Eire, Carlos. "Calvin and Nicodemism: A Reappraisal." *Sixteenth Century
Journal* 10 (1979): 44–69.

Ellero, Giuseppe. "Vergini christiane e donne di valore." In *Le Zitelle: Architettura, arte e storia di un'istituzione veneziana,* edited by Lionello
Pupi. Venice: Albrizzi, 1992.

Elukin, Jonathan M. "From Jew to Christian? Conversion and Immutabil-
ity in Medieval Europe." In *Varieties of Religious Conversion in the
Middle Ages,* edited by James Muldoon. Gainesville: University Press of
Florida, 1997.

Encyclopedia of Islam. New ed. Edited by H. A. R. Gibbs et al. Leiden:
Brill, 1979–.

Erdogan, Muzaffer. "Mîmar Davud Aga-nin Hayati ve Eserleri." *Türkiyat
Mecmuasi* 12 (1955): 179–204.

Esposito, John L. *Women in Muslim Family Law.* 2nd ed. Syracuse: Syracuse University Press, 2001.

Evangelisti, Silvia. "Wives, Widows, and Brides of Christ: Marriage and the Convent in the Historiography of Early Modern Italy." *Historical Journal* 43 (2000): 233–47.

Eyice, Semavi. "Gazanfer Ağa Külliyesi." *Türkiye Diyanet Vakfı Islam Ansiklopedisi* 13 (1996): 432–33.

Fabijanec, Florence Sabine. "Le développement commercial de Zadar et de Split aux XVe–XVIe siècles." Ph.D. diss., Université Paris I, 2002.

Faroqhi, Suraiya. "Crime, Women, and Wealth in the Eighteenth-Century Anatolian Countryside." In *Women in the Ottoman Empire: Middle Eastern Women in the Early Modern Era,* edited by Madeline C. Zilfi. Leiden: Brill, 1997.

———. "Crisis and Change, 1590–1699." In *An Economic and Social History of the Ottoman Empire,* vol. 2, *1600–1914,* edited by Halil Inalcik and Donald Quataert. Cambridge: Cambridge University Press, 1997.

———. *Subjects of the Sultan: Culture and Daily Life in the Ottoman Empire.* London: I. B. Tauris, 2000.

Félix, Ana Fernández. "Children on the Frontiers of Islam." In *Conversions islamiques: Identités religieuses en Islam méditerranéen,* edited by Mercedes García-Arenal. Paris: Maisonneuve et Larose, 2001.

Ferrante, Lucia. "Honor Regained: Women in the Casa del Soccorso di San Paolo in Sixteenth-Century Bologna." In *Sex and Gender in Historical Perspective,* edited by Edward Muir and Guido Ruggiero. Baltimore: Johns Hopkins University Press, 1990.

Ferraro, Joanne M. *Marriage Wars in Late Renaissance Venice.* Oxford: Oxford University Press, 2001.

———. "The Power to Decide: Battered Wives in Early Modern Venice." *Renaissance Quarterly* 48 (1995): 492–512.

Fetvaci, Emine Fatma. "Viziers to Eunuchs: Transitions in Ottoman Manuscript Patronage, 1566–1617." Ph.D. diss., Harvard University, 2005.

Fiorani, Luigi. "Verso la nuova città. Conversione e conversionismo a Roma nel Cinque-Seicento." *Ricerche per la storia religiosa di Roma* 10 (1998): 91–186.

Firpo, Massimo. "The Italian Reformation and Juan de Valdés."*Sixteenth Century Journal* 27 (1996): 353–64.

Fischer, Lucia Frattarelli, and Stefano Villani. " 'People of Every Mixture':

Immigration, Tolerance, and Religious Conflict in Early Modern Livorno." In *Immigration and Emigration in Historical Perspective,* edited by Ann Katherine Isaacs. Pisa: Edizioni Plus, 2007.

Fleischer, C. *Bureaucrat and Intellectual in the Ottoman Empire: The Historian Mustafā Ālī.* Princeton: Princeton University Press, 1986.

Foa, Anna. "Le donne nella storia degli ebrei in Italia." In *Le donne delle minoranze: Le ebree e le protesanti d'Italia,* edited by Claire E. Honess and Verina R. Jones. Turin: Claudiana, 1999.

———. "Il gioco del proselitismo: Politica delle conversioni e controllo della violenza nella Roma del cinquecento." In *Ebrei e cristiani nell'Italia medievale e moderna: Conversioni, scambi, contrasti,* edited by Michele Luzzati et al. Rome: Carucci, 1988.

———. "The Marrano's Kitchen: External Stimuli, Internal Response, and the Formation of the Marrano Persona." In *The Mediterranean and the Jews: Society, Culture, and Economy in Early Modern Times,* edited by Elliott Horowitz and Moises Orfali. Ramat Gan, Israel: Bar-Ilan University Press, 2002.

Fodor, Pál. "The Organisation of Defence in the Eastern Mediterranean (End of the 16th Century)." In *The Kapudan Pasha: His Office and His Domain,* edited by Elizabeth Zachariadou. Rethymon: Crete University Press, 2002.

Fondra, Lorenzo. *Istoria della insigne reliquia di San Simeone profeta che si venera in Zara.* Zadar: Fratelli Battara, 1855.

Forbes, Hamish. "Early Modern Greece: Liquid Landscapes and Fluid Populations." In *Between Venice and Istanbul: Colonial Landscapes in Early Modern Greece (Hesperia* supplement 40), edited by Siriol Davies and Jack L. Davis. N.p.: American School of Classical Studies in Athens, 2007.

Forsén, Björn. "Regionalism and Mobility in Early Modern Greece: A Commentary." In *Between Venice and Istanbul: Colonial Landscapes in Early Modern Greece (Hesperia* supplement 40), edited by Siriol Davies and Jack L. Davis. N.p.: American School of Classical Studies in Athens, 2007.

Fournel-Guérin, Jacqueline. "La femme morisque en Aragon." In *Les morisques et leur temps.* Paris: CNRS, 1983.

Franzoi, Umberto, and Dina di Stefano. *Le chiese di Venezia.* N.p.: Alfieri, 1976.

Frazee, Charles. *The Island Princes of Greece: The Dukes of the Archipelago.* Amsterdam: Adolf M. Hakkert, 1988.

Frejdenberg, Maren. "Venetian Jews and Ottoman Authorities on the Balkans (16th Century)." *Études balkaniques* 30, no. 3 (1994): 56–66.

Galanté, Abraham. *Esther Kyra d'après de nouveaux documents.* Constantinople: Société anonyme de papeterie et d'imprimerie, 1926.

Galasso, Giuseppe. "La mobilità delle persone nel mediterraneo: Qualche osservazione preliminare." *Mediterranea—Ricerche storiche* 3 (2006): 209–12.

Gauchat, Patrick. *Hierarchia catholica medii et recentioris aevi.* Vol. 4. Münster in Westfalen: Sumptibus et Typis Librariae Regensbergianae, 1935.

Gerber, Haim. "Social and Economic Position of Women in an Ottoman City, Bursa, 1600–1700." *International Journal of Middle East Studies* 12 (1980): 213–44.

———. *State, Society, and Law in Islam: Ottoman Law in Comparative Perspective.* Albany: State University of New York Press, 1994.

Gerouki, Ariadni. *Les excommunications à Corfou, XVIIe et XVIIIe siècles: criminalité et attitudes mentales.* Athens: Editions Ant. N. Sakkoulas, 1998.

Gibb, H.A.R., and H. Bowen. *Islamic Society and the West.* 2 vols. London: Oxford University Press, 1950.

Gil'adi, Avner. *Children of Islam: Concepts of Childhood in Medieval Muslim Society.* New York: St. Martin's, 1992.

Gilmore, David D., ed. *Honor and Shame and the Unity of the Mediterranean.* Washington, D.C.: American Anthropological Association, 1987.

Ginio, Eyal. "Childhood, Mental Capacity, and Conversion to Islam in the Ottoman State." *Byzantine and Modern Greek Studies* 25 (2001): 90–119.

Ginzburg, Carlo. *The Cheese and the Worms: The Cosmos of a Sixteenth-Century Miller.* Baltimore: Johns Hopkins University Press, 1992.

———. "Just One Witness." In *Probing the Limits of Representation: Nazism and the "Final Solution,"* edited by Saul Friedlander. Cambridge, Mass.: Harvard University Press, 1992.

Giotopoulou-Sisilianou, Helle. *Presveies tes Venetokratoumenes Kerkyras, 160s–180s ai.: Pege schediasma anasyntheses tes epoches.* Athens: G.A.K.–Archeia Nomou Kerkyras, 2002.

Gliubich, Simeone. *Dizionario biografico degli uomini illustri della Dalmazia*. Vienna: Rod. Lochner, 1836. Reprint, Bologna: Arnaldo Forni Editore, 1974.

Göçek, Fatma Müge, and Marc David Baer. "Social Boundaries of Ottoman Women's Experience in Eighteenth-Century Galata Court Records." In *Women in the Ottoman Empire: Middle Eastern Women in the Early Modern Era*, edited by Madeline C. Zilfi. Leiden: Brill, 1997.

Goffman, Daniel. *The Ottoman Empire and Early Modern Europe*. Cambridge: Cambridge University Press, 2002.

Goitein, S. D. *A Mediterranean Society*. Vol. 3, *The Family*. Berkeley: University of California Press, 1978.

Goodblatt, Morris S. *Jewish Life in Turkey in the XVIth Century: As Reflected in the Legal Writings of Samuel De Medina*. New York: Jewish Theological Seminary, 1952.

Goodman, Jennifer R. "Marriage and Conversion in Late Medieval Romance." In *Varieties of Religious Conversion in the Middle Ages*, edited by James Muldoon. Gainesville: University Press of Florida, 1997.

Goodwin, Godfrey. *A History of Ottoman Architecture*. London: Thames and Hudson, 1971.

Graizbord, David L. *Souls in Dispute: Converso Identities in Iberia and the Jewish Diaspora, 1580–1700*. Philadelphia: University of Pennsylvania Press, 2004.

Graovac, Vera. "Populacijski razvoj Zadra." *Geoadria* 9 (2004): 51–72.

Greenblatt, Stephen. *Renaissance Self-Fashioning: From More to Shakespeare*. Chicago: University of Chicago Press, 1980.

Greene, Molly. *A Shared World: Christians and Muslims in the Early Modern Mediterranean*. Princeton: Princeton University Press, 2000.

Gregory, Brad S. *Salvation at Stake: Christian Martyrdom in Early Modern Europe*. Cambridge, Mass.: Harvard University Press, 1999.

———. " 'To the Point of Shedding Your Blood': The Bible, Communities of Faith, and Martyrs' Resistance to Conversion in the Reformation Era." In *Conversions: Old Worlds and New*, edited by Kenneth Mills and Anthony Grafton. Rochester: University of Rochester Press, 2003.

Grubb, James S. "Elite Citizens." In *Venice Reconsidered: The History and Civilization of an Italian City-State, 1297–1797*, edited by John Jeffries Martin and Dennis Romano. Baltimore: Johns Hopkins University Press, 2000.

Guzzetti, Linda. "Separations and Separated Couples in Fourteenth-Century Venice." In *Marriage in Italy, 1300–1650,* edited by Trevor Dean and K.J.P. Lowe. Cambridge: Cambridge University Press, 1998.

Hacke, Daniela. *Women, Sex, and Marriage in Early Modern Venice.* Aldershot, U.K.: Ashgate, 2004.

Hale, J. R., and Michael Mallett. *The Military Organization of a Renaissance State: Venice c. 1400–1617.* Cambridge: Cambridge University Press, 1984.

Hamadeh, Shirine. "Splash and Spectacle: The Obsession with Fountains in Eighteenth-Century Istanbul." *Muqarnas* 19 (2002): 123–48.

Hammer, M. de. *Histoire de l'empire ottoman.* Translated by M. Dochez. 18 vols. Paris: Béthune et Plon, 1835–43.

Hanley, Sarah. "Engendering the State: Family Formation and State Building in Early Modern France." *French Historical Studies* 16 (1989): 4–27.

Hardwick, Julie. "Did Gender Have a Renaissance? Exclusions and Traditions in Early Modern Western Europe." In *A Companion to Gender History,* edited by Teresa A. Meade and Merry E. Wiesner-Hanks. Malden, Mass.: Blackwell, 2004.

Hartnup, Karen. *"On the Beliefs of the Greeks": Leo Allatios and Popular Orthodoxy.* Leiden: Brill, 2004.

Hasluck, F. W. *Christianity and Islam under the Sultans.* 2 vols. Oxford: Clarendon Press, 1929.

———. "Depopulation in the Aegean Islands and the Turkish Conquest." *Annual of the British School at Athens* 17 (1910–11): 151–81.

Hathaway, Jane. *The Politics of Households in Ottoman Egypt: The Rise of the Qazdaglis.* Cambridge: Cambridge University Press, 1997.

Hefner, Robert W. "Introduction: World Building and the Rationality of Conversion." In *Conversion to Christianity: Historical and Anthropological Perspectives on a Great Transformation,* edited by Robert W. Hefner. Berkeley: University of California Press, 1993.

Herzfeld, Michael. "Honour and Shame: Problems in the Comparative Analysis of Moral Systems." *Man* 15 (1980): 339–51.

———. "The Horns of the Mediterraneanist Dilemma." *American Ethnologist* 11 (1984): 439–54.

Heyberger, Bernard. "Se convertir à l'Islam chez les chrétiens de Syrie." *Dimensioni e problemi della ricerca storica* 2 (1996): 133–52.

Hocquet, Jean-Claude. "Commercio e navigazione in Adriatico: Porto di

Ancona, sale di Pago e marina di Ragusa." *Atti e memorie della deputazione di storia patria per le Marche* 82 (1977): 221–54.

———. *Le sel et la fortune de Venise.* Vol. 1, *Production et monopole.* 2nd ed. Lille: Université de Lille III, 1982.

Hoerder, Dirk. *Cultures in Contact: World Migrations in the Second Millennium.* Durham, N.C.: Duke University Press, 2002.

Hofmann, G. "La chiesa cattolica in Grecia (1600–1830)." *Orientalia christiana periodica* 2 (1936): 164–90, 395–436.

Horden, Peregrine, and Nicholas Purcell. *The Corrupting Sea: A Study of Mediterranean History.* Oxford: Blackwell, 2000.

———. "Four Years of Corruption: A Response to Critics." In *Rethinking the Mediterranean,* edited by W.V. Harris. Oxford: Oxford University Press, 2005.

———. "The Mediterranean and 'the New Thalassology.'" *American Historical Review* 111 (2006): 722–40.

Horodowich, Elizabeth. *Language and Statecraft in Early Modern Venice.* Cambridge: Cambridge University Press, 2008.

Horvat, Karlo. "Glagolaši u Dalmaciji početkom 17. Vijeka t. J. godine 1602–1603." *Starine* 33 (1911): 537–64.

Hrvatski biografski leksikon. Vol. 2. Zagreb: Jugoslavenski leksikografski zavod, 1989.

Hunt, Margaret R. "Women in Ottoman and Western European Law Courts: Were Western Women *Really* the Luckiest Women in the World?" In *Structures and Subjectivities: Attending to Early Modern Women,* edited by Joan E. Hartman and Adelle Seeff. Newark: University of Delaware Press, 2007.

Hurlburt, Holly S. "Columbus' Sister: Female Agency and Women's Bodies in Early Modern Atlantic and Mediterranean Empires." In *Conflict, Concord: Attending to Early Modern Women,* edited by Karen Nelson. Newark: University of Delaware Press, forthcoming.

Ibarra, Miguel A. de Bunes. "La figura del renegado en el Levante en la edad moderna." *AIESEE Bulletin* 26–7 (1996–97): 173–78.

———. "Reflexiones sobre la conversión al Islam de los renegados en los siglos XVI y XVII." *Hispania Sacra* 42 (1990): 181–98.

Imber, Collin. *The Ottoman Empire, 1300–1650.* New York: Palgrave Macmillan, 2002.

———. "Women, Marriage, and Property: Mahr in the *Behcetü'l-Fetāvā* of Yenişehirli Abdullah." In *Women in the Ottoman Empire: Middle*

Eastern Women in the Early Modern Era, edited by Madeline C. Zilfi. Leiden: Brill, 1997.

İnalcık, Halil. "Decision Making in the Ottoman State." In *Decision Making and Change in the Ottoman Empire,* edited by Caesar E. Farah. Kirksville, Mo.: Thomas Jefferson University Press, 1993.

———. *The Ottoman Empire: The Classical Age.* London: Weidenfeld and Nicholson, 1973.

———. "Ottoman Methods of Conquest." *Studia Islamica* 2 (1954): 104–29.

———. "The Ottoman State: Economy and Society, 1300–1600." In *An Economic and Social History of the Ottoman Empire,* vol. 1, *1300–1600,* edited by Halil İnalcık and Donald Quataert. Cambridge: Cambridge University Press, 1997.

Infelise, Mario. *Prima dei giornali: Alle origini della pubblica informazione.* Rome: Laterza, 2002.

Iorga [Jorga], Nicolae. "Contribuţiunĭ la istoria Munteniei în a doua jumătate a secoluluĭ XVI–lea." *Analele Academiei Române,* series 2, 18 (1895–96): 1–112.

———. *Geschichte des osmanischen Reiches.* 5 vols. Gotha: F. Perthes, 1908–13. Reprint, Darmstadt: Wissenschaftliche Buchgesellschaft, 1990.

———. *Histoire des roumains et de la Romanité orientale.* Vol. 4. Bucarest: n.p., 1940.

———. *Pretendenţi domnesci in secolulu al XVI-lea.* Bucharest: Institutul de Arte Grafice, Carol Göbl, 1898.

———. "Venezia ed i paesi romeni del Danubio fino al 1600." In *Scritti storici in onore di Giovanni Monticolo,* edited by C. Cipolla et al. Venice: Ferrari, 1915.

İpşirli, Mehmet. "Mustafa Selânikî and His History." *Tarih Enstitüsü Dergisi* 9 (1978): 417–72.

Isaacs, Ann Katherine. "Introduction." In *Immigration/Emigration in Historical Perspective,* edited by Ann Katherine Isaacs. Pisa: Edizioni Plus, 2007.

Iskowitz, Norman. *The Ottoman Empire and Islamic Tradition.* Chicago: University of Chicago Press, 1972.

Jennings, Ronald C. *Christians and Muslims in Ottoman Cyprus and the Mediterranean World, 1571–1640.* New York: New York University Press, 1993.

———. "Divorce in the Ottoman Sharia Court of Cyprus, 1580–1640." *Studia Islamica* 78 (1993): 155–67.

———. "Kadi, Court, and Legal Procedure in 17th-C. Ottoman Kayseri." *Studia Islamica* 48 (1978): 133–72.

———. "Women in Early-17th-Century Ottoman Judicial Records—The Sharia Court of Anatolian Kayseri." In *Studies on Ottoman Social History in the Sixteenth and Seventeenth Centuries: Women, Zimmis, and Sharia Courts in Kayseri, Cyprus, and Trabzon*. Istanbul: Isis, 1999.

Johnson, Walter. "On Agency." *Journal of Social History* 37 (2003): 113–24.

Juran, Kristijan. "Kad i u kojim povijesnim okolnostima Murterini i Betinjani dolaze na Kornate?" *Povijesni prilozi* 28 (2005): 135–50.

Kafadar, Cemal. *Between Two Worlds: The Construction of the Ottoman State*. Berkeley: University of California Press, 1995.

———. "A Death in Venice (1575): Anatolian Muslim Merchants Trading in the Serenissima." *Journal of Turkish Studies* 10 (1986): 191–218.

———. "The Ottomans and Europe." In *Handbook of European History, 1400–1600*, edited by Thomas A. Brady, Jr., Heiko A. Oberman, and James D. Tracy, vol. 1. Leiden: Brill, 1994.

———. "Les troubles monétaires de la fin du XVIe siècle et la prise de conscience ottomane du déclin." *Annales: ESC* 46 (1991): 381–400.

Kahf, Mohja. *Western Representations of the Muslim Woman*. Austin: University of Texas Press, 1999.

Kamen, Henry. "Strategies of Survival: Minority Cultures in the Western Mediterranean." In *Early Modern History and the Social Sciences: Testing the Limits of Braudel's Mediterranean*, edited by John A. Marino. Kirksville, Mo.: Truman State University Press, 2002.

Kaplan, Benjamin J. *Divided by Faith: Religious Conflict and the Practice of Toleration in Early Modern Europe*. Cambridge, Mass.: Harvard University Press, 2007.

Karant-Nunn, Susan C. "Continuity and Change: Some Effects of the Reformation on the Women of Zwickau." *Sixteenth Century Journal* 12 (1982): 17–42.

———. "The Reformation of Women." In *Becoming Visible: Women in European History*, 3rd ed., edited by Renate Bridenthal, Susan Mosher Stuard, and Merry E. Wiesner-Hanks. Boston: Houghton Mifflin, 1998.

Karapidakis, Nicolas. *Civis fidelis: L'avènement et l'affirmation de la citoyenneté corfiote (XVIème–XVIIème siècles)*. Frankfurt: P. Lang, 1992.

Karsten, Arne. "Die Gleichschaltung der Eminenzen? Venezianische Kardi-
nalsgrabmäler im Rom des 17. und 18. Jahrhunderts." In *Macht und
Memoria: Begräbniskultur europäischer Oberschichten in der Frühen
Neuzeit,* edited by Mark Hengerer. Cologne: Böhlau Verlag, 2005.

Kasdagli, Aglaia E. "Gender Differentiation and Social Practice in Post-
Byzantine Naxos." In *The Byzantine Tradition after the Fall of Constan-
tinople,* edited by John J. Yannias. Charlottesville: University Press of
Virginia, 1991.

———. *Land and Marriage Settlements in the Aegean: A Case Study of
Seventeenth-Century Naxos.* Venice: Hellenic Institute of Byzantine and
Post-Byzantine Studies, 1999.

Kedar, Benjamin Z. "Multidirectional Conversion in the Frankish Levant."
In *Varieties of Religious Conversion in the Middle Ages,* edited by James
Muldoon. Gainesville: University Press of Florida, 1997.

———. "Muslim Conversion in Canon Law." In *Proceedings of the Sixth
International Congress of Medieval Canon Law,* edited by Stephane Kutt-
ner and Kenneth Pennington, vol. 7, *Monumenta iuris canonici.* Rome:
Biblioteca Apostolica Vaticana, 1985.

Keddie, Nikki R. *Women in the Middle East: Past and Present.* Princeton:
Princeton University Press, 2007.

Kertzer, David I. *The Pope against the Jews: The Vatican's Role in the Rise
of Modern Anti-Semitism.* New York: Vintage, 2002.

———. *Sacrificed for Honor: Italian Infant Abandonment and the Politics
of Reproductive Control.* Boston: Beacon, 1993.

Kessler-Harris, Alice. "What Is Gender History Now?" In *What Is History
Now?,* edited by David Cannadine. New York: Palgrave Macmillan,
2004.

King, Margaret L. *Women of the Renaissance.* Chicago: University of Chicago Press, 1991.

Kirshner, Julius. "Introduction." *Jewish History* 16 (2002): 1–14.

Kissling, H. J. "Türkenfurcht und Türkenhoffnung im 15. 16. Jahrhun-
dert: Zur Geschichte eines 'Komplexes.'" *Südost-Forschungen* 23 (1964):
1–18.

Klapisch-Zuber, Christiane. *Women, Family, and Ritual in Renaissance Italy.*
Chicago: University of Chicago Press, 1987.

Kollmann, Nancy Shields. *By Honor Bound: State and Society in Early
Modern Russia.* Ithaca, N.Y.: Cornell University Press, 1999.

Kologu, Orhan. "Renegades and the Case [sic] Uluç/Kiliç Ali." In *Mediterraneo in armi (sec. XV–XVIII)*, edited by Rossella Cancila, vol. 4, tome 2, *Quaderni Mediterranea: Ricerche storiche*. Palermo: Associazione Mediterranea, 2007.

Kolumbić, Jelena. "Grbovi zadarskih plemićkih obitelji." *Radovi JAZU* 47 (2005): 27–98.

Kooi, Christine. "Converts and Apostates: The Competition for Souls in Early Modern Holland." *Archiv für Reformationsgeschichte* 92 (2001): 195–214.

Kortepeter, Carl Max. *Ottoman Imperialism during the Reformation: Europe and the Caucasus*. New York: New York University Press, 1972.

Kramer, J. H. "Mustafā I." *The First Encyclopedia of Islam*. New edition. Vol. 7. Leiden: Brill, 1993.

Krekić, Barisa. "Developed Autonomy: The Patricians in Dubrovnik and Dalmatian Cities." In *The Urban Society of Eastern Europe in Premodern Times*, edited by Barisa Krekić. Berkeley: University of California Press, 1987.

Krstić, Tijana. "Illuminated by the Light of Islam and the Glory of the Ottoman Sultanate: Self-Narratives of Conversion to Islam in the Age of Confessionalization." *Comparative Studies in Society and History* 51 (2009): 35–63.

Kunt, I. Metin "Ethnic-Regional (*Cins*) Solidarity in the Seventeenth-Century Ottoman Establishment." *International Journal of Middle East Studies* 5 (1974): 233–39.

———. *The Sultan's Servants: The Transformation of Ottoman Provincial Government, 1550–1650*. New York: Columbia University Press, 1983.

Kužić, Krešimir. "Osmanlijski zapovjedni kadar u turđavama Klis, Lončarić i Kamen oko 1630. Godine." *Zbornik Odsjeka za povijesne znanosti Zavoda za povijesne i društvene znanosti Hrvatske akademije znanosti i umjetnosti* 23 (2005): 187–214.

———. "Prilog biografiji nekih Kačićevih vitezova te podrijetlu stanovništva njihova kraja." *Radovi JAZU* 47 (2005): 191–224.

LaBalme, Patricia. "Venetian Women on Women: Three Early Modern Feminists." *Archivio Veneto* 117 (1981): 81–109.

Laiou, Sophia. "Christian Women in an Ottoman World: Interpersonal and Family Cases Brought Before the Shari'a Courts during the Seventeenth and Eighteenth Centuries (Cases Involving the Greek Community)."

In *Women in the Ottoman Balkans: Gender, Culture, and History,* edited by Amila Buturović and İrvin Cemil Schick. London: I. B.Tauris, 2007.

Lamdan, Ruth. "Malchi, Esperanza." In *Encyclopaedia Judaica,* 2nd ed., vol. 13. Detroit: Macmillan Reference, 2007.

Lane, Frederic C. *Venice, a Maritime Republic.* Baltimore: Johns Hopkins University Press, 1973.

Lassithiotakis, Michel. " «L'isola di Candia, piu d'ogn'altra lontana»: Aspects matériels et culturels de l'insularité en Crète à la fin de période vénitienne (1570 env.–1669)." In *Insularités ottomanes,* edited by Nicolas Vatin and Gilles Veinstein. Paris: Maisonneuve et Larose, 2004.

Lattes, Andrea Y. "Gli ebrei di Ferrara e le imposte per i catecumeni." *La rassegna mensile di Israele* 65, no. 3 (1999): 41–54.

Laven, Mary. *Virgins of Venice: Enclosed Lives and Broken Vows in the Renaissance Convent.* London: Penguin, 2002.

Lazar, Lance Gabriel. "Negotiating Conversions: Catechumens and the Family in Early Modern Italy." In *Piety and Family in Early Modern Europe,* edited by Marc R. Forster and Benjamin J. Kaplan. Aldershot, U.K.: Ashgate, 2005.

Le Gall, Dina. *A Culture of Sufism: Naqshbandis in the Ottoman World.* Albany: State University of New York Press, 2005.

Lendaki, Andrea. *E katastrophe tes Melou tou 18th aiona.* Athens: N.p., 1974.

Lever, Alison. "Honour as a Red Herring." *Critique of Anthropology* 6 (1986): 81–106.

Levi, Giovanni. "On Microhistory." In *New Perspectives on Historical Writing,* edited by Peter Burke. University Park: Pennsylvania State University Press, 1992.

Levin, Eve. *Sex and Society in the World of the Orthodox Slavs, 900–1700.* Ithaca, N.Y.: Cornell University Press, 1989.

Levtzion, Nehemia. "Toward a Comparative Study of Islamization." In *Conversion to Islam,* edited by Nehemia Levtzion. New York: Holmes and Meier, 1979.

Lewis, Bernard. *The Crisis of Islam: Holy War and Unholy Terror.* New York: Random House, 2003.

———. *Islam and the West.* Oxford: Oxford University Press, 1993.

Lewis, Laura A. "The 'Weakness' of Women and the Feminization of the

Indian in Colonial Mexico." *Colonial Latin America Review* 5 (1996): 73–94.

Lewis, Raphaela. *Everyday Life in Ottoman Turkey.* London: B. T. Batsford, 1971.

Lollino, Luigi. *Vita del cavaliere Ottaviano Bon.* Venice: P. Naratovich, 1854.

Lombardi, Daniela. "Fidanzamenti e matrimoni dal concilio di Trento alle riforme settecentesche." In *Storia del matrimonio,* edited by Michela de Giorgio and Christiane Klapisch-Zuber. Rome: Laterza, 1996.

Lopasic, Alexander. "The Bulgarian Moslems, or Pomaks." *Anglo Bulgarian Symposium* 2 (1985): 121–26.

———. "Islamization of the Balkans with Special Reference to Bosnia." *Journal of Islamic Studies* 5 (1994): 163–86.

———. "The Turks of Bosnia." *Research Papers: Muslims in Europe* 16 (1982): 12–23.

Lopes, Maria de Jesus dos Mártires. "A problemática da conversão ao cristianismo em Goa: Os catecúmenos de Betim (séculos XVIII–XIX)." *Anais de história de Além-Mar* 3 (2002): 277–305.

Luca, Cristian. "Călători și pribegi din țările române la Veneția în secolul al XVII–lea." In *Călători români în Occident: Secolele XVII–XX,* edited by Nicolae Bocșan and Ioan Bolovan. Cluj-Napoca: Institutul Cultural Român, 2004.

———. "Miscellanea italo-romena (XVI e XVII secolo)." In *Închinare lui Petre Ș. Năsturel la 80 de ani,* edited by Ionel Cândea, Paul Cernovodeanu, and Gheorghe Lazăr. Brăila: Editura Istros, 2003.

———. "Veneziani, levantini e romeni fra prassi politiche e interessi mercantili nell'Europa sud-orientale tra cinque e seicento." In *Romania e Romània: Lingua e cultura romena di fronte all'Occidente,* edited by Teresa Ferro. Udine: Forum, 2003.

———. "The Vlachs/Morlaks in the Hinterlands of Traù (Trogir) and Sebenico (Šibenik), Towns of the Venetian Dalmatia, during the 16th Century." In *Miscellanea Historica et Archaeologica in Honorem Professoris Ionel Cândea,* edited by Valeriu Sîrbu and Cristian Luca. Brăila: Editura Istros, 2009.

Lunardon, Silvia. "Le Zitelle alla Giudecca: Una storia lunga quattrocento anni." In *Le Zitelle: Architettura, arte e storia di un'istituzione veneziana,* edited by Lionello Pupi. Venice: Albrizzi, 1992.

Luria, Keith P. *Sacred Boundaries: Religious Coexistence and Conflict in Early-Modern France.* Washington, D.C.: Catholic University of America Press, 2005.

Luxardo de Franchi, Nicolò, ed. *Le fortificazioni venete in Dalmazia e Corfù.* Venice: Museo navale, 1975.

Lybyer, Albert Howe. *The Government of the Ottoman Empire in the Time of Suleiman the Magnificent.* Cambridge, Mass.: Harvard University Press, 1913.

Malcolm, Noel. *Bosnia: A Short History.* New York: New York University Press, 1994.

Malieckal, Bindu. "Slavery, Sex, and the Seraglio: 'Turkish' Women and Early Modern Texts." In *The Mysterious and the Foreign in Early Modern England,* edited by Helen Ostovich, Mary V. Silcox, and Graham Roebuck. Newark: University of Delaware Press, 2008.

Malliaris, Alexis. "Population Exchange and Integration of Immigrant Communities in the Venetian Morea, 1687–1715." In *Between Venice and Istanbul: Colonial Landscapes in Early Modern Greece (Hesperia supplement 40),* edited by Siriol Davies and Jack L. Davis. N.p.: American School of Classical Studies in Athens, 2007.

Mantran, Robert. *Istanbul au siècle de Soliman le Magnifique.* Paris: Hachette, 1994.

Marshall, Sherrin. "Childhood in Early Modern Europe." In *Children in Historical and Comparative Perspective,* edited by Joseph M. Hawes and N. Ray Hiner. New York: Greenwood Press, 1991.

Martin, John Jeffries. "*Renovatio* and Reform in Early Modern Italy." In *Heresy, Culture, and Religion in Early Modern Italy: Contexts and Contestations,* edited by Ronald K. Delph, Michelle Fontaine, and John Jeffries Martin. Kirksville, Mo.: Truman State University Press, 2006.

———. "Salvation and Society in Sixteenth-Century Venice: Popular Evangelism in a Renaissance City." *Journal of Modern History* 60 (1988): 205–33.

———. *Venice's Hidden Enemies: Italian Heretics in a Renaissance City.* Berkeley: University of California Press, 1993.

Maschietto, Francesco Ludovico. *Elena Lucrezia Cornaro Piscopia (1646–1684); prima donna laureata nel mondo.* Padua: Antenore, 1978.

Masters, Bruce. *Christians and Jews in the Ottoman Arab World.* Cambridge: Cambridge University Press, 2001.

Matar, Nabil. *Turks, Moors, and Englishmen in the Age of Discovery.* New York: Columbia University Press, 1999.

Maxim, Mihai. "I principati romeni e l'impero ottomano (1400–1878)." In *Una storia dei Romeni,* edited by Stephen-Fischer Galați et al. Cluj-Napoca: Fundația Culturală Română, 2003.

Maxim, Mihai, and Viorel Panaite. "Pax ottomanica et les pays roumains (I–II)." *Analele Universității București: Istorie* 35 (1986): 11–19; 36 (1987): 94–99.

Maynes, Mary Jo. "Age as a Category of Historical Analysis: History, Agency, and Narratives of Childhood." *Journal of the History of Childhood and Youth* 1 (2008): 114–24.

Mazza, Barbara Boccazzi. "Governare i 'luoghi pii': La casa delle Zitelle." *Studi veneziani* 50 (2005): 291–99.

Mazzarotto, Bianca Tamassia. *Le feste veneziane: I giochi popolari, le cerimonie religiose e di governo.* Florence: Sansoni, 1961.

McGinty, Anna Mansson. *Becoming Muslim: Western Women's Conversions to Islam.* New York: Palgrave Macmillan, 2006.

McGough, Laura. "Women, Private Property, and the Limitations of State Authority in Early Modern Venice." *Journal of Women's History* 14 (2002): 32–52.

McGowan, Bruce. "The Age of the Ayans, 1699–1812." In *An Economic and Social History of the Ottoman Empire,* vol. 2, *1600–1914,* edited by Halil İnalcık and Donald Quataert. Cambridge: Cambridge University Press, 1997.

McLean, Paul D. *The Art of the Network: Strategic Interaction and Patronage in Renaissance Florence.* Durham, N.C.: Duke University Press, 2007.

Mehmed, Mustafa. "La crise ottomane dans la vision de Hasan Kiafi Akhisari (1544–1616)." *Revue des études sud-est européennes* 13 (1975): 385–402.

Melammed, Renée Levine. "Crypto-Jewish Women Facing the Spanish Inquisition: Transmitting Religious Practices, Beliefs, and Attitudes." In *Christians, Muslims, and Jews in Medieval and Early Modern Spain: Interaction and Cultural Change,* edited by Mark D. Meyerson and Edward D. English. Notre Dame: University of Notre Dame Press, 2000.

Menchi, Silvana Seidel, and Diego Quaglioni, eds. *Coniugi nemici: La separazione in Italia dal XII al XVIII secolo.* Bologna: Il Mulino, 2000.

Meriwether, Margaret L. *The Kin Who Count: Family and Society in Otto-man Aleppo, 1770–1840.* Austin: University of Texas Press, 1999.

Meriwether, Margaret L., and Judith E. Tucker. "Introduction." In *Social History of Women and Gender in the Modern Middle East,* edited by Margaret L. Meriwether and Judith E. Tucker. Boulder, Colo.: Westview Press, 1999.

Meyerson, Mark D. "Aragonese and Catalan Jewish Converts at the Time of the Expulsion." *Jewish History* 6 (1992): 131–49.

Milan, Catia, Antonio Politi, and Bruno Vianello, eds. *Guida alle magistra-ture: Elementi per la conoscenza della repubblica veneta.* Verona: Cierre, 2003.

Miller, Alan S., and John P. Hoffman. "Risk and Religion: An Explanation of Gender Differences in Religiosity." *Journal for the Scientific Study of Religion* 34 (1995): 63–75.

Miller, William. "The Ionian Islands under Venetian Rule." *English Histori-cal Review* 18 (1903): 209–39.

———. *The Latins in the Levant: A History of Frankish Greece (1204–1566).* London: John Murray, 1908. Reprint, Cambridge: Speculum Historiale, 1964.

Mills, Kenneth, and Anthony Grafton. "Introduction." In *Conversions: Old Worlds and New,* edited by Kenneth Mills and Anthony Grafton. Rochester, N.Y.: University of Rochester Press, 2003.

Minkov, Anton. *Conversion to Islam in the Balkans: Kisve Bahası Petitions and Ottoman Social Life, 1670–1730.* Leiden: Brill, 2004.

Mocenigo, Mario Nani. *Storia della marina veneziana da Lepanto alla caduta della repubblica.* Rome: Ministero della Marina, 1935.

Moch, Leslie Page. *Moving Europeans: Migration in Western Europe since 1650.* 2nd ed. Bloomington: Indiana University Press, 2003.

Molho, Anthony. "Ebrei e marrani fra Italia e Levante ottomano." In *Storia d'Italia—Annali,* vol. 11, *Gli ebrei in Italia,* edited by Corrado Vivanti. Turin: Giulio Einaudi editore, 1997.

———. *Marriage Alliance in Late Medieval Florence.* Cambridge, Mass.: Harvard University Press, 1994.

———. "Review of *The Corrupting Sea,* by Peregrine Horden and Nicholas Purcell." *Journal of World History* 13 (2002): 486–92.

Monter, E. William. "Women in Calvinist Geneva (1550–1800)." *Signs* 6 (1980): 189–209.

Mordtmann, J. H. "Die jüdischen Kira im Serai der Sultane." *Mitteilungen des Seminars für orientalischen Sprachen* 32 (1929): 1–38.

Morris, Ian. "Mediterraneanization." *Mediterranean Historical Review* 18 (2003): 30–55.

Muir, Edward. *Mad Blood Stirring: Vendetta and Factions in Friuli during the Renaissance.* Baltimore: Johns Hopkins University Press, 1993.

———. *Ritual in Early Modern Europe.* Cambridge: Cambridge University Press, 2005.

Nashat, Guity. "Women in the Middle East, 8000 BCE to 1700 CE." In *A Companion to Gender History,* edited by Teresa A. Meade and Merry E. Wiesner-Hanks. Oxford: Blackwell, 2004.

———. "Women in the Middle East: 8000 B.C.E.–C.E. 1800." In *Women in the Middle East: Restoring Women to History,* edited by Guity Nashat and Judith E. Tucker. Bloomington: Indiana University Press, 1999.

Neagoe, Manole. *Mihai Viteazul.* Bucharest: Editura "Europa Nova," 1994.

Necipoğlu, Gülru. *The Age of Sinan: Architectural Culture in the Ottoman Empire.* Princeton: Princeton University Press, 2005.

———. *Architecture, Ceremonial, and Power: The Topkapi Palace in the Fifteenth and Sixteenth Centuries.* Cambridge, Mass.: MIT Press, 1991.

Neff, Mary Frances. "Chancellery Secretaries in Venetian Politics and Society, 1480–1533." Ph.D. diss., U.C.L.A., 1985.

Niero, Antonio. *I patriarchi di Venezia da Lorenzo Giustiniani ai nostri giorni.* Venice: Studium Cattolico Veneziano, 1961.

Nixon, Lucia. "Review of *The Corrupting Sea,* by P. Horden and N. Purcell, and of *The Mediterranean in the Ancient World,* by F. Braudel." *Journal of Roman Studies* (2002): 195–97.

Novak, Grga. *Povijest Splita.* 3 vols. Split: Čakavski sabor, 1978.

Nye, Robert A. *Masculinity and Male Codes of Honor in Modern France.* Oxford: Oxford University Press, 1993.

Oberling, Gerry, and Grace Martin Smith. *The Food Culture of the Ottoman Palace.* Istanbul: Republic of Turkey Ministry of Culture, 2001.

O'Connell, Monique. *Men of Empire: Power and Negotiation in Venice's Maritime State.* Baltimore: Johns Hopkins University Press, 2009.

Olteanu, Ştefan. *Les pays roumains à l'époque de Michel le Brave (l'union de 1600).* Bucharest: Editura Academiei Republicii Socialiste România, 1975.

Oris, Michel, and Emiko Ochiai. "Family Crisis in the Context of Different Family Systems: Frameworks and Evidence on 'When Dad Died.'" In *When Dad Died: Individuals and Families Coping with Family Stress in Past Societies,* edited by Renzo Derosas and Michel Oris. Bern: Peter Lang, 2002.

Orme, Nicholas. *Medieval Children.* New Haven: Yale University Press, 2001.

Ortega, Stephen. "'Pleading for Help': Gender Relations and Cross-Cultural Logic in the Early Modern Mediterranean." *Gender and History* 20 (2008): 332–48.

Paci, Renzo. *La scala di Spalato e il commercio veneziano nei Balcani fra Cinque e Seicento.* Venice: Deputazione di Storia Patria per le Venezie, 1971.

Pagratis, Gerassimos D. *Ekklesia kai krato sta venetika nesia tou Ioniou Pelagous: Martyries gia te drase Italon Phrankiskanon Missionarion apo ta archeia tes Propaganda Fide (17os aionas).* Athens: Ekdoseis Papazese, 2009.

———. "Sources for the Maritime History of Greece (Fifteenth to Seventeenth Century)." *Research in Maritime History* 28 (2004): 125–46.

———. "Tracce della presenza francescana in Levante: La chiesa e il convento di San Francesco dei frati minori di Corfù." *Il santo* 40 (2000): 99–119.

———. "Trade and Shipping in Corfu 1496–1538." *International Journal of Maritime History* 16, no. 2 (2004): 169–220.

Panaite, Viorel. "Power Relationships in the Ottoman Empire: Sultans and the Tribute Paying Princes of Wallachia and Moldavia (16th–18th Centuries)." *Revue des études sud-est européennes* 37 (1999): 47–78.

———. "The Voivodes of the Danubian Principalities—As Hâracgüzarlar of the Ottoman Sultans." *International Journal of Turkish Studies* 9 (2003): 59–78.

Parker, Geoffrey, and Lesley M. Smith, eds. *The General Crisis of the Seventeenth Century.* 2nd ed. London: Routledge, 1997.

Paspati, A. G. "Life of the Patriarch Cyril." *The Bibliotheca Sacra* 23 (1866): 452–85.

Pearl, David. *A Textbook on Muslim Personal Law.* 2nd ed. London: Croom Helm, 1987.

Pedani, Maria Pia. "Beyond the Frontier: The Ottoman-Venetian Border in the Adriatic Context from the Sixteenth to the Eighteenth Centuries." In *Zones of Fracture in Modern Europe: The Baltic Countries, the Balkans, and Northern Italy*, edited by Almut Bues. Wiesbaden: Harrossowitz Verlag, 2005.

————. "Dalla frontiera al confine." *Quaderni di studi arabi, studi e testi* 5. Rome: Herder editrice, 2002.

————. *I documenti turchi dell'archivio di stato di Venezia*. Rome: Ministero per i beni culturali e ambientali, 1994.

————. *In nome del Gran Signore*. Venice: Deputazione editrice, 1994.

————. "The Ottoman Venetian Frontier (15th–18th Centuries)." In *The Great Ottoman-Turkish Civilisation*, edited by Kemal Çicek et al. Ankara: Yeni Türkiye, 2000.

————. "Presenze islamiche a Venezia." *Levante* 35 (1993): 13–20.

————. "Safiye's Household and Venetian Diplomacy." *Turcica* 32 (2000): 9–32.

————. "Veneziani a Costantinopoli alla fine del XVI secolo." *Quaderni di studi arabi* 15, supplement (1997): 67–84.

Peirce, Leslie P. "Beyond Harem Walls: Ottoman Royal Women and the Exercise of Power." In *Gendered Domains: Rethinking Public and Private in Women's History*, edited by Dorothy O. Helly and Susan M. Reverby. Ithaca, N.Y.: Cornell University Press, 1992.

————. *The Imperial Harem: Women and Sovereignty in the Ottoman Empire*. Oxford: Oxford University Press, 1993.

————. *Morality Tales: Law and Gender in the Ottoman Court of Aintab*. Berkeley: University of California Press, 2003.

————. "Seniority, Sexuality, and Social Order: The Vocabulary of Gender in Early Modern Ottoman Society." In *Women in the Ottoman Empire: Middle Eastern Women in the Early Modern Era*, edited by Madeline C. Zilfi. Leiden: Brill, 1997.

Peri, Vittorio. "L'«incredibile risguardo» e l'«incredibile destrezza». La resistenza di Venezia alle iniziative postridentine della santa sede per i greci dei suoi domini." In *Venezia, centro di mediazione tra oriente e occidente (secoli XV–XVI): Aspetti e problemi*, vol. 2, edited by Hans-Georg Beck, Manoussos Manoussacas, and Agostino Pertusi. Florence: Olschki, 1977.

Peristiany, J. G., ed. *Honour and Shame: The Values of Mediterranean Society*. London: Weidenfeld and Nicolson, 1965.

Perry, Mary Elizabeth. "Behind the Veil: Moriscas and the Politics of Resistance and Survival." In *Spanish Women in the Golden Age: Images and Realities,* edited by Magdalena S. Sanchez and Alain Saint-Saens. Westport, Conn.: Greenwood Press, 1996.

———. "Contested Identities: The Morisca Visionary Beatriz de Robles." In *Women in the Inquisition: Spain and the New World,* edited by Mary Giles. Baltimore: Johns Hopkins University Press, 1999.

———. *The Handless Maiden: Moriscos and the Politics of Religion in Early Modern Spain.* Princeton: Princeton University Press, 2005.

———. "Moriscas and the Limits of Assimilation." In *Christians, Muslims, and Jews in Medieval and Early Modern Spain: Interaction and Cultural Change,* edited by Mark D. Meyerson and Edward D. English. Notre Dame: University of Notre Dame Press, 2000.

Peters, Christine. *Patterns of Piety: Women, Gender, and Religion in Late Medieval and Reformation England.* Cambridge: Cambridge University Press, 2003.

Pina-Cabral, João de. "The Mediterranean as a Category of Regional Comparison: A Critical View." *Current Anthropology* 30 (1989): 399–406.

Platon, Gheorghe. "Tra gli Imperi Ottomano, Austriaco e Russo (nei secoli XVI–XVII)." In *Una storia dei romeni: Studi critici,* edited by Stephen-Fischer Galaţi et al. Cluj-Napoca: Fundaţia Culturală Română, 2003.

Porter, Roy. *English Society in the Eighteenth Century.* London: Allen Lane, 1982.

Povero, Chiara. *Missioni in terra di frontiera: La controriforma nelle valli del Pinerolese secoli XVI–XVIII.* Rome: Istituto storico dei Cappuccini, 2006.

Povolo, Claudio. *L'intrigo dell'onore: Poteri e istituzioni nella republica di Venezia tra cinque e seicento.* Verona: Cierre Edizioni, 1997.

Power, Daniel. "Frontiers: Terms, Concepts, and the Historians of Medieval and Early Modern Europe." In *Frontiers in Question: Eurasian Borderlands, 700–1700,* edited by Daniel Power and Naomi Standen. New York: St. Martin's, 1999.

Praga, Giuseppe. *History of Dalmatia.* Pisa: Giardini, 1993.

Preto, Paolo. *Venezia e i turchi.* Florence: Sansoni, 1975.

Prodi, Paolo. "The Structure and Organization of the Church in Renaissance Venice: Suggestions for Research." In *Renaissance Venice,* edited by J. R. Hale. Totowa, Md.: Rowman and Littlefield, 1973.

Pullan, Brian. "The Inquisition and the Jews of Venice: The Case of Gaspare

Ribeiro, 1580–81." *Bulletin of the John Rylands Library of Manchester* 62 (1979): 207–231.

———. "La nuova filantropia nella Venezia cinquecentesca." In *Nel regno dei poveri: Arte e storia dei grandi ospedali veneziani in età moderna, 1474–1797*, edited by Bernard Aikema and Dulcia Meijers. Venice: Arsenale, 1989.

———. "The Old Catholicism, the New Catholicism, and the Poor." In *Timore e carità: I poveri nell'Italia moderna*, edited by Giorgio Politi, Mario Rosa, and Franco della Paruta. Cremona: Biblioteca Statale e Libreria Civica di Cremona, 1982.

———. *Rich and Poor in Renaissance Venice: The Social Institutions of a Catholic State, to 1620*. Cambridge, Mass.: Harvard University Press, 1971.

———. "Wage-Earners and the Venetian Economy, 1550–1630." In *Crisis and Change in the Venetian Economy in the 16th and 17th Centuries*, edited by Brian Pullan. London: Methuen, 1968.

Purcell, Nicholas. "The Boundless Sea of Unlikeness? On Defining the Mediterranean." *Mediterranean Historical Review* 18 (2003): 9–29.

———. "Fixity." In *Mobility and Travel in the Mediterranean from Antiquity to the Middle Ages*, edited by Renate Schlesier and Ulrike Zellmann. Münster: LIT Verlag Münster, 2004.

Queller, Donald E., and Thomas F. Madden. "Father of the Bride: Fathers, Daughters, and Dowries in Late Medieval and Early Renaissance Venice." *Renaissance Quarterly* 46 (1993): 685–711.

Rački, Franjo. "Prilozi za geografsko-statistički opis bosanskoga paša pašalika." *Starine* 14 (1882): 173–93.

Rambo, Lewis R. "Anthropology and the Study of Conversion." In *The Anthropology of Religious Conversion*, edited by Andrew Buckser and Stephen D. Glazier. Lanham, Md.: Rowman and Littlefield, 2003.

———. "Theories of Conversion: Understanding and Interpreting Religious Change." *Social Compass* 46 (1999): 259–71.

———. *Understanding Religious Conversion*. New Haven: Yale University Press, 1993.

Rangabé, Eugène Rizo. *Livre d'or de la noblesse ionienne*. Athens: Maison d'Éditions "Eleftheroudakis," 1925.

Rapley, Elizabeth. "Women and Religious Vocation in Seventeenth-Century France." *French Historical Studies* 18 (1994): 613–31.

Raukar, Tomislav. "Le città della Dalmazia nell XIII e XIV secolo." In *Le città del Mediterraneo all'apogeo dello sviluppo medievale: Aspetti economici e sociali.* Pistoia: Centro Italiano Studi di Storia, 2003.

———. "Venezia, il sale e la struttura economica e sociale della Dalmazia nel XV e XVI secolo." In *Convegno internazionale di studi su sale e saline in adriatico in età moderna,* edited by Antonio Di Vittorio and Sergio Anselmi. Naples: Giannini Editore, 1981.

———. *Zadar u XV stoljeću: ekonomski razvoj i društveni odnosi.* Zagreb: Sveučilište, Centar za povijesne znanosti, 1977.

Reid, Charles J. *Power over the Body, Equality in the Family: Rights and Domestic Relations in Medieval Canon Law.* Grand Rapids, Mich.: Eerdmans, 2004.

Reindl-Kiel, Hedda. "A Woman Timar Holder in Ankara Province during the Second Half of the 16th Century." *Journal of the Economic and Social History of the Orient* 40 (1997): 207–38.

Restall, Matthew. " 'He Wished It in Vain': Subordination and Resistance among Maya Women in the Post-Conquest Yucatan." *Ethnohistory* 42 (1995): 577–94.

Ricci, Giovanni. *Ossessione turca: In una retrovia cristiana dell'Europa moderna.* Bologna: Il Mulino, 2002.

Rigo, Angelo. "Giudici del Procurator e donne «malmaritate»." *Atti dell'Istituto Veneto di Scienze, Lettere ed Arti* 153 (1993): 241–66.

Rocciolo, Domenico. "L'archivio della pia casa dei catacumeni e neofiti." *Ricerche per la storia religiosa di Roma* 10 (1999): 545–82.

Roelker, Nancy. "The Appeal of Calvinism to French Noblewomen in the Sixteenth Century." *Journal of Interdisciplinary History* 2 (1972): 391–418.

Roper, Lyndal. *Oedipus and the Devil: Witchcraft, Sexuality, and Religion in Early Modern Europe.* London: Routledge, 1994.

Rossi, Ettore. "La sultana Nūr Bānū (Cecilia Venier-Baffo) moglie di Selīm II (1566–1574) e madre di Murād III (1574–1595)." *Oriente moderno* 33 (1953): 433–41.

Rostagno, Lucia. *Mi faccio turco: Esperienze ed immagini dell'islam nell'Italia moderna.* Rome: Istituto per l'Oriente C. A. Nallino, 1983.

Roth, Cecil. *The Duke of Naxos of the House of Nasi.* Philadelphia: Jewish Publication Society of America, 1948.

Rothenberg, G.E. "Christian Insurrections in Turkish Dalmatia 1580–96." *Slavonic and East European Review* 40 (1961): 136–47.

Rothman, E. Natalie. "Becoming Venetian: Conversion and Transformation in the Seventeenth-Century Mediterranean." *Mediterranean Historical Review* 21 (2006): 39–75.

———. "Between Venice and Istanbul: Trans-Imperial Subjects and Cultural Mediation in the Early Modern Mediterranean." Ph.D. diss., University of Michigan, 2006.

Rouillard, Clarence Dana. *The Turk in French History, Thought, and Literature.* Paris: Boivin, n.d.

Rozen, Minna. *A History of the Jewish Community of Istanbul: The Formative Years, 1453–1566.* Leiden: Brill, 2002.

Rudt de Collenberg, Wipertus Hugues. "Les «custodi» de la Marciana Giovanni Sozomenos et Giovanni Matteo Bustron: Relations familiales, sociales, culturelles et politiques au sein de la communauté chypriote." *Miscellanea marciana* 5 (1990): 9–76.

———. *Esclavage et rançons des chrétiens en Méditerranée (1570–1600).* Paris: Léopard d'Or, 1987.

Ruggiero, Guido. *The Boundaries of Eros: Sex Crime and Sexuality in Renaissance Venice.* Oxford: Oxford University Press, 1989.

———. " «Più che la vita caro»: Onore, matrimonio e reputazione femminile del tardo rinascimento." *Quaderni storici* 66 (1987): 753–75.

Safley, Thomas M. "Marital Litigation in the Diocese of Constance, 1551–1620." *Sixteenth Century Journal* 12 (1981): 61–77.

Sahlins, Peter. *Boundaries: The Making of France and Spain in the Pyrenees.* Berkeley: University of California Press, 1989.

Said, Edward W. *Orientalism.* New York: Vintage Books, 1979.

Salisbury, Neal. "Embracing Ambiguity: Native Peoples and Christianity in Seventeenth-Century North America." *Ethnohistory* 50 (2003): 247–59.

Sarti, Raffaella. *Europe at Home: Family and Material Culture, 1500–1800.* New Haven: Yale University Press, 2004.

Scaraffia, Lucetta. *Rinnegati: Per una storia dell'identità occidentale.* Rome: Laterza, 1993.

Schick, İrvin Cemil. "Christian Maidens, Turkish Ravishers: The Sexualization of National Conflict in the Late Ottoman Period." In *Women in the*

Ottoman Balkans: Gender, Culture, and History, edited by Amila Bu-turović and İrvin Cemil Schick. London: I. B. Tauris, 2007.

Schmidt, Jan. "The Egri-Campaign of 1596: Military History and the Problem of Sources." In *Habsburgisch-osmanische Beziehungen,* edited by Andreas Tietze. Vienna: Verlag des Verbandes der wissenschaftlichen Gesellschaften Österreichs, 1985.

———. *Pure Water for Thirsty Muslims: A Study of Muṣṭafā ʿĀlī of Gallipoli's "Künhü l-aḫbār."* Leiden: Het Oosters Instituut, 1991.

Schröeder, Franz. *Repertorio genealogico delle famiglie confermate nobili e dei titolati nobili esistenti nelle provincie Venete.* 2 vols. Venice: Alvisopoli, 1830–31. Reprint, Bologna: Arnaldo Forni Editore, 1972.

Schutte, Anne Jacobsen. "Legal Remedies for Forced Monachization in Early Modern Italy." In *Heresy, Culture, and Religion in Early Modern Italy: Contexts and Contestations,* edited by Ronald K. Delph, Michelle M. Fontaine, and John Jeffries Martin. Kirksville, Mo.: Truman State University Press, 2006.

———. "The Permeable Cloister." In *Arcangela Tarabotti: A Literary Nun in Baroque Venice,* edited by Elissa Weaver. Ravenna: Longo Editore, 2006.

Schwartz, Stuart B. *All Can Be Saved: Religious Tolerance and Salvation in the Iberian Atlantic.* New Haven: Yale University Press, 2008.

Scott, Joan W. "Gender: A Useful Category of Historical Analysis." *American Historical Review* 91 (1986): 1053–75.

———. "The Problem of Invisibility." In *Retrieving Women's History: Changing Perceptions of the Role of Women in Politics and Society,* edited by S. Jay Kleinberg. Oxford: UNESCO, 1988.

Scully, Sally. "Marriage or a Career?: Witchcraft as an Alternative in Seventeenth-Century Venice." *Journal of Social History* 28 (1995): 857–76.

Seeff, Adele F., and Joan Hartman, eds. *Structures and Subjectivities: Attending to Early Modern Women.* Newark: University of Delaware Press, 2007.

Semerdjian, Elyse. *"Off the Straight Path": Illicit Sex, Law, and Community in Ottoman Aleppo.* Syracuse, N.Y.: Syracuse University Press, 2008.

Semi, Francesco, and Vanni Tacconi, eds. *Istria e Dalmazia: Uomini e tempi.* Udine: Del Bianco Editore, 1992.

Sertoğlu, Midhat. *Osmanlı tarih lügatı.* Istanbul: Enderun Kitabevi, 1986.

Setton, Kenneth M. "Lutheranism and the Turkish Peril." *Balkan Studies* 3 (1962): 133–68.

———. *The Papacy and the Levant.* Vol. 4, *The Sixteenth Century.* Philadelphia: American Philosophical Society, 1984.

Sforza, Giovanni. "Un libro sfortunato contro i Turchi." In *Scritti storici in memoria di Giovanni Monticolo,* edited by C. Cipolla et al. Venice: Carlo Ferrari, 1922.

Shagan, Ethan H. *Popular Politics and the English Reformation.* Cambridge: Cambrige University Press, 2003.

Shatzmiller, Maya. "Marriage, Family, and the Faith: Women's Conversion to Islam." *Journal of Family History* 21 (1996): 235–66.

Shaw, Stanford. *History of the Ottoman Empire and Modern Turkey.* Vol. 1, *Empire of the Gazis.* Cambridge: Cambridge University Press, 1976.

Siebenhüner, Kim. "Conversion, Mobility, and the Roman Inquisition in Italy around 1600." *Past and Present* 200 (2008): 5–35.

Singleton, Fred. *A Short History of the Yugoslav Peoples.* Cambridge: Cambridge University Press, 1985.

Skendi, Stavro. "Crypto-Christianity in the Balkan Area under the Ottomans." *Slavic Review* 26 (1967): 227–46.

Skilliter, S. A. "Catherine de' Medici's Turkish Ladies-in-Waiting: A Dilemma in Franco-Ottoman Diplomatic Relations." *Turcica* 7 (1975): 188–204.

———. "The Letters of the Venetian 'Sultana' Nūr Bānū and Her Kira to Venice." In *Studia turcologica memoriae Alexii Bombaci dicata,* edited by Aldo Gallotta and Ugo Marazzi. Naples: Istituto universitario orientale, 1982.

Slot, B. J. *Archipelagus Turbatus: Les Cyclades entre colonisation latine et occupation ottomane, c. 1500–1718.* 2 vols. Istanbul: Nederlands Historisch-Archaeologisch Instituut te Istanbul, 1982.

Snyder, Jon R. *Dissimulation and the Culture of Secrecy in Early Modern Europe.* Berkeley: University of California Press, 2009.

Sokolnicki, Michel. "La Sultane Ruthène." *Belleten* 23 (1959): 229–39.

Spagni, Emilio. "Una sultana veneziana." *Nuovo archivio veneto* 19 (1900): 241–348.

Sperling, Jutta Gisela. *Convents and the Body Politic in Late Renaissance Venice.* Chicago: University of Chicago Press, 1999.

Sperling, Jutta Gisela, and Shona Kelly Wray, eds. *Across the Religious*

Divide: Women, Property, and Law in the Wider Mediterranean (ca. 1300–1800). New York: Routledge, 2009.

Sphyroeras, B. "Metanasteuseis kai epoikismoi Kykladiton eis Smyrnen kata ten tourkokratian." *Mikrasiatika chronika* 10 (1963): 164–99.

Stanivukovic, Goran V. "Cruising the Mediterranean: Narratives of Sexuality and Geographies of the Eastern Mediterranean in Early Modern English Prose Romances." In *Remapping the Mediterranean World in Early Modern English Writings,* edited by Goran V. Stanivukovic. New York: Palgrave Macmillan, 2007.

Stark, Rodney. *The Rise of Christianity.* New York: HarperCollins, 1997.

Stow, Kenneth. "Neofiti and Their Families; or, Perhaps, the Good of the State." *Leo Baeck Institute Year Book* 47 (2002): 105–13.

Strauss, Johann. "Ottoman Rule Experienced and Remembered: Remarks on Some Local Greek Chronicles." In *The Ottomans and the Balkans: A Discussion of Historiography,* edited by Fikret Adanır and Suraiya Faroqhi. Leiden: Brill, 2002.

Strocchia, Sharon T. "Gender and Rites of Honour in Italian Renaissance Cities." In *Gender and Society in Renaissance Italy,* edited by Judith C. Brown and Robert C. Davis. London: Longman, 1998.

Sturdza, Mihail-Dimitri. *Dictionnaire historique et gènéalogique des grandes familles de Grèce, d'Albanie et de Constantinople.* Paris: Chez l'Auteur, 1983.

Subrahmanyam, Sanjay. *Mughals and Franks.* Oxford: Oxford University Press, 2005.

Sugar, Peter F. *Southeastern Europe under Ottoman Rule, 1354–1804.* Seattle: University of Washington Press, 1977.

Süreyya, Mehmet. *Sicill-i Osmani.* Edited by Nuri Akbayar. Translated by Seyit Alikahraman. 6 vols. Istanbul: Kültür Bakanligi ile Türkiye Ekonomik ve Toplumsal Tarih Vakfi'nin ortak yayinidir, 1996.

Sutton, Susan B. "Liquid Landscapes: Demographic Transitions in Ermionidha." In *Contingent Countryside: Settlement, Economy, and Land Use in the Southern Argolid since 1700,* edited by Susan B. Sutton. Stanford: Stanford University Press, 2000.

Talbot, Michael. "The Italian Concerto in the Late Seventeenth and Early Eighteenth Centuries." In *The Cambridge Companion to the Concerto,* edited by Simon P. Keefe. Cambridge: Cambridge University Press, 2005.

Tamburini, Filippo. *Santi e peccatori: Confessioni e suppliche dai registri della penitenzieria dell'Archivio Segreto Vaticano (1451–1586)*. Milan: Istituto di Propaganda Libraria, 1995.

Tanindi, Zeren. "Bibliophile Aghas (Eunuchs) at Topkapi Saray." *Muqarnas* 21 (2004): 333–43.

———. "Transformation of Words to Images: Portraits of Ottoman Courtiers in the Diwans of Baki and Nadiri." *Res* 43 (spring 2003): 131–45.

Tassini, Giuseppe. *Curiosità veneziane*. 2nd ed. Venice: Grimaldo, 1872.

Tenenti, Alberto. *Naufrages, corsairs, et assurances maritimes à Venise, 1592–1609*. Paris: S.E.V.P.E.N., 1959.

Teter, Magdalena. "Jewish Conversions to Catholicism in the Polish-Lithuania Commonwealth of the Seventeenth and Eighteenth Centuries." *Jewish History* 17 (2003): 257–83.

Theunissen, Hans Peter Alexander. "Ottoman-Venetian Diplomatics: The ᶜAhd-Names." Ph.D. diss., University of Utrecht, 1991.

Thys-Şenocak, Lucienne. *Ottoman Women Builders: The Architectural Patronage of Hadice Turhan Sultan*. Aldershot, U.K.: Ashgate, 2006.

Tolan, John V. *Saracens: Islam in the Medieval European Imagination*. New York: Columbia University Press, 2002.

Topping, Eva C. "Patriarchal Prejudice and Pride in Greek Christianity Some Notes on Origins." *Journal of Modern Greek Studies* 1 (1983): 7–17.

Tóth, István György. "Between Islam and Christianity: Hungary as Religious Borderland in the Early Modern Period." In *Zones of Fracture in Modern Europe: The Baltic Countries, the Balkans, and Northern Italy*, edited by Almut Bues. Wiesbaden: Harrassowitz Verlag, 2005.

Toth, Lucio. "Per una storia della Dalmazia tra medioevo ed età contemporanea." *Clio* 38 (2002): 337–77.

Traljić, Seid M. "Tursko-mletačke granice u Dalmaciji u XVI. i XVII. stoljeću." *Radovi JAZU* 20 (1973): 447–58.

———. "Zadar i turska pozadina od XV do potkraj XIX stoljeća." *Radovi JAZU* 11–12 (1965): 203–27.

Tsitsas, A. Ch. *Venetokratoumene Kerkyra (thesmoi)*. Corfu: Hetaireia Kerkyraikon Spoudon, 1989.

Tucker, Judith E. "The Fullness of Affection: Mothering in the Islamic Law of Ottoman Syria and Palestine." In *Women in the Ottoman Empire: Middle Eastern Women in the Early Modern Era*, edited by Madeline C. Zilfi. Leiden: Brill, 1997.

———. *In the House of the Law: Gender and Islamic Law in Ottoman Syria and Palestine.* Berkeley: University of California Press, 1998.

———. "Rescued from Obscurity: Contributions and Challenges in Writing the History of Gender in the Middle East and North Africa." In *A Companion to Gender History,* edited by Teresa A. Meade and Merry E. Wiesner-Hanks. Malden, Mass.: Blackwell, 2004.

Twinam, Ann. "Women and Gender in Colonial Latin America." In *Women's History in Global Perspective,* vol. 2, edited by Bonnie G. Smith. Urbana: University of Illinois Press, 2005.

Vacalopoulos, Apostolos E. *The Greek Nation, 1453–1669: The Cultural and Economic Background of Modern Greek Society.* Translated by Ian Moles and Phania Moles. New Brunswick, N.J.: Rutgers University Press, 1976.

Valensi, Lucette. *The Birth of the Despot: Venice and the Sublime Porte.* Ithaca, N.Y.: Cornell University Press, 1993.

Vanzan, Anna. "In Search of Another Identity: Female Muslim-Christian Conversions in the Mediterranean World." *Islam and Christian-Muslim Relations* 7 (1996): 327–33.

Vatin, Nicolas. "L'empire ottoman et la piraterie en 1559–1560." In *The Kapudan Pasha: His Office and His Domain,* edited by Elizabeth Zachariadou. Rethymnon: Crete University Press, 2002.

———. "Îles grecques? Îles ottomanes? L'insertion des îles de l'Égee dans l'empire ottoman à la fin du XVIe siècle." In *Insularités ottomanes,* edited by Nicolas Vatin and Gilles Veinstein. Paris: Maisonneuve et Larose, 2004.

Vatin, Nicolas, and Gilles Veinstein. *Le Sérail ébranlé: Essai sur les morts, depositions et avènements des sultans ottomans XIVe–XIXe siècle.* Paris: Fayard, 2003.

Veinstein, Gilles. "Sur les conversions à l'Islam dans les Balkans Ottomans avant le XIXe siècle." *Dimensioni e problemi della ricerca storica* 2 (1996): 153–67.

Ventura, Angelo. "Scrittori politici e scritture di governo." In *Storia della cultura veneta dal primo Quattrocento al Concilio di Trento,* vol. 3/3, edited by Girolamo Arnaldi and Manlio Pastore Stocchi. Vicenza: Neri Pozzi Editore, 1981.

Vercellin, Giorgio. "Mercanti turchi e sensali a Venezia." *Studi veneziani* 9 (1980): 45–78.

Vilfan, Sergei. "Towns and States at the Juncture of the Alps, the Adriatic, and Pannonia." In *Cities and the Rise of States in Europe, A.D. 1000 to 1800,* edited by Charles Tilly and Willem P. Blockmans. Boulder, Colo.: Westview Press, 1994.

Vingopoulou, Ioli. *Le monde grec vu par les voyageurs du XVIe siècle.* Athens: Institut de Recerches Néohelléniques, 2004.

Viscuso, Patrick. "Marriage between Christians and Non-Christians: Orthodox and Roman Catholic Perspectives." *Journal of Ecumenical Studies* 31 (1994): 269–78.

————. "An Orthodox Perspective on Marriage: Demetrios J. Constantelos." In *Church and Society: Orthodox Christian Perspectives, Past Experiences, and Modern Challenges,* edited by George P. Liacopulos. Boston: Somerset Hall, 2007.

————. *Sexuality, Marriage, and Celibacy in Byzantine Law: Selections from a Fourteenth-Century Encyclopedia of Canon Law and Theology.* Brookline, Mass.: Holy Cross Orthodox Press, 2008.

Vitezić, Ivan. *La prima visita apostolica postridentina in Dalmazia (nell'anno 1579).* Rome: Pontificia Universitas Gregoriana, 1957.

Vitkus, Daniel J. "Early Modern Orientalism: Representations of Islam in Sixteenth- and Seventeenth-Century Europe." In *Western Views of Islam in Medieval and Early Modern Europe: Perception of Other,* edited by David R. Blanks and Michael Frassetto. New York: St. Martin's, 1999.

————. "Trafficking with the Turk: English Travelers in the Ottoman Empire during the Early Seventeenth Century." In *Travel Knowledge: European "Discoveries" in the Early Modern Period,* edited by Ivo Kamps and Jyotsna G. Singh. New York: Palgrave Macmillan, 2001.

Vryonis, Speros, Jr. "Byzantine and Turkish Societies and Their Sources of Manpower." In *Studies on Byzantium, Seljuks, and Ottomans.* Malibu: Undena, 1981.

Walter, Tony, and Grace Davie. "The Religiosity of Women in the Modern West." *British Journal of Sociology* 49 (1998): 640–60.

Warrraq, Ibn, ed. *Leaving Islam: Apostates Speak Out.* Amherst, Mass.: Prometheus Books, 2003.

Watt, Jeffrey. "Divorce in Early Modern Neuchâtel, 1547–1806." *Journal of Family History* 14 (1989): 137–55.

Weber, Alison. *Teresa of Avila and the Rhetoric of Femininity.* Princeton: Princeton University Press, 1996.

Weinstein, Donald. *The Captain's Concubine: Love, Honor, and Violence in Renaissance Tuscany.* Baltimore: Johns Hopkins University Press, 2000.

Weinstein, Roni. *Marriage Rituals Italian Style: A Historical Anthropological Perspective on Early Modern Italian Jews.* Leiden: Brill, 2004.

Weiss, Gillian. "Commerce, Conversion, and French Religious Identity in the Early Modern Mediterranean." In *The Adventure of Religious Pluralism in Early Modern France,* edited by Keith Cameron, Mark Greengrass, and Penny Roberts. Oxford: Peter Lang, 2000.

Wickersham, Jane. "Results of the Reformation: Ritual, Doctrine and Religious Conversion." *The Seventeenth Century* 18 (2003): 266–89.

Wiesner-Hanks, Merry E. *Christianity and Sexuality in the Early Modern World: Regulating Desire, Reforming Practice.* New York: Routledge, 2000.

———. *Gender, Church, and State in Early Modern Germany.* London: Longman, 1998.

———. *Women and Gender in Early Modern Europe.* 2nd ed. Cambridge: Cambridge University Press, 2000.

———. "Women's Response to the Reformation." In *The German People and the Reformation,* edited by R. Po-chia Hsia. Ithaca, N.Y.: Cornell University Press, 1988.

Wilson, Bronwen. "Reflecting on the Turk in Late Sixteenth-Century Venetian Portrait Books." *Word and Image* 19 (2003): 38–58.

Wolf, Eric. *Europe and the People without History.* Berkeley: University of California Press, 1982.

Wolff, Larry. *Venice and the Slavs: The Discovery of Dalmatia in the Age of Enlightenment.* Stanford: Stanford University Press, 2001.

Woodberry, J. Dudley. "Conversion in Islam." In *Handbook of Religious Conversion,* edited by H. Newton Malony and Samuel Southard. Birmingham, Ala.: Religious Education Press, 1992.

Wootton, David. "Lucien Febvre and the Problem of Unbelief in the Early Modern Period."*Journal of Modern History* 60 (1988): 695–730.

Yavari, Neguin. "The Conversion Stories of Shayk Abū Ishāq Kāzarūnī (963–1033)." In *Christianizing Peoples and Converting Individuals,* edited by Guyda Armstrong and Ian N. Wood. Turnhout: Brepols, 2000.

Zachariadou, Elizabeth A. "Co-Existence and Religion." *Archivium Ottomanicum* 15 (1997): 119–29.

———. "The Sandjak of Naxos in 1641." In *Festgabe an Josef Matuz:*

Osmanistik—Turkologie—Diplomatik, edited by Christa Fragner and Klaus Schwarz. Berlin: Klaus Schwarz Verlag, 1992.

Zagorin, Perez. *Ways of Lying: Dissimulation, Persecution, and Conformity in Early Modern Europe.* Cambridge, Mass.: Harvard University Press, 1990.

Zambelli, Paola. "Uno, due, tre, mille Menocchio?" *Archivio storico italiano* 137 (1979): 51–90.

Zannini, Andrea. *Burocrazia e burocrati a Venezia in età moderna: I cittadini originari (sec. XVI–XVIII).* Venice: Istituto Veneto di Scienze, Lettere ed Arti, 1993.

———. "Un censimento inedito del primo seicento e la crisi demografica ed economica di Venezia." *Studi veneziani* 24 (1993): 87–116.

Zhelyazkova, Antonina. "Islamization in the Balkans as a Historiographical Problem: The Southeast-European Perspective." In *The Ottomans and the Balkans: A Discussion of Historiography,* edited by Fikret Adanır and Suraiya Faroqhi. Leiden: Brill, 2002.

Zilfi, Madeline C. "Introduction." In *Women in the Ottoman Empire: Middle Eastern Women in the Early Modern Era,* edited by Madeline C. Zilfi. Leiden: Brill, 1997.

———. "The Kadizadelis: Discordant Revivalism in Seventeenth-Century Istanbul." *Journal of Near Eastern Studies* 45 (1986): 251–69.

———. "Muslim Women in the Early Modern Era." In *The Later Ottoman Empire, 1603–1839,* edited by Suraiya N. Faroqhi. Cambridge: Cambridge University Press, 2006.

———. " 'We Don't Get Along:' Women and *Hul* Divorce in the Eighteenth Century." In *Women in the Ottoman Empire: Middle Eastern Women in the Early Modern Era,* edited by Madeline C. Zilfi. Leiden: Brill, 1997.

Zorattini, Pier Cesare Ioly. "Battesimi «invitis parentibus» nella repubblica di Venezia durante l'età moderna: I casi padovani." In *Ebrei e cristiani nell'italia medievale e moderna: Conversioni, scambi, contrasti,* edited by Michele Luzzati et al. Rome: Carucci, 1988.

———. *I nomi degli altri: Conversioni a Venezia e nel Friuli veneto in età moderna.* Florence: Olschki, 2008.

abduction, 68
Agazzi, Agostino, 25–26
Agazzi, Bernardino, 25–26
agency, 56–57, 108, 110–11, 114, 115
Ahmed I, 60
Alberti, Gasparo, 29
Alberti, Giovanni Battista, 29
Alberti, Girolamo, 29
Albertino, Michele, 78, 95
Ali Ağa, 19–20, 25–26, 31
annulment, 9, 46
Antivouniotissa (Monastery of Our Lady), 87–88, 90, 113
apostasy: as dissolving marriage, 101; and Muslim women, 113. *See also* conversion
autonomy, of women, 8, 56–57

bailo/baili, 11, 23, 68, 90–91, 92, 96, 103
Balkans, 80, 81, 93
Barbarossa, 15
Bassadonna family, 60
Bekir Paşa, bey of Rhodes, 95, 96, 103
Belegno, Antonio, 68–69, 70
Benin, Filippo, 83, 91
Bernardo, Lorenzo, 12, 16
Bernardo, Perpetua, 57, 58–59
Bianchi, Angelo di, 5, 7, 8
Bianchi, Baldissare, 7, 24–25, 26–27, 28, 29, 32
Bianchi, Giacomo (Mehmed), 7, 24–25, 26–28, 29, 30, 32
Bogdan, Ioan (called Stefan), 50–53, 57, 58, 59

Bogdan, Voica, 50
Bollani, Giuseppe, 1
Bon, Francesca, 58
borders, 34, 36–40, 63, 65, 101, 108–10
Bosnia, 63, 80
Bragadin, Benedetto, 85, 86, 87
Budua, 1
Bulgaria, 52, 80
Burlion, Santo, 85, 86, 88, 89, 90, 98
Burlion family, 88
Bustrone, Zuanne, 27

Calichiopoulo, Orlando, 87, 88
Calvin, John, 17
Candia, 84, 98
Candia, War of, ix
Canea, 84, 98, 103
Capogrosso, Peregrino, 67
Cappello, Girolamo, 20, 21, 53
Casa delle Zitelle, 47–48, 56, 71–75, 94, 114
castration, 3
Catherine de' Medici, 15, 94
çavuş, 46, 60
chastity, 7, 60, 92, 93
children, 108; agency of, 56–57, 75, 114; custody of, 24, 81; legitimacy of, 94; parents and religious vows of, 142n76; religious status of, 100; saints as, 56
Christians/Christianity: and arranged marriages, 50; and confessional ambiguity, 80; and conversion and marriage, 100–101; and Dalmatia,

Mustafa Efendi, 81–83, 88, 91–94, 96–103
Mustafa Paşa, 52

Naima, Mustafa, 30, 31
nuns, 55, 56–57
Nurbanu, 4, 15

officials, Venetian, 49, 55
Omer Ağa: and Stefan Bogdan, 50, 51, 52, 53; and Isabetta Civalelli, 44–45, 46; and Gazanfer Ağa, 43–44; and marriage of Elena Civalelli (Suor Deodata), 50; origins of, 43; and plot to kidnap Elena Civalelli (Suor Deodata), 46; and Venetian officials, 49, 55
Osman II, 70
Othello and Disdemona, tale of, 15
Ottomans/Ottoman Empire: abductions in, 79; and Clissa, 63–64; and Dalmatia, 36; economic and social opportunity in, 13; honor in, 92, 94; imperial harem of, 111; information on, 14; and Milos, 77; and Moldavia, 51; political and economic distress in, 29–30; rioting by military of, 30; segregation of elite women by, 21; and Spalato, 63; and Veneto-Ottoman border, 36–38; women's favorable situation in, 13–14; and Zara, 40

Pago, 41
parents, 66–67, 69, 71–75, 114, 142n76
paternalism, 113
patriarchy, 13, 56, 108
Paul V, 86
Perović, Francesco, 66, 70
pilgrims, 40, 76
political distress, 29–30
Pomaks, 80
Ponzoni, Sfortia, 67
pregnancy, 90

Priuli, Lorenzo, 49, 54–55
property, 13
prostitution, 7, 94
provveditore dell'armata, 97
provveditore general da mar, 68–70
provveditori sopra li monasteri, 58, 70

Qur'an, 15

remarriage, 7, 8
restrictions, 20–21
ritual, 17
Roman Catholic Church/Roman Catholics, 77, 79, 80, 81
Romei, Annibale, 93

Safavids, 20
Saint Doimus, cathedral of, 67
Saint Raynerius, 66
sancak begs, 36, 39, 45, 59, 63–64, 67, 69
San Giacomo dall'Orio, 7
Sansonetto, Pietro, 27, 28
saray ağası, 43
Šatorović, Ahmed Ağa, 64, 65, 66–67, 68, 69, 71–75
Šatorović, Haisecaduna, 64, 65, 67, 69, 71, 72
Šatorović, Mihale (Catterina), 101, 105, 107; at Casa delle Zitelle, 70, 72; conversion of, 67, 115; flight of, 65–66, 68, 73; honor of, 66, 70; marriage of, 75; and Mediterranean world, 110, 113, 114, 116; and parents, 66–67, 69, 71–75
Šatorović family, 64–65
Savonarola, Girolamo, 7
segregation, of Ottoman women, 21
Selânikî, 20, 30, 43
Selim II, 1, 3, 4, 15, 51
Senate, Venice: and Elena Civalelli (Suor Deodata), 49, 58; and Gozzadini women, 89, 92, 95, 98, 99, 102; and Beatrice Michiel (Fatima